Comprehensive
Income Taxation

Studies of Government Finance: Second Series

TITLES PUBLISHED

Comprehensive Income Taxation

JOSEPH A. PECHMAN
Editor

*A Report of a Conference Sponsored by
the Fund for Public Policy Research
and the Brookings Institution*

Studies of Government Finance

THE BROOKINGS INSTITUTION

WASHINGTON, D.C.

Copyright © 1977 by
THE BROOKINGS INSTITUTION
1775 Massachusetts Avenue, N.W., Washington, D.C. 20036

Library of Congress Cataloging in Publication Data:

Main entry under title:

Comprehensive income taxation.

(Studies of government finance; 2d ser., book 8)
Bibliography: p.
Includes index.
1. Income tax—United States—Addresses, essays,
lectures. I. Pechman, Joseph A., 1918–
II. Brookings Institution, Washington, D.C. III. Se-
ries.
HJ4652.P427   336.2'42   77-24246
ISBN 0-8157-6982-2
ISBN 0-8157-6981-4 pbk.

9 8 7 6 5 4 3 2 1

THE BROOKINGS INSTITUTION is an independent organization devoted to nonpartisan research, education, and publication in economics, government, foreign policy, and the social sciences generally. Its principal purposes are to aid in the development of sound public policies and to promote public understanding of issues of national importance.

The Institution was founded on December 8, 1927, to merge the activities of the Institute for Government Research, founded in 1916, the Institute of Economics, founded in 1922, and the Robert Brookings Graduate School of Economics and Government, founded in 1924.

The Board of Trustees is responsible for the general administration of the Institution, while the immediate direction of the policies, program, and staff is vested in the President, assisted by an advisory committee of the officers and staff. The by-laws of the Institution state: "It is the function of the Trustees to make possible the conduct of scientific research, and publication, under the most favorable conditions, and to safeguard the independence of the research staff in the pursuit of their studies and in the publication of the results of such studies. It is not a part of their function to determine, control, or influence the conduct of particular investigations or the conclusions reached."

The President bears final responsibility for the decision to publish a manuscript as a Brookings book. In reaching his judgment on the competence, accuracy, and objectivity of each study, the President is advised by the director of the appropriate research program and weighs the views of a panel of expert outside readers who report to him in confidence on the quality of the work. Publication of a work signifies that it is deemed a competent treatment worthy of public consideration but does not imply endorsement of conclusions or recommendations.

The Institution maintains its position of neutrality on issues of public policy in order to safeguard the intellectual freedom of the staff. Hence interpretations or conclusions in Brookings publications should be understood to be solely those of the authors and should not be attributed to the Institution, to its trustees, officers, or other staff members, or to the organizations that support its research.

Foreword

MANY EXPERTS and laymen agree that the individual income tax—the cornerstone of the federal revenue system—has become unnecessarily complicated. Its basic structure remains progressive, but the proliferation of special deductions, exclusions, and tax credits has introduced wide disparities in tax liability among people with equal incomes and family responsibilities. Because the tax base has been narrowed so much, the marginal tax rates range from 14 percent to 70 percent, even though the revenue from the tax amounts to little more than 10 percent of total personal income.

The Internal Revenue Code has become so complex that almost every business must have technical tax advice before making major decisions. The tax forms have become so unwieldy that millions of low- and moderate-income Americans must pay others to have their tax returns prepared, and the firms that prepare tax returns have become large and profitable.

As a result of these developments, representatives of business, labor, and the general public are demanding tax reform to remove inequalities in the tax treatment of people with the same income and to simplify the tax structure. During the 1972 presidential campaign, influential members of both political parties expressed their support for a complete overhaul of the individual income tax. Members of Congress have also become more insistent on fundamental reform.

The basic approach to tax reform that has been embraced by these diverse groups is *comprehensive income taxation.* The idea is that all income should be taxed alike and that the revenue generated by the broader tax base should be used to lower the tax rates substantially. The removal of special provisions and the reduction of the high marginal rates, it is felt, would improve the equity of the income tax, minimize the influence of tax considerations on business decisions, and make the income tax easier to administer and more comprehensible to large numbers of taxpayers.

Although comprehensive income taxation is appealing, few understand its meaning. Even experts do not agree on the definition of comprehensive income and whether a tax system based on such a concept would in fact be simpler than the present one. How would transfer payments, pensions, and employee fringe benefits be treated under a comprehensive income tax? What deductions would be allowed? What is the appropriate unit of taxation? How would property and business incomes be determined?

To deal with these and other questions, the Brookings Institution and the Fund for Public Policy Research jointly sponsored a conference on comprehensive income taxation. The conference, held at Brookings on December 10 and 11, 1976, had as a basis for discussion a set of background papers prepared by experts on the major issues. The first was a general conceptual paper; the others dealt with such specific issues as transfer payments and employee benefits, personal deductions, homeowner preferences, capital gains and losses, business income, and the family unit.

The authors and discussants were asked to assume that the comprehensive tax would apply to income rather than consumption in a noninflationary economy and that corporation and individual income would be taxed separately. This was done not only to keep the discussion within manageable limits, but also because in 1976 Brookings published *Inflation and the Income Tax,* edited by Henry Aaron, and expects to publish other studies dealing with the consumption tax and integration of the corporation and individual income taxes.

This volume consists of the background papers, revised by the authors in the light of the conference discussions; a summary of the conference discussions; and an appendix that measures the comprehensive income tax base and illustrates the extent to which tax rates could be reduced without reducing the revenue yield of the present income tax. Its editor, Joseph A. Pechman, director of the Brookings Economic Studies program, also organized the conference.

The manuscript was checked for accuracy by Evelyn P. Fisher with the assistance of Kathleen Kane. The revenue estimates, other than those in the capital gains paper and in the appendix, were prepared by Robin Donaldson, Richard Booth, and Wing Thye Woo under the supervision of Joseph J. Minarik. Tadd Fisher edited the manuscript for publication; the index was prepared by Florence Robinson.

The project was supported by the Fund for Public Policy Research. Research on the revenue and distributional implications of changes in the structural features of the income tax was supported by a grant from the RANN program of the National Science Foundation.

This is the eighth publication in the second series of Brookings Studies of Government Finance. Both series are devoted to examining issues in taxation and public expenditure policy. The views expressed in this volume are those of the authors and discussants and should not be ascribed to the trustees, officers, or other staff members of the Brookings Institution, or to the Fund for Public Policy Research, the National Science Foundation, or any of the organizations with which the authors and other conference participants are affiliated.

BRUCE K. MAC LAURY
President

July 1977
Washington, D.C.

Contents

Text Tables

Appendix Tables

Figures

CHAPTER ONE

The Economic Definition of Income

RICHARD GOODE *

MUCH OF the discussion of the individual income tax in the United States over the past two decades has stressed inequities and economic defects due to the erosion of the tax base and has led up to recommendations for a broader-based tax. This approach implies that there is an income concept against which practice can be meaningfully appraised. While tax specialists have often stated a formal definition, they have not always paid heed to it in their policy prescriptions. Many other participants in the extensive talk and writing about the tax base appear to assume that everyone knows what income is, or that adjusted gross income as identified in the Internal Revenue Code or personal income as estimated by the Department of Commerce is a suitable measure.

Economic theorists have not agreed on the definition of income. There is an extensive and tedious literature on the subject, enlivened by a few notable contributions. Some of the keenest analysts have

* I gratefully acknowledge helpful comments received from Sijbren Cnossen, Federico Herschel, George E. Lent, Leif Mutén, Joseph A. Pechman, Stanley S. Surrey, and Vito Tanzi. They, of course, are not responsible for errors, omissions, or misjudgments, particularly since I did not—and could not—accept all their suggestions, which clashed on some points.

concluded that it may well be impossible to define income rigorously. Thus Henry Simons said: "That it should be possible to delimit the concept precisely in every direction is hardly to be expected"; in another passage he wrote about "insuperable difficulties to achievement of a rigorous conception of personal income."[1] Kaldor asserted that "the problem of *defining* individual Income, quite apart from any problem of practical measurement, appears in principle insoluble."[2]

But fortunately the total absence of ambiguity is not required to make a concept useful. If rigor were the ruling criterion, discourse on public policy would be short. Despite the difficulties, income is in practice measured and taxed, though unsatisfactorily in many respects. A premise of this paper is that individual income can be defined reasonably clearly in a sense that is relevant for taxation. If, as I believe is true, there is more than one definition that meets the requirements, a choice can be made by reference to general usage and, more important, to notions of justice and ability to pay. Measurability is also essential.

A good definition of income is an indispensable intellectual foundation for the evaluation of an income tax statute. It serves as a basis for the orderly consideration of specific questions about inclusions, exclusions, and deductions. Without such a basis, discussion is likely to be unnecessarily discursive and the ad hoc conclusions reached may lack force. But the definition should not be viewed as a Platonic ideal to which unquestioned deference is owed. Income, in the words of an able lawyer, is "a concept calling for creative elaboration to effectuate the practical implementation of the purposes of the [income] tax."[3] Few important issues can be resolved merely by appealing to a definition.

This paper is concerned with the economic definition of personal income for tax purposes. Definitions for use in the theory of capital, social accounting, and other fields may properly differ from that which is preferred for individual taxation. No systematic attention is given in the paper to special problems related to the definition and measurement of business income.

1. Henry C. Simons, *Personal Income Taxation: The Definition of Income as a Problem of Fiscal Policy* (University of Chicago Press, 1938), pp. 43, 110.
2. Nicholas Kaldor, *An Expenditure Tax* (London: Allen and Unwin, 1955), p. 70.
3. William D. Andrews, "Personal Deductions in an Ideal Income Tax," *Harvard Law Review,* vol. 86 (December 1972), p. 324.

Proposed Definitions

This section reviews several definitions of income that have been advanced by economists, sometimes explicitly for taxation but more often for other purposes, and briefly indicates some of their implications. One of the definitions has received far more support—from American specialists at least—than the others for use in taxation, and I shall try to explain why this is so. The preferred definition, nevertheless, is subject to a number of conceptual and practical difficulties that will be considered in later sections.

Definitions Stressing Capital Maintenance

Since 1976 was the bicentennial of *The Wealth of Nations* as well as of the Declaration of Independence, the filial piety proper for an economist impels me to begin my survey with Adam Smith. He wrote:

The gross revenue of all the inhabitants of a great country, comprehends the whole annual produce of their land and labour; the neat revenue, what remains free to them after deducting the expence of maintaining; first, their fixed; and, secondly, their circulating capital; or what, without encroaching upon their capital, they can place in their stock reserved for immediate consumption, or spend upon their subsistence, conveniences, and amusements.[4]

Smith's definition in form pertains to what would now be called national income or social income, but in content it resembles other definitions that are clearly intended to apply to individuals. While the two concepts are related and many common problems are involved in their quantification, important differences in purpose justify differences in coverage and in the treatment of particular items. In national income statistics the primary objective is to estimate the aggregate value of goods and services produced, whereas in individual income accounts the objective is to measure an individual's (or a family's) command over economic resources. It should not be expected that the summation of individual incomes, so conceived, will equal national income.[5]

4. *An Inquiry into the Nature and Causes of the Wealth of Nations,* Edwin Cannan, ed. (Modern Library, 1937), bk. 2, chap. 2, p. 271.

5. In the U.S. national accounts, personal income comprises factor incomes plus transfer payments from government and institutions but not from individuals, minus personal contributions for social insurance. In estimating factor incomes no deduction is made for depletion. Personal income includes the income of individuals, un-

The concept of income as what a person can consume without impairing his capital is a persistent one. It still appeals to economists. For example, J. R. Hicks in his influential treatise *Value and Capital,* first published in 1939 and revised in 1946, is reminiscent of Smith in the following:

The purpose of income calculations in practical affairs is to give people an indication of the amount which they can consume without impoverishing themselves. Following out this idea, it would seem that we ought to define a man's income as the maximum value which he can consume during a week, and still expect to be as well off at the end of the week as he was at the beginning. . . . I think it is fairly clear that this is what the central meaning must be.[6]

Behind Smith's dignified eighteenth-century prose and Hicks's self-consciously homely phrasing lie many complexities relating to the meaning of "encroaching upon . . . capital" or being "as well off at the end of the week as . . . at the beginning." Even the meaning and measurement of consumption are unclear on close examination, though this difficulty has received much less attention than has the problem of capital maintenance.

Moving out from the "central meaning" of income, Hicks elaborates three definitions, or approximations to the central concept, which differ in the interpretation of keeping capital intact. The third version—and the one he prefers but acknowledges to be imperfect—is "the maximum amount of money which the individual can spend this week, and still expect to be able to spend the same amount *in real terms* in each ensuing week."[7] By thus asserting that recurrence, or permanence, is an essential attribute of income, Hicks links his definition with an idea that has been common in Great Britain but less so in the United States. The idea, however, was endorsed in a presidential address to the American Economic Association entitled "The Concept of Income, as Recurrent, Consumable Receipts."[8]

---

incorporated enterprises, nonprofit institutions, private trust funds, and private pension, health, and welfare funds but does not include retained profits of corporations or capital gains and losses. See U.S. Department of Commerce, *National Income, 1954 Edition* (Government Printing Office, 1954), pp. 49–51. On the relationship between national income and individual income, see Simons, *Personal Income Taxation,* pp. 44–49, 58; and Joseph A. Pechman and Benjamin A. Okner, *Who Bears the Tax Burden?* (Brookings Institution, 1974), pp. 12–15.

6. *Value and Capital: An Inquiry into Some Fundamental Principles of Economic Theory,* 2d ed. (Oxford: Oxford University Press, 1946), p. 172.

7. Ibid., p. 174.

8. Carl C. Plehn, *American Economic Review,* vol. 14 (March 1924), pp. 1–12.

Although the central meaning of income, as seen by Hicks, can be reconciled with what I regard as the best definition of income for tax purposes, his own elaboration is different. Basically, income as defined by Hicks is subjective, dependent on the expectations of the individual, and hence not usable as a tax base.[9] If an effort is made to salvage the idea of recurrence or permanence by relating it to market values rather than to individual expectations, the outcome is not a measurable concept of income suitable for all individuals. What may be evolved is a rationalization for omitting capital gains and losses from income while including interest, dividends, and rent.[10] A distinction between change in capital value and yield may be meaningful in an agricultural society with certain legal institutions,[11] or in the world of abstract economic theory,[12] but it does not fit contemporary reality. There is in fact no clear difference between the function of changes in the market value of assets and the interest, dividend, or rental payments associated with them. Nor is it possible to distinguish for tax purposes between recurrent and nonrecurrent or expected and unexpected changes in market value. Another objection to Hicks's interpretation of income is that it concentrates on the yield of capital and applies awkwardly, if at all, to earnings from personal effort, which make up the greater part of what is commonly regarded as income and are taxed as such.

Source and Periodicity Concepts

Akin to definitions incorporating the criterion of recurrence or permanence are definitions that would restrict income to periodic flows from continuing sources.[13] This approach may have been influ-

9. Hicks cautioned against the use of the income concept in economic theory, characterizing income as a "very dangerous term" (*Value and Capital,* p. 180).

10. Strictly, part of the capital gain or loss should be reflected in current income, according to the Hicks definition, because it will affect the interest yield that can be obtained and spent in each future period. If the gain is not expected to recur, the amount that should be included is $rg/(1 + r)$, where g is the gain and r is the interest rate. See George F. Break, "Capital Maintenance and the Concept of Income," *Journal of Political Economy,* vol. 62 (February 1954), p. 59.

11. Lawrence H. Seltzer, *The Nature and Tax Treatment of Capital Gains and Losses* (National Bureau of Economic Research, 1951), pp. 25–46.

12. In addition to Hicks, *Value and Capital,* chap. 14, see Erik Lindahl, *Studies in the Theory of Money and Capital* (London: Allen and Unwin, 1939), pp. 96–111; and "The Concept of Gains and Losses," in *Festskrift til Frederik Zeuthen* (Copenhagen: Udgivet af Nationaløkonomisk Forening, 1958), pp. 208–19.

13. For reviews of these and other definitions, see Paul H. Wueller, "Concepts of Taxable Income," *Political Science Quarterly,* vol. 53 (March and December 1938),

enced by the origin of income taxation in several European countries
as partial taxes or groups of schedular taxes on income from particular sources, as distinguished from a unitary tax on an individual's
total income. The implications of the source and periodicity concepts
are similar to those connected with Hicks's version of the capital-
maintenance concept: the exclusion of capital gains and losses and
"casual" receipts such as gambling or lottery winnings and various
lump-sum payments on retirement or loss of employment. The weaknesses are also similar: the artificiality of the distinction between capital gains and other investment yields, the inconsistent treatment of
income from personal effort and income from other sources, and—
more generally—the omission of items that contribute to the ability
to pay taxes.

Fisher's Definition

Another definition that grew out of theorizing about capital and
its yield is that of Fisher. According to him, income is fundamentally
"yield," consisting of the services rendered by property or persons.
Since the only services desired for themselves are those that satisfy
consumers' wants, income, as defined by Fisher, is what others call
consumption.[14] Savings and increases or decreases in the value of
capital assets are explicitly excluded. Apart from the saving decisions
of owners, no provision is made for capital maintenance, and no
attention is paid to the question of permanence or recurrence. Income
is equivalent to consumption, regardless of whether spending is
financed out of current earnings or by using up capital.

Fisher developed his definition before the modern income tax was

---

pp. 83–110, 557–83, and vol. 54 (December 1939), pp. 555–76; Edwin R. A. Selig-
man, "Income Tax," *Encyclopaedia of the Social Sciences* (Macmillan, 1932), vol.
7, pp. 626–39; and Henry Laufenburger, "Die Einkommensbesteuerung," *Handbuch
der Finanzwissenschaft,* 2d ed. (Tübingen: J. C. B. Mohr [Paul Siebeck], 1956), vol.
2, pp. 460–69.

14. See the following works by Irving Fisher: *The Nature of Capital and Income*
(London: Macmillan, 1906); "Income," *Encyclopaedia of the Social Sciences* (Mac-
millan, 1932), vol. 7, pp. 622–25; "Income in Theory and Income Taxation in Prac-
tice," *Econometrica,* vol. 5 (January 1937), pp. 1–55; and "The Concept of Income:
A Rebuttal," *Econometrica,* vol. 7 (October 1939), pp. 357–61. See also Irving
Fisher and Herbert W. Fisher, *Constructive Income Taxation: A Proposal for Reform*
(Harper, 1942). Fisher objected at times to the assertion that he defined income as
merely consumption, calling this a "misrepresentation" of his views (see, for example,
"The Concept of Income," pp. 358–59); but this interpretation has been accepted by
all critics and, finally, by Fisher himself (*Constructive Income Taxation,* p. 51).

adopted in the United States and, he assures us, independently of any views that he came to hold on social policy and taxation.[15] He later, however, enthusiastically advocated its use for taxation and argued that an "income" tax based on his definition would be fairer and economically superior to the existing tax.

For a long time Fisher insisted that the meaning of income should be restricted to his concept, but finally he gave up this point and conceded that in addition to "services" or "yield" income, as he defined it, there was another useful concept, "enrichment" income or "accretion," consisting of consumption plus capital increase (or minus capital decrease).[16] Indeed he remarked: "While yield is the more fundamental concept, accretion is, for some purposes (other than taxation), the more useful."[17]

Although Fisher's argumentation sometimes appears to be reducible to the proposition that the correct base for the income tax must be "income" as he defined it for another purpose—and in a sense different from common usage—his writings are intellectually far superior to many others on the subject. When he does discuss tax policy Fisher makes a respectable case for preferring an expenditure tax (personal consumption tax) to a conventional income tax. He also deserves credit for addressing many of the practical problems that would have to be solved in order to put into effect an expenditure tax. I am not persuaded that the expenditure tax is better than the income tax, but I shall reserve for my discussion of the accretion concept the few comments on the advantages of the income tax for which there is space in this paper.

The Schanz-Haig-Simons Definition

The income definition that has received most support from American tax specialists is usually called the Haig-Simons concept but more accurately and less parochially could be named the Schanz-Haig-Simons (S-H-S) concept or definition.[18] Developed explicitly for tax

15. *Constructive Income Taxation,* p. x; and "The Concept of Income," p. 360.

16. "The Concept of Income," p. 357; and *Constructive Income Taxation,* pp. 48–51.

17. *Constructive Income Taxation,* p. 50. Fisher said that accretion may be more useful in that it conveys information about future yields as well as the yield of the period under consideration.

18. Georg von Schanz (1853–1931) was a German economist and founder and editor of *Finanz-Archiv.* His definition is set forth in his important article, "Der

purposes, this is the accretion concept, which defines personal income as the sum of consumption and accumulation.

Haig stated that income is "the increase or accretion in one's power to satisfy his wants in a given period in so far as that power consists of (*a*) money itself, or, (*b*) anything susceptible of valuation in terms of money. More simply stated, the definition of income which the economist offers is this: Income is the *money value of the net accretion to one's economic power between two points of time.*"[19] He emphasized that the definition is in terms of the power to satisfy economic wants rather than the satisfactions themselves and pointed out that this means that income is received when the power is obtained and not when it is exercised. This is to say, income includes savings as well as consumption.

Simons defined personal income for tax purposes as "the algebraic sum of (1) the market value of rights exercised in consumption and (2) the change in the value of the store of property rights between the beginning and end of the period in question." He added, "In other words, it is merely the result obtained by adding consumption during the period to 'wealth' at the end of the period and then subtracting 'wealth' at the beginning."[20]

In an enumeration that may have appeared deliberately provocative in 1896 in the light of much doctrine and tax practice, Schanz made clear that his definition included not only ordinary profits but also the usufruct of property, gifts, inheritances, legacies, lottery winnings, insurance proceeds, annuities, and windfall gains of all kinds and that all interest paid and capital losses should be deducted.[21]

As noted above, the S-H-S definition can be reconciled with a concept going back at least as far as Adam Smith. Income is the amount that one could consume without experiencing any increase or decrease

---

Einkommensbegriff und die Einkommensteuergesetze," *Finanz-Archiv*, vol. 13, no. 1 (1896), pp. 1–87. See the article on Schanz by Hans Teschemacher in *Encyclopaedia of the Social Sciences* (Macmillan, 1934), vol. 13, pp. 563–64. According to Leif Mutén (*On the Development of Income Taxation Since World War I* [Amsterdam: International Bureau of Fiscal Documentation, 1967], p. 25), Schanz was anticipated by David Davidson, writing in Swedish in 1889.

19. Robert Murray Haig, "The Concept of Income—Economic and Legal Aspects," in Haig, ed., *The Federal Income Tax* (Columbia University Press, 1921), p. 7, reprinted in Richard A. Musgrave and Carl S. Shoup, eds., *Readings in the Economics of Taxation* (Irwin for the American Economic Association, 1959), p. 59.

20. *Personal Income Taxation*, p. 50.

21. As quoted in ibid., p. 61.

in his capital. The reconciliation is valid, however, only on the basis of a particular and relatively simple view of the meaning of maintaining capital intact: capital comprises only nonhuman wealth, and it is intact if its money value does not change within the period.[22] In this sense, capital is equivalent to what is commonly called net worth in accounting statements.

Adherents to definitions stressing capital maintenance, however, usually have in mind a quite different interpretation. Only rarely is this clearly stated, and reliance is frequently placed on figures of speech—often a harvest metaphor—rather than on accounting statements. The intention is to exclude from income capital gains and losses and many nonrecurrent accretions to capital. Hicks has provided the sophisticated version of this interpretation of maintaining capital intact. As argued above, Hicks's version is unusable for taxation because it cannot be objectively measured; even if it could be approximated its policy implications would be unacceptable. The emphasis on the permanence of the real level of consumption accords with the rentier's aspiration in a world of uncertainty and inflation. A parallel concept can hardly be applied to entrepreneurs or recipients of income from personal effort. A definition of taxable income that omits capital gains and nonrecurrent or "casual" receipts will favor investors and speculators in securities, real estate, and commodities.

The Fisher definition, in contrast, is objective and measurable in principle (although there would be practical difficulties in applying it). Concern about capital maintenance and permanence or recurrence drop out of the formal requirements, or more accurately, the tax authorities would accept whatever provision the individual thought it appropriate to make for capital maintenance. But I do not believe that legislators or the public thought that a direct tax on consumption was being imposed when the income tax was enacted.

The reasons for preferring the S-H-S concept to Fisher's concept are really the reasons for preferring an income tax to an expenditure tax. This is not the place to elaborate the arguments, but a brief statement is essential, even at the risk of dogmatism. As I see it the income tax is superior in principle to the expenditure tax, first because income is generally a better index of ability to pay than is consumption. Both the amount of income obtained and the amount consumed depend on the decisions and opportunities of the individual, but con-

22. Break, "Capital Maintenance and the Concept of Income."

sumption reflects an additional choice, that is, the disposal of the power to consume that accrues to one within a period of time. It is intuitively appealing to say that an individual's ability to pay is measured by the whole set of his additional consumption opportunities rather than by the subset that he elects to utilize currently.[23] Another reason for preferring the income tax is that accumulation itself is an objective and a source of satisfaction distinguishable from current or future consumption. To the extent that progressive taxation is regarded as a means of preventing excessive inequality, total income or wealth is preferable to consumption as a tax base because accumulation enhances the economic and political power and the social status of the individual. The proposition sometimes advanced that a tax on consumption is superior because it is apportioned according to the use of resources rather than according to one's contribution to production is misleading. Savers and investors direct the use of economic resources no less than do consumers. Whether private consumption or private investment should be displaced to make room for government expenditure is an important question of economic policy that ought to be debated on its merits.[24]

Although the S-H-S definition has been accepted by most American specialists as the best available for tax purposes, a number of conceptual and practical questions are encountered in trying to apply it. I turn now to some of these issues. Before doing so, however, I should like to emphasize that my concentration on issues relating to the S-H-S concept should not be taken to imply that the difficulties could be avoided by adopting one of the other definitions. Many of the problems to be discussed would arise in connection with the other definitions, and there would be some special difficulties as well.

Conceptual Questions about the S-H-S Definition

This section considers several questions related to the meaning or acceptability of the S-H-S definition; questions that mainly concern

23. In any given year some persons will consume more than their current income, but in a system that has imposed an income tax based on the S-H-S definition for a generation or longer, the consumption power used in the current year will have been part of the taxable income of an earlier year.

24. The best case for the expenditure tax is made in Kaldor, *An Expenditure Tax*. I state my own position in Richard Goode, *The Individual Income Tax*, rev. ed. (Brookings Institution, 1976), chaps. 2, 3.

difficulties of administration and compliance are discussed in the next section.

Price-Level Changes

A leading cause of changes in the money value of net worth, and hence a source of positive or negative income according to S-H-S, is fluctuations in the average price level. This presents some conceptual questions and important issues of policy and administration. They are outside the scope of this conference, however, and will not be discussed here.[25]

Double Counting in Relation to Capital Gains

An objection to including in income changes in the value of capital assets, as required by the S-H-S definition, is that such gains and losses merely reflect future income increases or decreases and that including them in both present and future income results in double counting and in double taxation or double deductions.[26] This objection is closely related to the general argument that an income tax results in double taxation of savings but is narrower in scope.

If one accepts the proposition that in taxing income the objective is to apportion the liability with reference to accretions in the power to consume rather than actual consumption, there is no irrationality or inequity in taxing both a capital gain and the subsequent income that it foretells. These are distinct though not independent accretions to consumption power. Where the increase in yield is of finite duration—for example, where it relates to a building or a piece of machinery—a full accrual system should permit the gain to be written off over the remaining life of the asset through periodic valuations or increased depreciation allowances. Thus the decline in consumption power associated with the diminishing value of the asset will reduce taxable income. (Under a system that taxes capital gains only when realized, a similar result will obtain if the asset is sold and the buyer depreciates his cost over the remaining life.) Where the increased yield is for an asset with an unlimited, or indefinite, life—for example, a share of corporate stock—adjusting future income will be un-

25. See Henry J. Aaron, ed., *Inflation and the Income Tax* (Brookings Institution, 1976).

26. See Fisher, "Income in Theory and Income Taxation in Practice," p. 47.

necessary unless the expected yield and market value of the asset change again.

A highly simplified illustration may help clarify the case of an unexpected increase in the yield of a depreciable asset, with full accrual accounting according to the S-H-S definition. Assume a discount rate of 15 percent a year and consider an asset with a two-year life that throws off its yield in equal installments of $50 on the last day of each of the two years. In a perfect market the cost of the asset on the first day of year 1 and an investor's expected gross yield, depreciation allowance (straight-line), and net taxable income in years 1 and 2 will be as shown in column 1 below (all columns are in dollars):

	1	*2*	*3*
Year 1			
Cost	81.29	81.29	81.29
Capital gain	. . .	81.29	. . .
Gross yield	50.00	100.00	100.00
Depreciation allowance	40.65	81.29	40.65
Net taxable income	9.35	100.00	59.35
Year 2			
Gross yield	50.00	100.00	100.00
Depreciation allowance	40.64	81.29	40.64
Net taxable income	9.36	18.71	59.36
Years 1 and 2			
Net taxable income	18.71	118.71	118.71

If on the second day of year 1 it is discovered that the yield of the asset will be twice what was expected on the previous day, the position of an investor who bought on the first day will be approximately as shown in column 2. Column 3 shows the outcome if capital gains are included in taxable income only when realized rather than when accrued. It will be seen that the aggregate taxable income is the same in columns 2 and 3, though distributed differently between the years.

Human Wealth

The S-H-S concept does not include human wealth in capital or net worth, and changes in the value of human wealth are not taken into account in measuring accumulation. Thus, for example, a professional athlete is not seen as having experienced a gain in net worth when his skill is "discovered" and his future earning power is enhanced, nor is he permitted to deduct a depreciation allowance to reflect the decrease of the capitalized value of his expected future earnings with the passage of time and the shortening of his remaining career. In contrast, the owner of a racehorse has a capital gain in analogous circumstances and is entitled to depreciation allowances. The difference arises from the political and legal system, which classifies as property a horse but not a human being. It is entirely appropriate that this fundamental distinction be reflected in the definition of taxable income. No one appears to have contested the exclusion of increases in the value of human capital, but depreciation allowances to cover the disappearance of human earning capacity have often been advocated. These, however, would be unjustified except for deductions to recoup the cost of education and training and other investments that add to earning power.[27]

Interest Rate Changes

A frequent source of capital gains and losses is changes in the interest rate at which expected future yields are discounted. For example, if the relevant interest rate falls from 9 percent to 8 percent, a perpetual stream of yields of $100 a year will increase in value from $1,111 to $1,250. A bond with twenty years to run to maturity, bearing a coupon rate of 9 percent, will increase in value from $1,000 to $1,099. An increase in the interest rate from 9 percent to 10 percent will cause the value of the perpetual stream to fall to $1,000 and the value of the bond to fall to $914.

The S-H-S definition requires that these increases or decreases in capital values be included in taxable income, but the question arises whether this is correct, since by assumption there has been no change in the expected stream of future yields of the assets. Concentrating on the case of the increase in capital values due to a decline in interest rates, one notes that the increment represents an immediate increase in the consumption power of the owner in the sense that he could command more consumption goods if he liquidated his capital. But a person who decided to "realize" his additional income by selling part of his assets would find that, other things being equal, he would

27. Depreciation allowances have the function of (1) spreading the cost of an asset over its useful life; and (2) under a full accrual system, permitting the amortization of capital gains on depreciable assets that have been included in taxable income.

receive less money income in the future. Clearly, this is another aspect of the problem of capital maintenance and permanency.

Kaldor argued that an increase in capital value due to a decline in the interest rate is fictitious in the sense that it represents nominal capital accumulation rather than real capital accumulation. Real capital accumulation, he asserted, occurs only when an individual secures "increased command over both consumption goods and income yielding resources." It would not be possible to correct for this kind of fictitious capital increment, even if one wished to do so, because all that can be observed is changes in market values. These may reflect either a change in the expected future yields or a change in the relevant discount rate, and the two cannot be separated. It was these considerations that led Kaldor to the pessimistic conclusion that the problem of defining income is "in principle insoluble."[28]

If capital maintenance is interpreted in Kaldor's exacting way (in which he resembles Hicks), the considerations just recited constitute a damaging criticism of the S-H-S definition. I think, however, that such a stringent standard for capital maintenance is unnecessary. The immediate increase in consumption power that occurs when interest rates decline represents a new opportunity for asset owners that merits inclusion in the index of ability to pay. The capital gain obtained by those who invested before the decline in interest rates reflects a genuine advantage they enjoy that is not obtained by those who invest later or by other income recipients. To argue that this capital gain should be excluded from income is tantamount to saying that old investors should be allowed to retain in perpetuity a preferred position compared with that of new investors and of recipients of income from labor and other sources. Furthermore, capital gains and losses due to changes in the interest rate, as Kaldor noted, cannot be unambiguously distinguished from other gains and losses that represent clear additions to economic power.

Over time, some of the apparent anomalies associated with changes in capital values due to interest rate changes will disappear. Thus, for example, an investor who immediately consumes his capital gain that is due to an interest rate decline will have less taxable income in the future than another investor who refrains from doing so. In the case of a bond the increase in capital value will be temporary and will be gradually reversed as the maturity of the bond approaches.

28. Kaldor, *An Expenditure Tax*, pp. 54–78 (quotations on pp. 69 and 70).

Definition of Consumption

The definition of consumption presents a fundamental problem of such complexity as to elicit Simons's concession that a rigorous conception of personal income cannot be achieved.[29] There are two aspects of the problem: first, the distinction between consumption and the costs of obtaining income; and second, the treatment of goods and services produced and used within the household. In a broad sense a large fraction of what is called consumption may be considered a cost of production in that it is necessary in order to sustain an efficient labor force. The impossibility of distinguishing clearly between the part of household expenditure that serves to make possible further production and the part that constitutes, in Adam Smith's phrase, "the sole end and purpose of all production,"[30] raises philosophical questions. It means that income from personal effort cannot be measured as precisely as property income and suggests that costs are less fully deductible for the former than for the latter.

Generally the classification of an item as a cost of production or as consumption depends on the intention of the spender, supplemented in practice by rules based partly on custom but with arbitrary elements. Many administrative questions arise about travel and entertainment and other expenditures that may plausibly be viewed as either a source of immediate gratification or a means of obtaining additional income. The difficulties are particularly acute in connection with income from self-employment, but they exist also for salary and wage earners.

The performance of services for oneself or one's household, such as housekeeping, repairs, and gardening, provides a series of illustrations of the problem of identifying and valuing income and consumption that do not pass through the market. While these services have economic value, any effort to include this in taxable income would fail and would discredit the tax law and its administration. Unavoidable inequities and economic distortions arise when some people work at paid employment and use their money income to buy services that others perform for themselves. The widespread bartering of personal services, allegedly a growing practice in certain countries

29. Simons, *Personal Income Taxation*, pp. 110–24.
30. *Wealth of Nations*, bk. 4, chap. 8, p. 625.

with high marginal tax rates, could result in similar or worse distortions.

Leisure is sometimes classified as consumption[31] and hence by implication as part of S-H-S income. While in a broad sense this is correct, it would be impossible to make any allowance for leisure in assessing income for taxation. To the extent, however, that the performance of services within a household competes with leisure rather than with outside work that is compensated by money payments, the distortions due to the taxation of the latter are mitigated.[32]

It should be emphasized that the defects of an income tax based on the S-H-S definition that are due to the difficulties just discussed could not be avoided by adopting any of the other definitions of income that have been proposed or by going over to an expenditure tax.

A specific point that may be noted here is the argument of Andrews that medical expenses may appropriately be deducted from taxable income, even if the S-H-S definition is accepted, on the grounds that these outlays are not really consumption. Differences in the amount spent for medical care, he argues, reflect differences in need rather than choices among gratifications.[33] Acceptance of this conclusion would require recognizing that in addition to consumption goods and services and capital goods, there is another category comprising final utilization of economic resources in ways that are not pleasurable. While agreeing with Andrews that most people may derive little conscious gratification from medical expenditures, I do not accept his conclusion. For one thing, the same is true of many other outlays that are classified as consumption expenditures. Thus one buys an umbrella not as a source of gratification per se but for the purpose of avoiding the unpleasantness of getting wet when it rains. Also, the distinction between trying to stay in good health, for example, by spending for a nutritious diet and by paying for periodic checkups by a physician is not as clear as either the Andrews argument or the present tax law implies. Furthermore, a considerable part of medical expenditures strictly defined reflects voluntary choices about the need for treatment and its nature and cost. The high fees paid to prestigious physicians for the treatment of fashionable illnesses resemble the outlays that the patients make for other services. My disagreement with

31. Simons, *Personal Income Taxation*, p. 52.
32. Goode, *The Individual Income Tax*, pp. 142–43.
33. "Personal Deductions in an Ideal Income Tax," pp. 331–43.

Andrews's rationalization of the medical expense deduction does not pretend to demonstrate that the provision cannot be justified on other grounds.

Andrews also argues that charitable contributions should be deducted because they are not part of the donor's consumption and suggests that the interest deduction may be justifiable on the same grounds.[34] His reasoning is too complex to summarize briefly. As to charitable contributions, my view is that they should be included in adjusted gross income because they are part of the economic resources subject to the disposal of the taxpayer but that a personal deduction for them can be supported for traditional reasons of public policy. My comments on interest payments are given below.

Taxes and Government Expenditures

Curiously, the public finance literature on the definition of income contains only infrequent references to the treatment of government. The formal definition of income as equal to consumption plus accumulation takes no explicit account of direct or indirect taxes. Literally, the S-H-S definition applies to income net of direct personal taxes; however, it has generally been interpreted to mean income before personal taxes, or perhaps more accurately no account has been taken of the existence of personal taxes.[35] Presumably consumption goods and services are valued at market prices, including indirect taxes. The treatment of direct personal taxes poses no conceptual issue, though for policy reasons taxes other than the personal income tax and income taxes levied by other jurisdictions may be deducted or credited. The treatment of indirect taxes involves no special problems as long as the income tax is based on nominal values, but if an adjustment for price level changes were introduced, it would be necessary to decide whether fluctuations corresponding to changes in indirect taxes should be excluded.

The question whether the value of government services should be included in individual income is a conceptual issue. Bittker argues that consistent application of the S-H-S definition would require the inclusion of these items and that the failure to do so "compromises" the tax reformers' aim of "taxing all income alike." His conclusion is

34. Ibid., pp. 344–76.
35. See Henry Aaron, "What is a Comprehensive Tax Base Anyway?" *National Tax Journal,* vol. 22 (December 1969), pp. 543–49.

not that an effort should be made to value the benefits but that the impossibility of doing so is evidence for his judgment that a comprehensive tax base is not a feasible or desirable objective.[36] Musgrave agrees that "ideally" a comprehensive definition of income would include the imputed value of the benefits from public services, along with cash transfers received from government, but holds that the impossibility of doing so does not destroy the usefulness of the comprehensive income concept or justify the exclusion of cash transfers.[37]

The question of the treatment of the benefits from government services is, in my opinion, less important than it may seem when first encountered. Expenditures for national defense, general government administration, and other so-called public goods cannot be allocated to individual beneficiaries. They represent a part of the general social environment in the same way that climate is part of the physical environment. No inequity or inefficiency results from failure to take account of the substantial fraction of total government expenditures falling in this category.

In a number of areas, however, close substitutability exists between benefits in kind and cash transfers. Medical services and education are important examples. Strict adherence to the S-H-S definition, as usually interpreted, would require that the cash grants be included in income, but this may be unfair and inefficient so long as the in-kind benefits are ignored. Since many of the in-kind benefits cannot be accurately valued and taxed, the exclusion from taxable income of cash grants for similar purposes may be justifiable as a means of avoiding arbitrary differences in taxation.[38] This argument would not justify the exclusion of cash transfer payments, such as unemployment compensation and old-age and survivors' benefits, which the recipient may spend as he pleases and for which there are no close counterparts in the form of in-kind benefits. Public assistance payments can be used for many purposes, but their limitation to persons

36. Boris I. Bittker, "A 'Comprehensive Tax Base' as a Goal of Income Tax Reform," *Harvard Law Review,* vol. 80 (March 1967), pp. 935–38; reprinted in Bittker and others, *A Comprehensive Income Tax Base? A Debate* (Federal Tax Press, 1968), pp. 11–14.

37. Richard A. Musgrave, "In Defense of an Income Concept," *Harvard Law Review,* vol. 81 (November 1967), pp. 54–55; reprinted in Bittker and others, *A Comprehensive Income Tax Base?* pp. 72–73.

38. See Aaron, "What is a Comprehensive Tax Base Anyway?"

who pass a means test may justify their exclusion from taxable income.

Gratuitous Receipts

The S-H-S concept calls for including in income gratuitous receipts in the form of gifts and inheritances (also bequests and devises). Simons argued that the donor should not be allowed a deduction because making a gift presumably provides satisfaction to him and is a form of consumption by him.[39] Only a few tax specialists have agreed that these items should be included in the taxable income of the recipients.[40] Generally transfers at death are subject to special taxation on the estate or the heir, and in the United States and some other countries inter vivos gifts are taxed.

One source of difficulty is the diverse nature of the transfers that legally qualify as gratuitous. Some of them appear to have an important element of quid pro quo and to be similar to transactions that are generally agreed to give rise to income. In the relatively trivial cases of tips, noncontractual bonuses and severance pay, and other voluntary payments by employers to employees, the present practice is to include the item in taxable income.

Many other gratuitous transfers, however, particularly those between family members, appear to be of a different nature. Often these transfers may accurately be viewed as a sharing of consumption power rather than the creation of new income. This is related to the question of the appropriate definition of the taxable unit.

Transfer taxes on donors may have some advantages over income taxes on gratuitous receipts. It can be argued that donors should be subjected to special taxation because gifts and bequests represent a significant exercise of economic power. Under the income tax, large differences in taxation might occur between cases where wealth is transferred by a series of gifts and cases where it is transferred in a

39. *Personal Income Taxation*, pp. 125–47.
40. At a conference held at the Brookings Institution in 1965, a few participants favored replacing the estate and gift taxes by including the transfers in the donee's taxable income, but "no substantial support for this proposal developed." See Carl S. Shoup, *Federal Estate and Gift Taxes* (Brookings Institution, 1966), p. 118. The proposal was supported by the Carter Commission in Canada (*Report of the Royal Commission on Taxation* [Ottawa: Queen's Printer, 1966], vol. 3, pp. 465–519), but was not accepted by the government.

lump sum at the death of the donor, a possibility that is generally considered to be a weakness of unintegrated transfer taxes.[41] On both social and economic grounds, higher rates may be acceptable for transfer taxes than for the income tax. Estate and gift taxes apply to transfers to residents and nonresidents alike; if these taxes were replaced by income taxation, some special problems would arise in the treatment of nonresident beneficiaries, whose circumstances would not be known or easily verifiable by the domestic tax authorities.

Administration and Compliance Questions

This section identifies several items that pose difficulties in applying the S-H-S definition without involving conceptual issues of the same complexity as those reviewed in the preceding section. Space limitations allow only a cursory treatment.[42]

Accrued Capital Gains and Losses

A major problem associated with the use of the S-H-S concept concerns the time at which capital gains and losses should be taken into account. Although the concept requires that changes in the value of capital assets be reflected annually on an accrual basis, the majority of experts think that this would not be feasible and are willing to settle, at least at present, for the recognition of capital gains and losses at the time of realization through sale, exchange, gift, or bequest. The application of the realization principle for capital gains and losses substantially reduces the equity and efficiency of the income tax, even if gains are taxed at regular rates and losses are fully

41. While holding that the income tax should be regarded as "the basic form of levy upon inheritance," Simons favored a supplementary tax in the form of "a cumulative personal tax on beneficiaries with respect to gifts, inheritances, and bequests . . . , with a credit for all amounts paid as personal income tax" with respect to the gratuitous receipts (*Personal Income Taxation,* p. 144). This compromise greatly weakens the case for including gratuitous receipts in taxable income. See Alan A. Tait, *The Taxation of Personal Wealth* (University of Illinois Press, 1967), pp. 102–04. At the end Simons was "open-minded and uncertain" about the taxation of gifts and inheritances and speculated that "a quite different and better approach . . . may be available and awaiting early discovery" or rediscovery (Henry C. Simons, *Federal Tax Reform* [University of Chicago Press, 1950], pp. 138–39).

42. I have dealt with the questions covered in this section at greater length in *The Individual Income Tax*—and have discussed some of them in still more detail in other publications—but have not thought it necessary to give specific citations of the relevant passages.

deductible. The impairment of the income tax is of course greater when gains are taxed at lower rates than other income and limitations are imposed on the deductibility of capital losses. Under a realization system the taxation of many gains is postponed for a long time, and this greatly reduces the effective tax rate. Probably the inflation and high nominal interest rates prevailing in the recent past have stimulated economists to attach more importance to the effect of postponement.[43]

Taxes on capital gains have been increased in recent years but remain below those on other income. Further increases in the taxation of capital gains would be the most important step that could be taken to lessen the tilt of the income tax in favor of property income. There is a strong case for full taxation of gains realized by a sale or other exchange and those constructively realized by gift or at death. Although in principle capital losses should be fully deductible, it may be expedient to continue limitations on their deductibility against ordinary income so long as capital gains are taxed only at realization, in order to prevent taxpayers from realizing their losses while deferring their gains. Further consideration needs to be given to the feasibility of measures that would reduce the advantages of deferring gains.[44]

Imputed Income from Dwellings and Durables

A comprehensive income tax base would have to include the imputed rental value of owner-occupied dwellings. Substantial problems would be involved in estimating this item, but I think they could be coped with in a reasonably satisfactory way. Imputed rent is taxed in the Scandinavian countries, Germany, and some other countries,

43. It is interesting to contrast the equanimity with which Simons viewed the postponement question (*Personal Income Taxation,* pp. 168–69) with the recent treatment by Roger Brinner in "Inflation, Deferral and the Neutral Taxation of Capital Gains," *National Tax Journal,* vol. 26 (December 1973), pp. 565–73.

44. William Vickrey's cumulative averaging plan is one suggestion for reducing the attractiveness of deferral and is intended to deal also with other problems. See his *Agenda for Progressive Taxation* (Ronald Press, 1947), pp. 172–95; and his "Cumulative Averaging after Thirty Years," in Richard M. Bird and John G. Head, eds., *Modern Fiscal Issues: Essays in Honor of Carl S. Shoup* (University of Toronto Press, 1972), pp. 117–33. However, I see major weaknesses in this scheme that cannot be discussed here. An idea that appears promising is Brinner's suggestion that realized gains be "written up" by a factor to reflect in a rough way the advantages of deferral ("Inflation, Deferral and the Neutral Taxation of Capital Gains," pp. 570–71).

but in the United Kingdom the previous practice of including it in taxable income has been discontinued. In principle, owner-users of consumer durables should also have to reflect in their taxable income an imputed return on their equity. My judgment is that it would not be practicable to assess this latter item and that its omission must be accepted as a shortcoming of the income tax in comparison with an ideal one.

Life Insurance

The S-H-S definition indicates that life insurance death benefits should be included in the income of beneficiaries and implies that interest accruing on life insurance policy reserves should be included in the income of policyholders. In the United States at present both are omitted, though some interest earnings are taxed when insurance proceeds are paid for reasons other than the death of the insured (when a policy matures or is surrendered). Death benefits resemble bequests and other gratuitous receipts and should be treated in the same way as these. Interest accruing on policy reserves, in my judgment, should be currently taxed to policyholders, and I believe that this would be feasible, although so far as I know no country does so. Since casualty insurance usually does not involve substantial policy reserves, a comparable provision would not be needed for it.

Interest Paid

Interest payments may be either a cost of obtaining income or a consumption expense. In my opinion the former but not the latter payments should be deducted in computing income.[45] There is, however, no fully satisfactory way of distinguishing between the two. One approach (followed in Canada) is to allow the deduction only of interest paid on debts formally connected with business operations, professional practice, or income-producing property. This is too narrow because an individual's economic power can be properly evaluated only by taking a comprehensive view of his income and outgo and his balance sheet. In a broad sense any interest he pays is a cost of obtaining the yield of any capital assets he holds, because by contracting the interest-bearing debt he avoids disposing of the income-

---

45. Schanz favored the deduction of all interest payments (quoted in Simons, *Personal Income Taxation*, p. 61). Simons and Haig did not explicitly address the subject.

yielding assets. Thus, for example, interest paid on consumer installment debt may be viewed as a cost of obtaining interest income on
bonds owned by the same individual. On the other hand, if the individual holds no income-yielding assets and is not engaged in business
or professional activity, the interest paid on the installment debt
appears to be part of the cost of consumer goods. It is similar to a
price supplement paid for buying a consumer good early or to rental
payments for a leased car or other durable consumer good. A complication arises because the yield of certain assets—for example, owner-
occupied dwellings, consumer durables, and municipal bonds—is not
included in taxable income in the United States. Interest paid to carry
such assets should not be deductible.

All things considered, I think that the least arbitrary solution
would be to allow interest to be deducted only against taxable property income, defined as investment income and the part of business
and professional income attributable to capital according to conventional rules. Interest payments would no longer be deductible by persons who report only salary and wage income. The last feature would
no doubt be criticized as discriminatory and regressive.

Costs of Earning Labor Income

In order to reduce differences in the treatment of labor income and
property income, the liberalization and rationalization of the rules
for deducting the costs of education and training that are intended to
enhance earning capacity would be desirable. It would be hard—
though in my judgment possible—to devise acceptable rules and procedures to distinguish these costs from other educational costs. Similar problems arise in classifying moving expenses as costs of earning
income or as consumption. Some would argue that commuting expenses are also of a mixed nature and should be partly deductible.

Pension Rights

The expectation of receiving a pension on retirement has an important bearing on the economic welfare of employed persons, and
the appropriate treatment of pensions poses difficult questions for the
income tax or for a wealth tax. Many pension plans in the United
States call for contributions by employees and employers to a trustee
who is not currently taxable on the interest obtained by investing the
reserves. Employees do not obtain a deduction for their contributions

and are not required to include in their current income employers' contributions and interest accruals. They are taxable on the benefits when received but are allowed to recover their own contributions free of tax.

It seems clear that the accrual of a pension right is a form of accumulation and hence a part of income according to the S-H-S concept. Significant questions of interpretation arise, however. If the accumulation is attributed to the employee only to the extent that he acquires a fully vested right to it, arbitrary distinctions may be made between plans calling for vesting and other plans, and the former kind of plan may be discouraged. On the other hand, if vesting is not considered a criterion, individuals may be taxed on hypothetical benefits they never obtain. While legislation enacted in 1974 requires a greater degree of vesting for tax-exempt pension plans than was customary in the past,[46] vesting is far from universal.

Assessment Procedures

The S-H-S income definition is a conceptual guide, not an assessment formula. In practice, net income is measured primarily by reference to transactions classified according to accounting conventions and not by the aggregation of consumption and accumulation. The U.S. Internal Revenue Code, like other tax statutes, identifies taxable income by enumerating items to be included, excluded, or deducted; however, it goes on to say that income is not limited to the enumerated items but includes income "from whatever source derived."

Comprehensively defined income—which may be regarded as an approximation of S-H-S income—could be assessed as follows:

$$Y_c = G - E + S - K + A,$$

where G = gross receipts other than the proceeds of sale of capital assets, E = costs of obtaining G, S = proceeds of sale of capital assets (plus the value of capital assets transferred by gift or bequest), K = the cost or other basis of capital assets sold (or otherwise transferred), and A = change in the value of capital assets held throughout the year. G should be interpreted to include the imputed rental value of owner-occupied dwellings and E to include interest, depreciation, maintenance, property taxes, and other expenses relating to such dwellings. G should also include certain income received in kind by

46. Employee Retirement Income Security Act of 1974 (Public Law 93-406).

employees and others. *E* should include interest paid up to the amount of nonlabor income received. If capital gains and losses are taxed only when realized, *A* is dropped from the equation above. According to Simons, *G* should include gifts and inheritances received, but many others who generally favor the S-H-S approach would exclude these items.

In comparing U.S. practice with the formula, it is helpful to distinguish between adjusted gross income and taxable income. Adjusted gross income is net of most allowable costs of obtaining income and may be compared with Y_c. Taxable income is adjusted gross income less personal deductions, *P,* and personal exemptions. If this distinction were carefully observed, *P* would not include the costs of obtaining income but would consist of allowances that are granted for policy reasons other than the improvement of the definition of income. While this is broadly true, *P* now includes some items that might properly be regarded as part of *E*: for example, certain interest payments, certain investment expenses, part of educational expenses, union dues, and miscellaneous employment expenses.[47] A sharp distinction between *P* and *E* would help clarify discussion and would suggest the elimination of inequities that now arise when persons who elect the standard deduction are denied deductions for some items that would qualify as part of *E*.

In the present U.S. law, *G* omits imputed income receipts, interest on tax-exempt bonds, most transfer payments received from government, and other gratuitous receipts. *E* is understated because it fails to include most of the costs of education and training that contribute to earning capacity and certain other costs of earning labor income but may be overstated in regard to travel and entertainment expenses and perhaps some other items. *S* omits half of the proceeds of the sale of capital assets held for certain minimum time periods (for 1976, six months; for 1977, nine months; and for 1978 and later, twelve months) as well as the value of assets transferred by gift or bequest. *K,* on the other hand, is in effect understated in certain cases by virtue of the limitation on the deductibility of capital losses against

47. The deduction for child-care expenses was formerly in this category, but the Tax Reform Act of 1976 (Public Law 94-455) replaced the deduction with a tax credit. In my opinion, this change was inconsistent with the rationale for tax relief for these expenses on the grounds that they are costs of earning income. Costs should be *deducted* from income and not treated as the base for a tax credit.

other income (and because of inflation, which is not being covered in this paper). *A* is wholly omitted.

Tax Expenditures

Closely related to the question of how taxable income compares with comprehensively defined income is the concept of "tax expenditures." Proposed originally by Assistant Secretary of the Treasury Stanley Surrey in 1967 and soon quantified by the Treasury Department, the idea won rapid acceptance in public and congressional debates on taxation.[48] It was incorporated in the Congressional Budget Act of 1974, which requires a listing of tax expenditures in the annual budget.

In his 1967 speech Surrey spoke of "deliberate departures from accepted concepts of net income and . . . various special exemptions, deductions and credits" that he considered equivalent to government expenditures.[49] The Treasury study, published in the 1968 annual report of the secretary of the treasury, gave estimates of the revenue reductions due to "the major respects in which the current income tax bases [i.e., the corporation and individual tax bases] deviate from widely accepted definitions of income and standards of business accounting and from the generally accepted structure of an income tax."[50] The Congressional Budget Act of 1974 defines tax expenditures as "revenue losses attributable to provisions of the federal tax laws which allow a special exclusion, exemption, or deduction from gross income or which provide a special credit, a preferential rate of tax, or a deferral of tax liability."[51]

The estimates of tax expenditures prepared by the Treasury Department are based on a broad income concept but not on the S-H-S definition or a close approximation of it. The standard is vaguer and more pragmatic. Thus the list of tax expenditures comprehends the

48. William F. Hellmuth and Oliver Oldman, eds., *Tax Policy and Tax Reform, 1961–1969: Selected Speeches and Testimony of Stanley S. Surrey* (Commerce Clearing House, 1973), pp. 573–641; Stanley S. Surrey, *Pathways to Tax Reform: The Concept of Tax Expenditures* (Harvard University Press, 1973); and *Annual Report of the Secretary of the Treasury on the State of the Finances for the Fiscal Year Ended June 30, 1968*, pp. 322–40.

49. Hellmuth and Oldman, *Tax Policy and Tax Reform*, p. 576.

50. Ibid., p. 588; and *Annual Report of the Secretary of the Treasury, 1968*, p. 327.

51. Public Law 93-344, sec. 3(a)(3).

exclusion from taxable income of social security benefits and public assistance benefits but not the exclusion of food stamp and Medicaid benefits or private gifts and inheritances; the deduction of mortgage interest and property taxes on owner-occupied dwellings is classified as a tax expenditure, but the omission of imputed net rent is not so classified; the exclusion of interest accruing on life insurance policy reserves, but not the exclusion of death benefits, is considered a tax expenditure; the low tax rate on long-term capital gains is viewed as a tax expenditure, but not the failure to tax unrealized gains or gains constructively realized by transfer through gift or bequest.[52]

Some of the differences between the official list of tax expenditures and a list based on a rigorous application of the S-H-S definition are due to estimating difficulties.[53] However, Surrey and Hellmuth, replying to criticism of the tax expenditure budget by Bittker,[54] explicitly denied that the Treasury Department followed the Haig-Simons definition of income. No effort was made to cover exclusions "where the case for their inclusion in the income base stands on relatively technical or theoretical arguments" such as those for including imputed net rent. Surrey and Hellmuth appeal to the idea of a broad consensus about tax equity and to the implication that a special provision is a departure from accepted equity criteria that "must be defended on terms other than its rightful place in the tax structure—terms that in essence make it a 'tax expenditure.' "[55]

The term "tax expenditure" has undoubtedly stimulated many people to think about certain tax issues and the budget in a new way, and the regular publication of tax expenditure estimates provides useful information. In my opinion, however, the present tax expenditure budget rests on a shaky conceptual foundation and for this reason is less convincing to skeptics than it would be if more rigorously derived. The Surrey-Hellmuth defense assumes a broader and more

52. Some of the congressional analyses have classified as a tax expenditure the exclusion of accrued capital gains on assets transferred at death. See the publications cited in note 56.

53. *Special Analyses, Budget of the United States Government, Fiscal Year 1977*, pp. 116–22.

54. Boris I. Bittker, "Accounting for Federal 'Tax Subsidies' in the National Budget," *National Tax Journal*, vol. 22 (June 1969), pp. 244–61.

55. Stanley S. Surrey and William F. Hellmuth, "The Tax Expenditure Budget—Response to Professor Bittker," *National Tax Journal*, vol. 22 (December 1969), pp. 529, 537.

exact consensus on tax equity than I detect, and the tax expenditure estimates are less firmly based than would be desirable for official statistics.[56]

Two alternatives to the present tax expenditure budget, either of which could be more easily defended in my judgment, would be (1) a broader tabulation showing, as far as feasible, the estimated effects on tax liability of all differences between S-H-S income and adjusted gross income and of all personal deductions and credits; or (2) a narrower tabulation including only those provisions for which there is evidence in the legislative history that the dominant motivation was to encourage or reward certain behavior or to compensate for a particular hardship by reducing income tax liability. The term "tax expenditure" could appropriately be reserved for the latter items. The test of motivation should be critically applied since there is hardly any provision that has not sometimes been supported on the grounds that it induces desirable behavior or relieves hardship. The examination of the legislative history, however, should not be confined to that of the original enactment but should extend to any later systematic consideration of the provisions by the congressional tax committees of the two houses.

Conclusion

This review leads me to the conclusion that the S-H-S definition of income is much better for tax purposes than other definitions. All definitions are subject to conceptual problems and practical difficulties of application that prevent the attainment of a fully accurate and noncontroversial measurement. The S-H-S definition, however, is more objective than definitions of the Hicks-Kaldor type, which depend on subjective factors in determining whether capital is being maintained. The latter definitions and the source and periodicity con-

---

56. In addition to *Special Analyses, Budget, Fiscal Year 1977,* see *Estimates of Federal Tax Expenditures,* prepared for the Committee on Ways and Means and the Committee on Finance by the staff of the Joint Committee on Internal Revenue Taxation (GPO, 1976); Committee on the Budget, U.S. Senate, *Tax Expenditures: Compendium of Background Material on Individual Provisions,* 94 Cong. 2 sess. (GPO, 1976); and U.S. Bureau of the Census, *Statistical Abstract of the United States, 1975* (GPO, 1975), p. 231. In the last source, many of the items classified as tax expenditures are included in a table headed "Gross Budgetary Cost of Major Federal Tax Subsidies."

cepts place undue emphasis on recurrence and permanence and thus omit accretions to economic power that are highly significant in modern economies. They favor investors and speculators over recipients of income from personal effort. The Fisher definition avoids the difficulties to which the other definitions are subject in regard to capital maintenance and timing, but it relates to consumption and not to income as ordinarily conceived. For the reasons briefly stated above, I believe that an income tax should be preferred to a consumption tax.

The S-H-S definition is a valuable guideline for tax policy and administration. There is a presumption that in assessing the income tax all the constituents of income as identified by S-H-S should be brought into the calculations. But a definition is not enough to establish policy. Those who wish to depart from the S-H-S definition should be expected to advance persuasive arguments for doing so, but they need not be asked to carry an extraordinary burden of proof.

The principal departures from the S-H-S definition that seem to me to be warranted are the exclusion from adjusted gross income of gifts and inheritances received, life insurance proceeds, accrued but unrealized capital gains and losses, and government transfer payments that are either close substitutes for in-kind benefits or subject to a means test.

The S-H-S definition gives guidance with respect to inclusions and exclusions from adjusted gross income. It calls for the deduction of all costs of obtaining income but is not particularly helpful in identifying these. The definition implies that income should be taxed at the time when an accretion to economic power accrues, but its adherents have not consistently stressed this point. The formulators of the definition and its users, it seems to me, implicitly assume that the consumer unit and the income unit for tax purposes coincide. Otherwise, the importance attached to consumption power is hard to interpret, and the recommendations on the treatment of gifts and inheritances are untenable. On the other hand, the S-H-S definition in itself does not tell which personal deductions are advantageous for policy purposes (as distinguished from the allowance of costs of obtaining income). It has nothing to say about personal exemptions or tax rates.

If it is not possible to move all the way to a comprehensive concept of income, the question arises whether a clear gain would be obtained by moving part of the way. Partial measures could make matters worse. This might well be true of action to include in adjusted gross

income some of the government transfer payments that are now excluded. It has been contended that the base-broadening actions that
are likely to be taken would accentuate an alleged discrimination
against earned income, compared with investment income, and
would therefore be undesirable.[57]

One's reaction to this criticism depends in part on a political fore-
cast of what measures are likely to be enacted and also on one's view
of the role of experts. Although tax experts should not be oblivious
to the harm that may be done by the partial adoption or modification
of their recommendations, I think that this should cause them to re-
double their efforts at explanation and persuasion rather than to give
up the attempt to formulate proposals for a good income tax and a
good tax system. Leaving aside the question of short-run political
acceptability, my opinion is that the reforms needed to approach
more closely the S-H-S version of a comprehensive income definition
would not, on balance, discriminate against earned income. Prominent among these reforms are measures that would increase taxes on
investment income, including the full taxation of capital gains on a
realization basis and the inclusion in income of the imputed rental
value of owner-occupied dwellings, interest earned on life insurance
policy reserves, and interest on tax-exempt bonds. Furthermore, in
appraising the relative taxation of income from labor and income
from property, account should be taken not only of the individual
income tax but also of the corporation income tax, the property tax,
estate and gift taxes, and payroll taxes.

Comments by Henry Aaron

We were informed that this is a conference about how to define a
comprehensive income tax base, not whether it is desirable to do so.
This stricture is rather confining; Richard Goode spends a good deal
of time explicitly defending the accretion base against the consumption base and even more time on aspects of accretion that raise the
same issues that divide advocates of consumption from those of
accretion.

57. Bittker, "A 'Comprehensive Tax Base' as a Goal of Income Tax Reform,"
p. 983. Economists should be embarrassed that it was left for a lawyer to introduce
into the debate "the theory of second best."

Goode has written a nearly perfect introduction to a conference on comprehensive income taxation. He provides a lucid survey of the major issues that have occupied a copious literature for generations. He presents alternative positions clearly and is candid and forthright in expressing his own views. The serious reader of Goode's paper will learn much and will be driven to rethink a wide range of issues, some of which he may have thought cut and dried but which he discovers are not. Furthermore, I agree with many of the positions Goode has taken, which makes my admiration for his perspicacity all the greater.

Goode raises five specific issues on which I would like to comment. First, I agree with his evaluation of tax expenditures. The tax expenditure concept is invaluable for complete analysis of alternative ways to achieve desired public purposes. It is impossible to formulate policy sensibly in such fields as health care, housing, and income security if one fails to include in one's deliberations such provisions of the Internal Revenue Code as deductions for medical expenditures, mortgage interest and property taxes, the exclusion of transfer payments, and many other provisions. Many provisions of the tax code would be revised, repealed, or replaced with direct expenditures if this approach were consistently applied.

But it is futile to dream of a "grand budget" that sums direct expenditures—a set of affirmative actions *actually* taken—and tax expenditures—a set of actions *not* taken or revenues *not* collected. The list of things we have chosen not to do is infinite and unspecifiable. The futility of such an endeavor is revealed by the fact that if we try correctly to estimate the aggregate level of tax expenditures, the level of each particular tax expenditure depends on the number of tax provisions that are *defined* as tax expenditures. The level of social security outlays does not depend on whether we define, say, Federal Home Loan Bank Board advances to be in or out of the budget; but the revenue implications of, say, permitting the deduction of property taxes does depend on the fact that unemployment insurance is excluded. The impossibility of constructing an unambiguous grand tax expenditure budget should not divert attention from the immense value of program analysis that includes both direct and tax expenditures.

Second, I agree with Goode's conclusion, but not with his reasoning, about the exclusion of the imputed value of government services from income. The practical difficulties of imputing such income are decisive. In principle, however, the imputed value of parks, schools, or national defense should be included in income as surely as the imputed value of owner-occupied homes. The income would be equal to the value of each public service at the margin multiplied by the quantity of each service enjoyed. Such income may differ by very large amounts across and within income classes. But it is no more abstract than the services that households receive from private schools or nondeductible gifts. The trouble is that the value of public services cannot be estimated with the precision necessary for taxation. For practical reasons, not for analytical ones, Goode is correct.

Third, Goode observes that tax rates on capital gains have increased in recent years but remain below taxes on other income. As a statement about statutory rates, this observation is undoubtedly correct. As a statement about effective rates, it is not generally true for realized gains because of the presence of inflation gains; the effective rates of real realized gains may now exceed those on ordinary income for many taxpayers. The real problem is that most gains entirely escape taxation through a variety of channels.

Fourth, Goode's defense of the income base on the ground that accumulation is a source of satisfaction is odd. It is the stock of wealth, not additions to it, that is usually thought to give utility.

Fifth, the issue of what to do when fluctuations in interest rates generate capital gains and losses is probably insoluble within the framework of the comprehensive income tax. A household, inextricably locked into its present asset holdings, enjoys no gains and suffers no losses on its assets from changes in real interest rates, although it may alter its savings and consumption decisions. Another household that is teetering on the edge of whether to sell a bond and that decides to sell because of a change in interest rates assuredly does experience a gain or loss from the change. In general, changes in interest rates are precisely equivalent to other changes in relative prices. In this case the relative price of present and future consumption is altered. As Edward M. Gramlich has observed, whether such a change in relative prices results in meaningful gains and losses depends on the substitution possibilities of the taxpayer.[58] My inclination is to recognize a gain if it is realized but to ignore it otherwise.

58. See "Comments and Discussion," *Brookings Papers on Economic Activity, 1:1976*, p. 62.

Comments by *Charles Davenport*

Richard Goode's paper captures the issues that need to be discussed in arriving at an economic definition of income. My comments are limited to a critique of his discussion of tax expenditures.

Goode suggests two interrelated problems. First, he has difficulty in finding a workable definition of income to serve as a basis for measuring tax expenditures. Second, he is uncertain of the use to which the concept can be put. I begin with the second problem because a discussion of uses will aid in the definitional problem.

The tax system is composed of two sets of rules. One set is designed to measure income and establish principles for the application of an income tax. In effect it establishes a normative tax system. The second set gives selective relief to encourage certain behavior or to relieve hardships. These rules provide financial assistance in the form of tax relief. Because this financial assistance has some of the qualities of direct spending programs, the special tax relief is called a tax expenditure.

Tax expenditures are defined in the Congressional Budget Act of 1974 as revenue losses that can be attributed to special exclusions, exemptions, or deductions or that provide a special credit, a preferential rate of tax, or a deferral of tax liability. The emphasis in this definition is on the words "special," "preferential," and "deferral."

The tax expenditure concept that identifies those provisions is useful to two kinds of people—those who make or assist in the development of tax policy and those who are interested in budget policy. The tax policy analyst must have some guidelines, criteria, or principles from which to begin an analysis of a problem. If he does not, he is entirely at sea. Without any premise on which to begin, the results may be irrational and unpredictable. The tax expenditure concept is useful because it forces the tax policy analyst to focus on a proper definition of income for tax purposes and how that income is to be taxed. For those who are interested in government spending, the concept helps to identify preferential assistance, and it tells the budget-maker who is obtaining funds that are not generally available to taxpayers. Without this knowledge, the amount of government aid flowing to the beneficiaries through the tax system is unknown, and rational decisions about direct expenditures cannot be made.

With these uses in mind, two practical guidelines may help identify the provisions to which the term should be applied.

First, does the provision work as a subsidy? If it does, it should be included in the tax expenditure budget. Often the nature of the subsidy will be clear, as in the case of the investment credit, for example. The subsidy element may not be so clear in other cases, but if a tax provision is defended in terms of economic need rather than in terms of a proper measure of income, it is very likely a tax expenditure.

Second, should the provision be considered when Congress is considering other nontax programs? A good example of this kind of provision is the exclusion of social security benefits from the tax base. In establishing the level of these benefits, Congress needs to consider the exemption of the benefits from tax. Another example lies in the tax preferences for rental housing units. When Congress considers the low-income housing program, it invariably considers the tax preferences attached to housing. The low-income housing program may not be workable without the tax preferences that go with it.

On the basis of these guidelines, Goode's definitional problem can be considered. He argues that either a broader or narrower definition can be more easily defended than the present definition.

Under the broader definition the tax expenditure concept would parallel, if not precisely coincide with, the Schanz-Haig-Simons definition of income. Goode lists twelve items that concern him under this broader definition of income. Of these twelve, the congressional tax expenditure budget includes only one item (public assistance) that Goode excludes from the comprehensive tax base, and he includes in the comprehensive tax base three items that are not in the tax expenditure budget (net imputed rental income from owner-occupied homes, death benefits from life insurance policies, and accrued gains on capital assets). Most of the published budgets have noted that these items were not included and have suggested that they might be. Thus there is very little difference between Goode's comprehensive tax base and the items appearing in the tax expenditure budgets.

The narrower definition would encompass only those provisions that were intended to encourage or reward certain behavior or to compensate for hardships. Goode notes that nearly every provision in the published tax expenditure budgets has been so defended at one time. Thus this test would not narrow the list unless the test of motivation were "critically applied," but Goode does not provide a definition of critical application. Lacking that guideline, one must return to the grounds on which these provisions are defended. When that is done, I believe it will be found that all the items in the budget have been defended as incentives or as compensation for hardship. Hence I am not sure that the list would be much different if the narrower definition were applied.

The tax expenditure estimates have frequently been criticized as being unreliable. This comes about because often the text accompanying the published estimates, if not read carefully, suggests that the estimates are unreliable. The estimating techniques are said to be limited by six factors: (1) each expenditure is measured in isolation and therefore the elimination of combinations would produce different results from the mere totaling of each estimate; (2) the effect on induced behavior is not measured; (3) Congress might desire to replace the tax subsidy with other assistance; (4) the elimination of a provision would not immediately terminate the tax expenditure, because revenue losses would continue from previous behavior—for example, accelerated depreciation on housing; (5) tax expenditures fluctuate with levels of income; and (6) for some unspecified items, the data base is poor.

Except for the last of these, not one factor bears on the integrity of the estimates. The estimates do tell us what is being spent through the tax system. Obviously they do not tell us what would be spent if several items, including other provisions of the tax law, were changed at the same time. Spending estimates as well as revenue estimates suffer from this law. For example, if food stamps were eliminated, the outlays for aid to families with dependent children might increase, but no one suggests that estimates for the food stamp program are in error for this reason. Each of the other "limitations" are equally conjectural. As to the last limitation, nearly all spending estimates are based on information taken from whatever sources are available and assumptions are made on which to base the estimates. In fact, some tax expenditure estimates are based on hard information from tax returns—a better source than for some spending programs.

In conclusion, the tax expenditure concept is not as vague as Goode suggests. For the most part, it is not controversial. In the last two or three years, more than eighty items have been included in the tax expenditure budgets. There were only three or four differences between the budgets published by the Ford administration and by the various congressional committees. The Ford administration acknowledged the exclusion of these items and seemed ready to agree that they be included. Thus interpretation of the definition of tax expenditures seems to be fairly uniform among those preparing the various budgets.

CHAPTER TWO

Personal Deductions

JOHN F. DUE

A TRULY comprehensive income tax would apply to all income, net of the expenses of earning the income, without deductions for any type of consumption expenditure. The primary justification for non-deductibility is that any deduction discriminates in favor of persons making greater than average expenditures on the deductible items and is equivalent to a governmental expenditure for that particular purpose. Expenditures of this nature may be regarded as objectionable in principle in two ways: they are not subject to annual budgetary review, and their disguised nature may result in much higher levels than Congress would ever vote outright. Since the deductions reduce tax revenue, a higher tax rate is necessary to raise a given sum of revenue, with the possibility of greater adverse effects on incentives in the economy. Under usual theories of governmental decisionmaking, the likely result is that tax rates are somewhat higher and other governmental expenditures somewhat lower than they would be if the deductions were not provided. The deductions increase family expenditures for deductible items to the extent that families will substitute these expenditures for others.

There are other general objections as well to any such deductions. Because the deductible amounts may differ by income level, the net effect may be to alter the overall pattern of distribution of the tax burden by income group from that regarded as optimal. The chances

37

for avoiding taxes by converting into deductible form items of expenditure that were not designed to be covered under the intent of the law are increased, as well as the likelihood of tax evasion, in view of the difficulty of checking the accuracy of all reported deductions. The granting of some deductions inevitably leads to political pressure for more.

In this aspect as in others the U.S. income tax in practice is far from comprehensive; in fact, the American personal deduction system is one of the most generous in the world. The personal deductions fall into two general groups, on the basis of motive:

1. *Those designed to refine the concept of income.* First are expenditures that are regarded as necessary to gain income but that are not deductible as business expenses under the structure of the U.S. income tax. These are not truly personal deductions but are adjustments to arrive at net income. With some of these items, however, there is no clear-cut line between the amounts necessary to gain income and the amounts that are essentially consumption expenditures. The major categories that are deductible, or that have been proposed for deduction, as expenditures necessary to gain income, are care of children and other dependents; education; moving and travel; and miscellaneous work-related items such as union dues, special work clothing, and so on.

Second are negative income items—the value of occurrences that constitute negative income and therefore are appropriately deductible under the Simons definition because they reduce net wealth without yielding consumer satisfaction. The principal example is uninsured casualty loss.

2. *Consumption expenditures deliberately favored.* These include:

(a) Expenses necessitated by ill fortune or catastrophe that do not reflect the preference of the taxpayer for the items and therefore are considered to reduce taxpaying capacity. The primary example is medical expenses. The deductibility of interest on money borrowed to finance expenditures necessitated by misfortune is partly justified on this basis, as are state and local tax payments in part because they are regarded as necessary payments over which an individual has no control.

(b) Expenditures the government wishes to encourage as a matter of social policy, in part because governmental spending would be greater if the expenditures were not made. Contributions to religious, educational, charitable, and related organizations constitute the prime example. A second type, found in many developing countries and being discussed in the United States, consists of certain (or all) forms of savings made during the year, in order to encourage saving and discourage consumption. Complete deductibility of net savings would convert the tax from an income tax to an expenditure tax.

(c) Deductions for intergovernmental fiscal coordination purposes. To the extent that taxes paid to subordinate governments are deductible, the ability of these governments to finance their activities is increased.

(d) Deductions provided for administrative considerations. While in general any deduction creates administrative complications, certain deductions may facilitate the operation of the tax. The deductibility of interest was partly designed to avoid the complication of distinguishing between interest on loans made for production and consumption purposes, although a distinction is now required between "excess investment" interest and other types.

The major personal deductions, whose details have been changed frequently, were introduced at various times, as shown below:

Taxes	1913
Interest	1913
Contributions	1917
Medical expenses	1942
Standard deduction	1944
Child care	1954

These deductions are the result of the favorable attitude of Congress and the various administrations—in part at least, reflecting the wishes of the voters; the strong lobbying pressure of interested groups, particularly charitable organizations, private colleges, and churches, all of which fear a drastic loss in revenue without the contributions deduction; and the urging of state and local governments that desire the continuation of the deduction of taxes paid to them. One of the few general political theories of personal deductions is that advanced by C. M. Lindsay, who argues that the deductions arise because various groups have widely divergent interests in various potential deductible items; consensus can be reached only when concessions in the form of deductions are made to those who have high preferences for the categories and therefore have a lower demand for governmental services.[1] In addition, people are more willing to support higher expenditure and tax levels when they know that if certain events (catastrophic loss, for example) occur in the future, their tax burden will fall accordingly. The remainder of this paper is devoted to a more detailed consideration of each deduction.

Adjustments to Refine the Determination of Income

Two related types of deductions are designed to bring income into closer conformity with the Simons concept of income—the sum of consumption and increase in net wealth during the period.

Expenses to Gain Income

The first consists of the deduction of certain items necessary to gain income. As noted, for employees and to some extent the self-employed, business deductions per se are drastically restricted, primarily to keep the tax returns and the calculation of tax simpler. Therefore certain elements are made deductible as personal deductions even though they are of the nature of business deductions. Others are often proposed.

Complete, exact attainment of the exclusion of all expenses necessary to gain income is difficult, primarily because no sharp line divides expenditures for consumption and expenditures to gain an income. This problem arises even with goods typically regarded as capital equipment for business use only; a farmer buys a much larger and more expensive combine than he needs simply because he enjoys using such a machine (and impressing his neighbors with it). But in other types of activities the lack of a clear delineation is more significant. The entire spectrum of consumption spending is very broad. At the one extreme are expenditures that are purely of a consumption nature, such as the purchase of whiskey and cigarettes. Next come expenditures that may make some contribution to earning an income but that are primarily consumption—vacations at luxury hotels and visits to expensive night clubs, for example. Housing, automobiles, and luxury foods fall into an intermediate category as expenditures that exceed the amounts necessary to live and to earn an income. At the other extreme is basic food necessary for sustaining life, necessary

1. "Two Theories of Tax Deductibility," *National Tax Journal,* vol. 25 (March 1972), pp. 43–52.

clothes, and medicines. Other expenditures are "necessary," given a person's circumstances (commuting to work), but have some voluntary element; one does not have to live in the suburbs. Still others, depending on type of employment, may be of a more necessary nature—union dues for a worker in a union shop, for example.

The basic philosophy of the U.S. income tax, like that of the tax in most countries, is that the exemptions and credits, plus the low-income allowance (formerly called the minimum standard deduction), are designed to exclude from tax the income necessary to sustain life on a minimum scale. Thus the expenditures on basic food, clothing, and so on, do not qualify as personal deductions. But certain items more directly related to earning income are deductible or have been proposed for deductibility:

Child-care and other dependent-care expenses. Before 1954 no deduction was allowed for the care of children while the parents were employed. The deduction has gradually been liberalized under strong pressure from women's groups. It now (1977) takes the form of a credit against tax equal to 20 percent of the dependent-care expenses up to $2,000 for one dependent and $4,000 for more than one dependent, subject to a maximum of the amount of the person's earned income, or the lesser of the spouses' individual incomes. To be eligible, the expenses must be incurred to allow the taxpayer to be gainfully employed, and the taxpayer must maintain a household with a dependent child under fifteen, an adult dependent, or a spouse who is incapacitated.

While justification can be advanced for this adjustment, particularly on the grounds of facilitating the entry of women into the labor market and of minimizing hardships for households with only one adult or an incapacitated adult, it does remove substantial consumption expenditures from the tax base, particularly for persons in higher income levels. The shift in 1976 from a deduction to a credit against tax, although designed to lessen the gain to the higher income groups, is criticized on several grounds, as noted in a subsequent section. The alternative, to tax the imputed income of housewives, is so repugnant to Congress that it is unlikely to be considered seriously.

Educational expenses.[2] The deduction of educational expenditures

2. For a detailed discussion, see John K. McNulty, "Tax Policy and Tuition Credit Legislation: Federal Income Tax Allowances for Personal Costs of Higher Education," *California Law Review*, vol. 61 (January 1973), pp. 1–80.

has long been debated. The law did not provide for such deductions, but the Internal Revenue Service authorized certain items in 1958, following several court decisions. These deductions, however, are severely limited and almost impossible to delineate clearly. At present they are essentially limited to expenses necessary to maintain or improve skills required by an individual in his employment or required by an employer or by law for an employee to retain his job, status, or salary. But expenditures to meet the minimum requirements for a position or to advance to a higher level are not deductible. An example of an expenditure that is deductible is the cost to teachers of required attendance at summer sessions to maintain their teaching certificates. Few provisions of the income tax create more arbitrary delineations than this section.

The case for general deductibility is that education contributes to a person's future earning capacity—that investment in education is equivalent to investment in capital equipment, for which full deductibility of depreciation is allowed. But educational expenditures are made for both consumption and income-producing objectives. A college education may result in higher future income, but it also conveys other benefits to the recipient as well. There is no clear-cut line between the two results.

Even if the principle of broad deduction is accepted, serious problems arise in devising a suitable type of adjustment. The first question is whether the deductible amount should cover only tuition fees and other direct charges; or these items plus the costs of residence, which in private colleges are typically about equal to the tuition fees; or these two plus income forgone by attending college. Consideration of the third category is not justifiable, since the amounts are not included in taxable income. The costs of residence (room and meals) in part merely replace similar costs that would be incurred anyway, and to determine the additional amount (if any) due to attending college is difficult. Thus if adjustment is to be made, it should be confined to tuition charges, fees, and related items. The second issue is who gets the deduction, the student or the parents? The answer clearly is that it must be the student if the deduction is to be allowed on the grounds of the cost of earning income. Since the student lacks current income in many instances, the deduction could be established on a capitalization and depreciation basis over some reasonable period of years (ten perhaps). Giving the parents the deduction could be justified only on the basis of deliberately encouraging this type of expenditure.

Distinguished from college educational expenses are those of various technical or professional courses taken during the years in which a person is working. These could justifiably be made deductible on a current basis, provided the education is related to gaining income (as distinguished from adult classes in flower display, home cooking, or dancing).

In general, the present treatment is unsatisfactory, and broadening the deduction would not only simplify the operation of the tax but would also adjust taxable income more satisfactorily to a net basis exclusive of the costs of earning the income. To avoid the complications of the depreciation approach, as a second-best solution tuition and fees for both college and special adult education should be made deductible to the student on a current basis against the labor income of the student or spouse, provided the education is related to current or future income, with a carry-forward provision of perhaps ten years.[3] This change would eliminate many of the current arbitrary distinctions, although the one between income-related education and other education would remain, and would represent a compromise between operational and equity-incentive considerations.

Moving and commuting expenses. The costs of commuting to and from work have never been deductible and moving expenses have been only since 1964. Congress and the Internal Revenue Service (IRS) have always taken the view that commuting expenses are personal consumption expenses—that commuting is undertaken voluntarily and in part is offset by lower living expenses. This is not an unreasonable rule, and there is little merit in deliberately encouraging commuting. The deductibility of expenses of moving to another area has been defended because the expenses are a necessary cost of accepting a new position and thus are an expense of gaining income. Under present legislation virtually all expenses related to moving are deductible, provided that the move is at least thirty-five miles in distance and is related to employment income. The deduction is not entirely without merit and offers the economic advantage of increasing the mobility of labor. The primary objection is that the move may

---

3. The deduction would be allowed regardless of the source of the funds.

not have been undertaken for employment-related reasons but because the family wished to change location for purely personal reasons, such as climate. Families are encouraged to move before retirement rather than after. The thirty-five-mile rule obviously encourages people moving within large metropolitan areas to select a new residence at least this far from the old.

Travel and entertainment expenses. Some travel expenses are obviously necessary to earn income (for example, those of a lawyer who travels to another city to conduct a case). Certain entertainment expenses are also necessary for earning income—a salesman taking a client to lunch, for example. But this category typically involves a combination of business and consumption activity. A major travel issue relates to professional persons who attend conventions away from home, thereby gaining both professional and personal benefit, the former often being very limited. The fondness of various groups for holding conventions at Banff or on Caribbean cruise ships demonstrates this combination of benefits. The deductibility of travel expenses encourages the use of more expensive accommodations. Entertaining customers involves the same issues; the deductibility of expensive dinners allows both the persons themselves and their clients to enjoy meals on a tax deductible basis. Quite apart from the question of the propriety of the deduction has been the tendency to pad the figures, reporting charges that were not actually made or that were made for other members of the taxpayer's family.

Although major limitations and even the denial of this deduction have been proposed, Congress has imposed relatively few limitations. Legislation passed in 1976 does restrict deductible expenses for foreign conventions to two conventions a year and contains other restrictions as well,[4] plus the incredible rule that the taxpayer must attach to his return a statement signed by the sponsor of the convention that the person has attended two-thirds of the total hours of scheduled sessions each day. Such control cannot possibly be implemented to attain the objective, and the rule will most likely become a mere formality.

4. One consequence, already apparent, is the increase in the number of conventions being held in Puerto Rico and Hawaii. The failure to exclude conventions in Canada from the "foreign conventions" rule was unfortunate, since the two principal Canadian convention cities, Montreal and Toronto, are conveniently close to major U.S. metropolitan areas.

The simplest solution, although somewhat arbitrary, would be to limit the deduction of expenses of attending foreign conventions to a specified sum—perhaps $1,000 a year—and to apply a separate limit to domestic conventions as well. A schedule of maximum amounts deductible for meals and accommodations and travel would also have merit.

Miscellaneous deductions related to the expenses of gaining an income. A limited list of items directly related to gaining an income, including union dues and membership in professional organizations, the cost of certain types of necessary work uniforms and tools, and the like, is deductible. There is little objection to such deductions; the only difficulty is that they are treated as personal deductions and thus are not available to a person using the standard deduction. The reason for not treating them as business deductions per se is for simplification; the typical employee does not have other business deductions.

Casualty Losses

Casualty losses are essentially negative incomes; by reducing net wealth, under the Simons definition they reduce the amount of positive income during the period. U.S. law authorizes the deduction of personal casualty losses (in excess of insurance received) in excess of $100. This floor is designed to avoid the nuisance of handling many small deductions and is also justified on the grounds that all families have some losses.

In principle, the deduction is justifiable. The major objection raised is that most of these losses are insurable risks; therefore, since insurance premiums are not deductible, the uninsured are favored and incentive is given not to carry insurance.

Deductions of Personal Consumption Expenditures

The true personal deductions relate strictly to consumption expenditures.

Medical Expenses

The deduction for medical expenses in excess of 3 percent of adjusted gross income was introduced in 1942 at the time the coverage of the tax was greatly expanded. The limitation to expenses above 3 percent was established on the grounds that since all families have certain health expenses there is no need to allow a deduction until the expenditures become significant relative to income. The category of deductible medical expenses is broad, but only those for drugs and medicines in excess of 1 percent of adjusted gross income are eligible. Up to $150 of premiums paid for health insurance is deductible without regard to the 3 percent ceiling.

The medical expense deduction is based on the philosophy that medical expenditures are essentially involuntary, that they are necessitated by misfortune, and that their magnitude may be such as to reduce tax capacity drastically. The very uneven incidence of medical expenses by family suggests the importance of need rather than choice. Health insurance makes the problem less serious but by no means eliminates it, and the more rapid rise in hospital costs than in incomes in the last decade has aggravated the problem. In a sense the government becomes a partial insurer of medical expenses not covered by other insurance.

While the argument for this deduction is strong, certain objections can be raised. The most basic is that a substantial voluntary element is involved in the actual expenditures, however necessary medical care may be. A person may have little choice about having an appendicitis operation, but he can choose the type of medical and hospital care that he receives. For many ailments the type of treatment varies substantially in cost, at the patient's discretion. Second, the deduction inevitably increases the amounts that people, especially in the higher income groups, spend on medical care. To a degree this may be defended on social policy grounds, but much of the additional spending generated by the deduction is likely to be made for "luxury" aspects of medical care. A third problem is the delimitation of medical expenditures from other expenses, since the category is not easily defined. Goode provides a number of examples of seemingly conflicting interpretations by the Internal Revenue Service.[5] It can be argued that the current interpretation of medical expenses is unnecessarily broad and that only major necessary items, such as physicians' charges, expensive drugs, X-rays, and hospital expenses, should be deductible. (The issue of deduction versus tax credit will be discussed below.)

The deduction as it stands favors the uninsured over the insured in

5. Richard Goode, *The Individual Income Tax,* rev. ed. (Brookings Institution, 1976), pp. 158–59.

a sense, despite the $150 insurance deduction that is not subject to the 3 percent limit. But it in no way compensates for all the medical expenses in the event of major illness and is hardly likely to alter one's decision about carrying insurance, particularly with the $150 deduction authorized.

Contributions

The most important deduction, dollarwise, and the most debated, is that of contributions to charitable, religious, educational, and similar institutions, and governmental units. The organizations must be recognized by the IRS as eligible institutions; they may not spend any of the money for the benefit of private shareholders and they are limited as to propaganda and lobbying activities. Limits are set on the amounts of the contributions: for most types, the total cannot exceed 50 percent of adjusted gross income, with a lower limit of 20 percent on contributions to certain foundations and other organizations. By far the largest amount—$10.3 billion in 1973—is given for religion. In 1973 education received $4.4 billion, health $3.9 billion, social welfare $2.1 billion, the arts and humanities $1.7 billion, and all other $3.2 billion.[6]

There are several ways of looking at this deduction, but primarily it reflects the desire of Congress to encourage people to make gifts to these organizations, whose activities contribute to the welfare of society. In part these activities would otherwise be undertaken by federal, state, and local governments, and government spending would be higher. There is widespread acceptance of the point of view that not all higher education, welfare, scientific research, and related activity should be financed and controlled by government. Much of the total money contributed is given for religious activity—a function that the government by constitutional prohibition cannot finance, yet many, though certainly not all, regard it as an activity that government should encourage. It may also be argued that from the standpoint of the donor, making a contribution reduces taxpaying capacity. The greatest organized support for the deduction comes from churches, charities, foundations, and the like, that benefit; their officials are convinced that without the deduction total giving would be very much less.

6. *Giving in America: Toward a Stronger Voluntary Sector,* Report of the Commission on Private Philanthropy and Public Needs (The Commission, 1975), p. 15.

On the other hand, the deductibility of such contributions has received substantial criticism. A basic objection is that giving is a voluntary act on the part of the donors—a preferred type of consumption expenditure yielding satisfaction in the same fashion as other expenditures. Another issue centers on the type of activity carried on by the recipients, particularly by various organizations designed in fact to propagate a particular point of view that society generally may regard as trivial or objectionable—the preservation of field mice or the establishment of rights for homosexuals, for example. A number of extreme right-wing groups take the form of fundamentalist religious organizations. Some of the criticisms may be regarded as unwarranted because they reflect the particular biases of the critics, but others have widespread support. Yet evaluation of the importance of the recipient organization to society by the IRS is open to question, and on the few occasions when it was attempted it led to strong complaints. The result, however, is that the government, through forgone tax revenue, is essentially subsidizing activities that Congress could not or would not consider financing directly. The defenders of deductibility counter with the argument that the need for minority expression and innovational ideas more than offsets these objections.

Many contributions serve to support activities such as luxurious suburban churches and expensive private colleges that primarily benefit the upper income groups. In the past at least, and to some extent at present, contributions to foundations have been a device to reduce the contributors' tax liability. The funds would be used to acquire income-yielding property for the use of the donors; they would not have title to this property, but they would benefit from its use. Legislation now seeks to prevent this abuse.

The amount of outright evasion is limited because the taxpayer can be required to provide evidence. The rule that deduction is denied if the funds are designated by the donor for the benefit of a particular recipient is difficult to enforce, but in many cases the inability to control does little harm since the persons benefiting would qualify for assistance under general rules.

A major question is the effectiveness of the deduction in encouraging additional contributions.[7] Clearly, elimination of the deduction

---

7. This aspect has been of particular concern in recent years because contributions by individuals as a percentage of personal income have been declining—by about 15 percent, from 2.0 to 1.7 percent of personal income between 1960 and 1972. *Giving in America*, p. 71.

would reduce gifts by very wealthy persons because they would simply have less to give. The controversy centers on incentive effects. In a study in 1967 Michael Taussig concluded that the effects on giving are very limited and confined to high-income taxpayers.[8] But in more recent studies Martin Feldstein concluded the opposite: that the effect is substantial, and that the organizations would lose more in revenue than the Treasury would gain in taxes if the deduction were eliminated.[9] The overall effects would be to reduce giving by about 20 percent, but with widely different effects on various types of organizations—a 50 percent fall in giving to hospitals and educational institutions but a decline of only 14 percent in giving to religious organizations. Two reasons account for the differences: giving to churches is more heavily concentrated in the lower and middle income groups that are subject to lower tax rates, and many people feel more strongly impelled to give regularly to their churches. Most of the contributions to religious organizations come from people having an adjusted gross income (AGI) of under $15,000, while 70 percent (1962) of the gifts to educational institutions and hospitals come from those with an AGI of over $15,000.[10]

Both Feldstein and Robert Schwartz have concluded that the incentive effects per se are much the same in the lower and higher income groups, although the dollar magnitudes are greater in the higher income groups.[11] It must be remembered, however, that many people in the lower income groups use the standard deduction and are not affected by the deduction of contributions.

The provision of a ceiling on contributions is designed to prevent the wealthy from diverting too much of their income away from taxes in support of activities of their own choices. The present 50 percent figure may be regarded as excessively high, though few people reach it.

8. Michael K. Taussig, "Economic Aspects of the Personal Income Tax Treatment of Charitable Contributions," *National Tax Journal*, vol. 20 (March 1967), pp. 1–19.

9. See Martin Feldstein, "The Income Tax and Charitable Contributions," pt. 1: "Aggregate and Distributional Effects," *National Tax Journal*, vol. 28 (March 1975), pp. 81–100; and pt. 2: "The Impact on Religious, Educational and Other Organizations," ibid. (June 1975), pp. 209–26. See also Martin Feldstein and Charles T. Clotfelter, "Tax Incentives and Charitable Contributions in the United States," *Journal of Public Economics*, vol. 5 (January-February 1976), pp. 1–26.

10. Feldstein, "The Income Tax and Charitable Contributions," pt. 2, p. 214.

11. Robert A. Schwartz, "Personal Philanthropic Contributions," *Journal of Political Economy*, vol. 78 (November-December 1970), pp. 1264–91.

There would be substantial merit, from the standpoint of protecting revenue, in allowing a deduction of only the amount over a certain percentage of AGI. This would continue to supply incentive for giving large amounts, in fact perhaps increasing the incentive for those near the eligibility line. It would also eliminate large numbers of small claimed deductions, which are difficult to check. A 3 percent floor, near the average of contributions relative to AGI but far below the figure at the higher income levels, would increase tax revenues by $4.2 billion, with possibly little effect on actual giving. A more complex but more satisfactory system, in terms of equity and incentive effects, would establish the floor on a graduated basis, with higher percentages in the upper income levels than in the lower. Any floor system does lead to bunching of gifts in certain years.

Another issue relates to gifts made in kind. Gifts of property are deductible; those of personal services are not, since no taxable income is involved. The law now seeks to prevent the deduction of the "value" of personal papers and similar items produced by the donor. But gifts of property that has increased in value are valued on a current basis, while the accrued capital gain involved is not taxed, with minor exceptions. The result is to encourage giving in this form and in effect to allow the escape of appropriate payment of tax on capital gains. A related problem is evasion through overstatement of the values of items that do not have an easily ascertained market value. The simplest solution is to allow only the original cost to be deducted; the donor can always sell the property and give the proceeds if he prefers.

State and Local Taxes

The deductibility of taxes paid to states and local governments is based on two objectives. The first is that of intergovernmental fiscal relations—the desire to facilitate financing state and local government activities in view of the lesser overall financial resources of these levels of government. The second is the argument that taxes paid by individuals to state and local governments reduce their tax capacity, constituting compulsory obligations rather than discretionary expenditures for consumption purposes. The granting of the deduction was also encouraged by acceptance of the nonsensical notion that failure to do so results in a "tax on a tax."

Present legislation allows the deduction of state and local property, income, sales, and gasoline taxes. Taxes that are not deductible include excises on liquor, tobacco, and other products other than gasoline; motor vehicle and driver's license charges; and other state and local levies such as admissions and transfer taxes. Death and gift taxes and special assessments are likewise nondeductible. Real property taxes constitute the major deductible item, in dollar terms, followed by income, sales, gasoline, and personal property taxes in that order.[12]

The intergovernmental argument is not without merit. The deduction does avoid the possible confiscatory income taxation that could otherwise occur if the combined marginal rates exceeded 100 percent or approached it, although they do not currently do so. The deduction provides an element of coordination of the taxes of the various levels of government and to some extent increases the taxing capacity of the states and local governments. In particular it should lessen resistance to the introduction of state income taxes, but the extent to which the resistance to these taxes and to state and local taxes generally is lessened is unknown. Does a person voting on a local school property tax rate increase take into consideration the deductibility of the property tax?

Justification on the "obligatory payment" basis is much weaker. It is true that state and local taxes are mandatory payments, and particular individuals may strongly object to the amounts they must pay because the level of governmental services may far exceed their demand for the services at existing tax prices. But for the community as a whole, state and local tax payments constitute voluntary payments for services rendered and are as discretionary as the purchase of new cars or suits of clothes.

The strongest case can be made for the deductibility of state income taxes because the gains from fiscal coordination are greatest in this field, and the potential effect in lessening opposition to increases in state taxes is greater with this levy than with others because of the progressive rate structure. The deductibility of sales taxes probably has little effect on voter choices and is little more than a windfall gain to the taxpayers. But the argument is advanced that failure to provide it would discriminate against taxpayers in those states that rely primarily on this form of tax. One solution is to disallow the deduction of the sales tax and the portion of income tax payments under 2 percent of AGI. This would avoid possible confiscatory combined rates

12. The personal property tax deduction is a relatively small item and is not discussed further.

and would lessen the opposition of the wealthy to state income taxes.

The real property tax is the most debatable category. On the one hand, the deduction favors the homeowner over the tenant, who has no equivalent deduction and who presumably bears part or all of the property tax burden on the property, at least under widely accepted views of the incidence of the tax.[13] But the property tax is by far the heaviest state-local tax on typical middle-income taxpayers and the one about which they are most conscious. For many people in the lower middle-income groups, the tax constitutes a substantial percentage of income, and disallowance of the deduction would add materially to their tax burdens, even though they are subject to relatively low income tax rates. Nondeductibility would in all likelihood increase the resistance to property tax rate increases and aggravate still more the financing of local government activity, particularly of education. The standard deduction offers some assistance to the lower-income tenants.

Deductibility of the gasoline tax, a road-user charge, has no justification whatever—certainly no more than for highway tolls or the cost of gasoline. Congress quite legitimately places the cost of the federally financed highway system on the road users and then takes part of it off for those subject to federal income taxes. Furthermore, by reducing the cost of car travel, the deduction may affect one's choice between driving and using public transport and hence be contrary to the public policy of seeking to lessen energy use, pollution, and congestion. Attempts to eliminate this deduction always encounter the argument that doing so would increase the cost of driving to work. This is nonsense, given the accepted system of road financing and the general disallowance of a deduction for commuting expenses.

Interest

The deduction of interest on debt for consumption purposes, one not found in other countries, reflects two motives: the desire to avoid the need to distinguish between interest on loans for production pur-

13. The tenant does not bear the burden under more recently advanced theories of incidence that conclude that the tax rests on all capital owners. But this argument is based on a number of assumptions that are open to question. A summary of the issues relating to incidence is presented in George F. Break, "The Incidence and Economic Effects of Taxation," in Alan S. Blinder and others, *The Economics of Public Finance* (Brookings Institution, 1974), pp. 154–68. See also Henry J. Aaron, *Who Pays the Property Tax? A New View* (Brookings Institution, 1975).

poses and those for consumption purposes (the original motive for congressional action), and the argument that interest payments are obligatory and reduce tax capacity. The deduction also equalizes somewhat between a family that owns its home but has a heavy mortgage and a family with a home of equivalent value but with full equity. In this sense the deduction is an adjustment to bring tax liability more in line with tax capacity. It should be noted that in the United States all interest is deductible regardless of the purpose of the loan, except on loans to acquire tax-free securities, on loans on certain life insurance premiums, and in part on loans for financial investments.

The deduction does help to bring tax payments more closely in line with capacity when, for example, a homeowner having 100 percent equity is compared with one having 20 percent. But the deduction creates serious inequity between homeowners and tenants, whose rent payments presumably cover the landlord's interest (actual or implicit), yet tenants are allowed no deduction. The source of the difficulty is the failure to include the imputed value of owner-occupied homes in taxable income; if this were included, the deduction of interest would create no inequities. But such a change is most unlikely.

Logically, interest on money borrowed for business purposes should be deductible and that for consumption use should not be. But drawing a line between the two is difficult, as has been demonstrated by Canadian experience with such a rule. One person may borrow with the security of a mortgage on his home in order to expand his business, while another may borrow with the security of his store to build a home. The security used is not conclusive. The result in Canada has been substantial litigation and obvious inequity. Attempts have been made to trace the use of the particular borrowed funds, but this has proved to be very troublesome. Whether the interest is deductible or not depends primarily on the particular form of the transaction—whether the taxpayer tied the loan funds to a particular business purpose.[14] Efforts to substantiate this purpose lead to manipulation of borrowing policy. U.S. taxpayers, however, must already separate investment interest from other interest because of the limitations on the deductibility of the former. It appears feasible, though admittedly there would be problems, to apply the same rule to interest on home and other nonbusiness loans, with deductibility up to the

14. This is explained in Gordon Bale, "The Interest Deduction Dilemma," *Canadian Tax Journal,* vol. 21 (July-August 1973), pp. 317–36.

amount of property income plus a specified figure, perhaps $3,600. This rule would still allow the deduction of interest on the typical home (roughly up to a $45,000 mortgage), yet would prevent the deduction of very large sums.

The argument that interest payments are obligatory is technically true, but a large portion of borrowing is discretionary—to buy a new home, car, or other consumer durable sooner than otherwise, for example. The amount of borrowing arising out of dire emergency (serious illness, for example) is only a small portion of the total.

Alimony

The deductibility of alimony payments reflects the fact that the payments are mandatory; the amounts are available to the recipient, not to the payer, for personal purposes. This is not essentially a deduction in any usual sense but recognition of the legal reassignment of income, and alimony is appropriately deductible in the same fashion as business expenses.[15]

Political Contributions

A relatively new deduction is that for political contributions, up to a maximum of $100 ($200 for a married couple), or an alternative of a credit of $25 ($50 for a married couple). This deduction reflects the objective of Congress in seeking wider support for political campaigns in lieu of large contributions from wealthy donors.

Possible Deductions to Stimulate Saving

The United States offers no deductions that have the objective of increasing savings and lessening consumption,[16] a policy followed in some developing countries where, for example, premiums paid on life insurance and amounts deposited in savings accounts may be totally or partially deducted, a practice designed to encourage people both to save and to carry insurance. To allow the deduction of net amounts saved would convert the levy to an expenditure tax, a change beyond the scope of this paper. To allow the deduction of certain types of savings not only encourages the use of this particular form of keeping

15. This was recognized by Congress in the Tax Reform Act of 1976, which allowed the deduction of alimony from gross income in addition to the use of the standard deduction.

16. The provision allowing the assignment of income to individual retirement accounts and Keogh accounts could be regarded as an incentive for saving but is not a personal deduction in the usual sense.

savings, but is discriminatory according to personal preferences for outlets for accumulated savings. Any system other than one allowing the deduction of net savings creates opportunities for avoiding the intent of the law by adding to savings in the specific deductible forms and reducing other savings.

The Standard Deduction

The standard deduction, first provided in the United States in 1944, was designed to simplify the filling out of tax returns by people in the lower income groups. Beginning in 1977, the deduction is a flat $2,200 for single persons and $3,200 for married couples. For years the figure was 10 percent of AGI, with a maximum of $1,000 for both single or married persons.

The underlying philosophy of the standard deduction is somewhat ambiguous; essentially the law says that a taxpayer may deduct certain items; if he does not have actual deductions as large as the standard figure, he can deduct the latter anyway. The justification is that this simplifies tax returns, although the provision does have the incidental advantage of somewhat offsetting the discrimination against tenants, who are unable to benefit from the property tax or the interest deduction. The standard deduction was used on about two-thirds of all returns in 1974, primarily those of the lower income groups. From a high of 80 percent in 1945, the figure fell steadily for a number of years because of rising money incomes and the long-frozen $1,000 maximum. The most objectionable feature of the rule is that the maximum for a married couple is less than twice that for a single person; thus when a couple marry, their standard deduction falls. This is one of the major ways in which the income tax discriminates against marriage, by increasing the tax of a couple if they marry under circumstances that make the standard deduction preferable to the itemization of deductions.

The lack of rationale for the standard deduction, coupled with the desire to maximize revenue, has led to the suggestion of a floor under all deductions so that only totals in excess of a specified percentage of adjusted gross income would be deductible. But on a blanket basis such a floor is questionable because of the unlike nature of the various deductible items, even though it can be used satisfactorily for particular categories. When proposed to Congress in the 1960s by the Treasury Department, it received no serious consideration.

Deductions versus Tax Credits

The feature of the deduction system subjected to the most severe criticism is the so-called upside-down-subsidy aspect: the tax reduction, and thus in a sense the tax subsidy, is inversely related to income. A person in the 70 percent bracket will bear only 30 percent of the cost of additional charitable contributions; one in the 14 percent bracket will bear 86 percent. Or conversely, the government in a sense matches any contribution by persons in the top bracket to the extent of 70 percent of the amount, but only 14 percent for persons in the lowest bracket and not at all for those who are not subject to tax. The same is true of taxes; the federal government absorbs 70 percent of the cost of property tax payments in the top bracket, but only 14 percent in the lowest.

A solution would be to authorize tax credits instead of deductions, as provided for child care. For example, taxpayers might be authorized to credit against tax liability 25 percent of all contributions made. Thus the tax saving and the "tax subsidy" would be the same percentage of the contribution at all income levels. If a figure equal to the average ratio of contributions to incomes were used, those in the lower brackets would be allowed to deduct more per dollar of contribution or state and local taxes paid than at present and those in the top income brackets much less.

Two objections may be raised against this approach. First, it is clearly inappropriate for deductions designed to allow more correct determination of taxable income (moving expenses, such educational expenses as are deductible, casualty losses, and so on). Ironically, the one use made of the credit in lieu of a deduction is for dependent care, essentially an adjustment to arrive at correct taxable income. Second, the credit may reduce the incentive effect when the deduction is designed to encourage a particular expenditure—for example, charitable contributions. The greatest incentive effect is presumably in the upper income groups, and the incentive for such groups is presumably less with the credit. Similarly, when the objective is fiscal coordination, the credit is less effective; combined marginal income tax rates could exceed 100 percent. Despite these limitations, however, further consideration of the credit approach is warranted, particularly for medical expenses, because there is no public benefit in encouraging higher expenditures for health care by the higher income groups.

Allocation of Personal Deductions

A common criticism of personal deductions is that they are allowed in total regardless of whether the income is gained entirely from taxable sources or not. To take an extreme example, a family receives $100,000 in exempt state and local bond interest and $20,000 in taxable interest, and contributes $20,000 to charities. Accordingly, the family pays no tax at all on the $20,000 of normally taxable income. The plan has been advanced at times to allow the deduction of only the fraction of total deductions equal to the fraction of total income that consists of taxable income. Thus in the example above only one-sixth of the $20,000 contribution, or $3,333, would be allowed as a deduction, under the presumption that it was made proportionately from exempt and taxable income.

Clearly this rule should not be applied to deductions allowed to attain a more satisfactory definition of income. Otherwise, it has merit in the interests of equity. The one objection against the allocation of charitable contributions would be the loss of incentive effects. Only a fraction would be deductible if the family had much nontaxable income. But the principal objection that should be raised, however, is not related to equity but to compliance and administration. Serious problems would be encountered in determining the amounts of some of the nontaxable income items—particularly various tax deferral techniques where the current value is not known. The elements in the minimum tax could of course be used as a rough guide, which would be better than none at all. The one attempt made by the Treasury (1969) to get Congress to introduce this rule was approved by the House but not by the Senate.

Distribution Pattern of Gains from Deductions

Two analyses were made of the distribution of the benefits of deductions by income class. The results of the first are summarized in table 2-1, which is based on data from the IRS *Statistics of Income* for 1973, the latest available. The second was based on the Brookings MERGE File data.

Regressive Deductions

A deduction is regarded as regressive if the tax saving from it constitutes a higher percentage of income in high-income groups than in

Table 2-1. Personal Deductions as Percentage of Adjusted Gross Income, by Income Class, 1973

Adjusted gross income class (thousands of dollars)	Interest paid		Medical and dental expenses	Contributions[b]	Taxes paid					Miscellaneous		
	Home mortgage	Total[a]			Real estate	State and local gasoline	Sales	State and local income	Total taxes[a]	Casualty losses	Child- and dependent- care expenses	Total miscellaneous[e]
1–3	17.9	14.9	19.3	8.5	21.2	2.3	2.6	2.1	14.4	[d]	...	5.8
3–5	13.0	12.5	14.0	6.1	9.0	1.8	2.5	2.2	11.4	12.0	16.1	6.4
5–7	10.9	10.1	8.8	5.0	6.9	1.3	2.2	2.1	9.8	8.6	14.7	4.8
7–9	9.1	9.6	6.5	3.8	4.9	1.1	2.0	2.4	8.6	4.8	8.8	3.8
9–11	7.7	9.1	4.9	3.1	4.2	1.0	1.9	2.4	8.3	5.2	6.0	3.3
11–13	7.0	8.7	3.8	2.8	3.6	0.9	1.8	2.6	8.2	4.1	5.6	3.1
13–15	6.4	8.1	3.1	2.8	3.4	0.8	1.8	2.7	8.1	3.7	4.9	2.9
15–20	5.6	7.2	2.2	2.4	3.2	0.7	1.6	2.9	8.0	2.6	4.3	2.5
20–25	5.1	6.5	1.7	2.4	3.0	0.6	1.5	3.3	7.9	1.9	2.9	1.9
25–50	4.3	5.8	1.4	2.5	2.9	0.4	1.2	4.1	7.9	1.6	2.8	2.1
50–100	2.9	5.5	1.0	3.2	2.3	0.2	0.8	5.2	7.7	1.8	1.0	2.3
100–200	1.8	6.0	0.7	4.4	1.8	0.1	0.6	5.8	7.5	1.7	0.9	2.6
200–500	1.1	7.2	0.5	6.9	1.5	*	0.4	6.4	7.4	1.4	0.2	3.1
500–1,000	0.7	6.8	0.2	9.9	1.2	*	0.2	6.6	7.2	1.3	0.0	3.1
1,000 and over	0.3	5.3	*	14.0	0.8	*	0.2	6.9	7.0	1.2	0.0	3.2
All classes	5.5	7.1	2.6	2.9	3.2	0.6	1.5	3.5	8.0	2.7	5.3	2.6

Source: U.S. Internal Revenue Service, *Statistics of Income—1973, Individual Income Tax Returns* (Government Printing Office, 1976), tables 2.4, 2.5, 2.6, 2.7, 2.9. Data are taken from taxable individual income tax returns with itemized deductions.

a. Percentages are computed on the basis of adjusted gross income for persons itemizing each deduction. Therefore, percentages for total deductions in any category may be lower than the percentage for particular deductions in that category.

b. Does not include political contributions, which are included in total miscellaneous.

c. Includes deductions not shown separately.

d. Not shown separately because of small size of sample.

* 0.05 or less.

low-income groups, that is, if the deduction lessens the progressivity of the income tax. The contributions deduction, which is steeply regressive in the upper income brackets, begins to rise above the $25,000 income bracket. But in the lower and middle income ranges, which include most taxpayers, the deduction is nearly proportional, constituting from 2.4 to 2.8 percent of AGI for those with incomes between $11,000 and $50,000.[17] Below $11,000, the deduction is progressive, revealing in part the contributions made by elderly persons who have low current taxable incomes but substantial wealth and in part the use of the standard deduction by persons who make small contributions. Of necessity state and local income taxes, which are progressive in effect (and most are progressive in rate), rise steadily as a percentage of income as income rises, and therefore are regressive in effect.

There are no other regressive deductions.

The Most Progressive Deductions

Most of the deductions are progressive in effect, constituting declining percentages of AGI as AGI rises. The effect, therefore, is to make the tax structure more progressive relative to AGI than otherwise.

Three categories are steeply progressive:

—Child care, with the cutoff feature that denied the deduction in 1973 to families in higher income groups.

—Medical care, continuously and remarkably progressive throughout. Though the wealthy may obtain more luxurious medical care, the deduction constitutes a declining percentage of AGI. This is attributable to greater difficulty in exceeding the 3 percent floor at higher incomes.

—Sales taxes and gasoline taxes, reflecting the declining percentage of expenditures subject to tax in relation to income.

Deductions with Moderate Progression

The two categories related to home ownership—real property taxes and interest on home mortgages—are moderately progressive over a wide range of income, more steeply at the lower income ranges.

17. Figures indicate lower end of bracket.

Deductions with a Substantial Proportional Range

Total interest payments are steeply progressive at the lower income levels, close to proportional with only a slight degree of progression from the $7,000 to $50,000 income brackets, slightly regressive from $50,000 to $200,000, and then progressive again. Casualty losses are nearly proportional from $20,000 to the top income levels and are progressive at lower levels.

By far the most important items, percentagewise, to the lowest income group are interest, medical, and real estate tax deductions, while at the highest income levels contributions are the top item, followed by taxes and interest.

The basic difficulty with these figures is that they reflect itemized deductions only, and therefore the lower income group sample consists of only those who have relatively high individual deduction items, particularly, homeowners. There is no satisfactory way to introduce standard deductions into the tables. Were the standard deduction not available, the deductions as percentages of AGI at the lower levels would be much lower than at present, and the deductions would be less progressive or more regressive than they now are. The standard deduction system thus materially improves the distributional effects of the personal deductions, given the present structure.

The lower income groups include a number of retired persons whose current incomes are lower than their average lifetime incomes; accordingly the regressive distributive impact of random deductions is less serious than it would be under usual standards of equity.

The progressivity or regressivity of a deduction is certainly not the sole criterion for evaluation. The deductions that are essentially costs of earning an income cannot be appropriately judged on this basis, any more than business deductions can be. The state income tax deduction, designed primarily to lessen resistance to the introduction of, and increases in, state income taxes and to avoid confiscatory marginal rates, is inevitably regressive in effect. The high regressivity of the contributions deduction at the upper income levels suggests that the deduction may be attaining its objective of encouraging contributions by the wealthy.

Table 2-2 shows the amount of tax saving from the various deductions expressed as a percentage of tax that would be paid without present personal deductions, in various comprehensive income

Table 2-2. Tax Savings from Deductions Expressed as Percentage of Tax That Would Be Paid under 1976 Law without Deductions but with a Comprehensive Income Base, by Income Class

| Comprehensive income class (thousands of dollars) | Interest paid | | Contri- butions | Taxes paid | | | All personal deduc- tions |
	Home mort- gage	Other		Real estate	State and local gasoline	State and local income	
2.5–5	1.4	0.3	9.2	18.2	2.7	0.4	23.8
5–7.5	1.0	0.5	2.3	1.8	0.5	0.3	8.1
7.5–10	1.5	0.5	1.7	1.5	0.5	0.4	7.0
10–15	2.3	0.8	2.1	1.9	0.6	0.7	9.0
15–20	3.2	0.8	2.6	2.5	0.7	1.2	9.1
20–25	4.0	0.9	2.7	3.1	0.8	1.7	8.5
25–30	4.2	1.3	3.0	3.5	0.8	2.2	10.3
30–50	4.4	1.4	3.7	4.0	0.7	3.1	13.5
50–100	3.0	2.4	4.9	3.9	0.4	5.0	20.2
100–200	1.3	2.8	4.8	2.5	0.1	6.4	21.9
200–500	0.5	4.3	5.2	1.5	0.1	4.8	19.8
500–1,000	0.3	4.4	8.2	1.3	0.1	5.0	23.8
1,000 and over	0.1	2.6	7.3	0.5	*	2.7	15.6

Source: Brookings MERGE File.
* Less than 0.05.

classes, based on the Brookings MERGE File. The data differ from those of table 2-1 in several ways.

First, the tax savings from the deductions are expressed as a percentage of the total *tax* that would be paid under the present income tax but without personal deductions. By contrast, table 2-1 shows the amount of the deductions expressed as a percentage of reported AGI. But both measures show the effect of the deductions on the progressivity of the tax.

Second, the income brackets in table 2-2 are based on estimates of comprehensive income, those in table 2-1 on AGI. Since total income is much greater than AGI, the brackets are not at all equivalent; total comprehensive income is roughly 25 percent greater than total AGI. Furthermore, nontaxable income as a percentage of total income rises as income rises; thus the gap between the two measures of income is greater at higher income levels.

The basic results are comparable in many respects. Tax savings from contributions fall sharply in the lower income ranges and then rise steadily until the over-$1 million bracket. Savings from the income tax deduction rise steadily to the $100,000 bracket and then move irregularly, with a decided fall at the top bracket. The fall occurs because so much income at this level is nontaxable. The gasoline tax, however, while much lower in percentage at the top levels, is roughly proportional to total tax payments over much of the comprehensive income range. Real estate taxes fall initially, then rise to the $50,000 income level, probably reflecting the increased percentage of home ownership, and then fall above this figure. The high figure for real estate taxes in the first income bracket is attributable to the fact that taxpayers in this bracket who itemize deductions are typically homeowners. Table 2-1 data show proportionality in the range in which table 2-2 data show a rise in the percentage, in part a result of progressive rates. Home mortgage interest, a declining percentage throughout in table 2-1, shows an increase up to $50,000 in income, and then a decline. Other interest rises throughout, except at the top income bracket.

Total deductions show a rising trend, except for a sharp drop from the first bracket, but with some irregularities, and a drop in the top bracket—the over-$1 million bracket, roughly equal to the $500,000–$1 million and over-$1 million brackets combined in table 2-1.

Proposed Changes

The changes proposed in this paper are based on the assumption that although Congress is unwilling to alter the basic concessions that have been made for certain types of expenditures, despite the varying degree of justification for them on usual standards, it would be both worthwhile and possible to reduce the total deductions, thus allowing lower tax rates. The specific proposals are as follows:

1. Establish a floor under the contributions deduction, preferably on a graduated scale as shown below:[18]

AGI	*Percentage*
(thousands of dollars)	*floor*
Under 5	1
5–10	2
10–50	3
50–100	4
100 and over	5

18. To avoid a notch problem, the floor for an AGI of $5,000–$10,000 would be calculated as $50 (1 percent of $5,000) plus 2 percent of the excess over $5,000, and so on.

This system seeks to acknowledge that lower-income people typically give lower percentages of their incomes than those in the highest income groups, and thus the incentive to give can be maintained only if a lower floor is used.

2. Eliminate the deduction of the gasoline tax. As explained above, this deduction makes no sense; there is no more reason to allow the deduction of the gas tax than of the cost of gasoline.

3. Eliminate the sales tax and the income tax deductions, except the portion of the income tax in excess of 2 percent of adjusted gross income. The deductibility of larger percentages of income tax is desirable to avoid excessive marginal income tax rates and to lessen the opposition by the wealthy to state income taxes. There is no need to allow the deduction of smaller payments or the sales tax.

4. Limit the entire interest deduction on personal loans and investment loans to $3,600 plus the sum of property income. The $3,600 would take care of the typical taxpayer paying interest on his home mortgage and thus would equalize the tax burden according to equity in the home but would restrict the gains to people with higher incomes and large interest payments.

5. Limit deductions for foreign convention travel to $1,000 a year and eliminate the current restrictions on the deductibility of the cost of attending foreign conventions because these restrictions are difficult to implement. Exempt conventions in Canada from the foreign convention rule. Limit meals and accommodations figures to specified amounts.

6. Reduce the standard deduction to 10 percent or less.

The revenue gain from the changes is estimated to be as follows in billions of dollars:[19]

Establishment of floor under contributions deductions	4.2
Elimination of gas tax deduction	1.1
Elimination of sales tax and income tax deductions, except for portion of income tax in excess of 2 percent of AGI	5.7
Limitation of interest deduction on personal loans	0.2
Limitation on convention deduction	negligible
Reduction in standard deduction	8.1
Total	20.5

In addition, those deductions related to earning income or constituting negative income (child care, casualty losses, educational de-

19. The total exceeds the sum of the items because increases in taxable incomes due to the elimination of deductions push taxpayers into higher rate brackets.

ductions, moving expenses, and deductible interest, plus miscellaneous items), should be separated and listed as business deductions, which the taxpayer would receive in addition to the standard deduction. This would reduce liabilities by about $0.2 billion.

One change is recommended for the educational deduction: to allow a deduction from the current wage income of the taxpayer or spouse of tuition and educational fees related to earning present or future income. It is difficult to estimate the revenue loss.

Conclusions

The personal deductions were introduced for a variety of reasons and have been retained and modified under diverse influences. One group consists of items that are essentially business deductions—the expenses of earning income—but that masquerade under the heading of personal deductions. The most controversial of these is the expense of gaining an education. Closely related is the category of casualty losses, which essentially constitute negative income. Eliminating the Big Four truly personal deductions—contributions, taxes, interest, and medical expenses—would appear to be politically impossible and, in complete form, doubtful in terms of equity and accepted policy. Strong pressure groups support them, and the philosophy underlying most of them is widely accepted. But their objectives could be attained in substantial measure even if the scope of the deductions were to be sharply curtailed, a step that would also increase revenue and allow lower tax rates. Only medical deductions would escape largely unscathed, primarily because they contribute most to progressivity and to the alleviation of hardships.

Providing a sliding scale for a ceiling under contributions, limiting the deduction for interest on nonbusiness (investment and personal) loans to property income plus $3,600, and limiting the tax deductions to real estate taxes and income tax in excess of 2 percent of AGI, while by no means free of problems and inequities, would materially increase tax revenue without significantly impeding the attainment of the objectives. But the expectation of even these changes is not too high: the basic problem is that those who gain most, directly or indirectly, from present deductions are well aware of the gains and fight to retain them, while the taxpayers as a whole, who would be the beneficiaries of the lower rates, are unaware of the potential gain or may fear that the rates would not be lowered, and they are not organized to fight for the curtailment of the deductions.

Comments by Donald C. Lubick

John Due's paper on personal deductions covers the subject admirably, stating the theoretical underpinnings of each one and the logical and practical difficulties inherent in proposals to make changes in each of them.

As a practitioner-lawyer rather than an academic, I have strong feelings that the time is ripe for a substantial move toward simplification—not only for the high-income taxpayer, but especially for the middle-income taxpayer. An essential ingredient of any tax reform program aimed at producing an income tax that achieves both horizontal and vertical equity is a radical reduction of available itemized personal deductions. It is also the logical way to raise revenue to permit the drastically lower rate scale across the board that will give the impetus needed to make major tax reform salable.

Although capital gains reform is not the subject of this discussion, a program to tax capital gains as ordinary income (with taxation of gains realized by gratuitous disposition) will permit a top marginal rate considerably below today's 70 percent. I would look to the elimination of personal deductions along with capital gains reform and other base-broadening to bring the top rate down to 40 percent, not very different from the current top capital gains rate. Lower marginal rates, made possible by reduced personal deductions, would in themselves help make uneconomical many tax shelter transactions that have been marketed in recent years.

A radical limitation of personal deductions would make it possible for the average taxpayer to prepare his own return, a return that would be shorter and more understandable. It would reduce the need for much recordkeeping by the average taxpayer. It would also reduce audit problems and permit the resources of the Internal Revenue Service to be allocated more efficiently.

Due identifies the special-interest groups that would be aroused—the charities, the homebuilders, the automobile clubs, and the like. They were heard from in 1963 when the administration proposed a 5 percent floor on itemized deductions. But they never had to face a proposal that promised truly major rate cuts and simplification. A program that showed deviations from present tax liabilities within a range of less than $100 for substantially all middle-income taxpayers just might be salable. Another factor today is the support for tax reform of public-interest groups that were not active fifteen years ago.

Due states in capsule form all the arguments for and against the deduction for charitable contributions. I come out where he does—that a floor is appropriate. I would not use a variable floor, because it introduces unnecessary complexity and hits harder at the top incomes where the tax incentive seems to be most productive of charitable giving. A 2 or 3 percent floor would eliminate most audit and record-keeping problems and leave the incentive where it is effective. It is hard to believe that taxes play any role for incentive to give at incomes below $10,000. I would not change the deductibility of appreciation for gifts of property. Especially if it is proposed to tax gains at gratuitous disposition, an exemption for charitable giving will provide a substantial incentive for the charities. I would want to limit the fight over the incentive argument to situations in which the historical evidence shows the tax incentive is unnecessary—hence the 3 percent floor.

Medical expenses and casualty losses are less difficult to deal with than others. The casualty floor of $100 might be changed to 2 or 3 percent of adjusted gross income if the loss is over $100, thus reducing the incentive not to carry insurance. Incidentally, lower marginal rates would also have the effect of reducing the insurance provided by the tax law.

I agree with Due on retaining the medical expense deduction for hardship cases. I might return to the 5 percent floor and put health insurance premiums back with other medical expenses.

I largely agree with Due on his evaluation of the deduction for taxes. I am glad to see he would retain the deductibility of income taxes, so that perhaps my agreement with him is not based solely on my desire to see New York State, with its 15 percent income tax, avoid disaster. One argument for the deductibility of income taxes is that the deductible items are in a sense an expense related to earning the income to be taxed by the federal government. I do not agree with Due's proposed 2 percent floor but would accept it to carry the day on eliminating the deductibility of sales and gasoline taxes.

I find it hard to include deductions for sales and gasoline taxes in a category of progressive deductions, as Due does. Although they may be progressive, if one's definition relates only to percentage of adjusted gross income, they are as good an illustration of giving relief to the wrong people as can be found in the tax code. At a time of energy crisis, subsidizing 70 percent of the gasoline taxes of low-miles-per-gallon gas guzzlers and only minimal amounts for thirty-miles-per-gallon small cars does not deserve the label of progressive.

I would also propose to eliminate the property tax deduction, which causes Due a great deal of anguish. Disallowance would not add materially to the tax burden of middle-income groups, as he suggests, because of concomitant rate reduction. Due's argument was used effectively against the 5 percent floor in 1963—that the proposal was cutting back on benefits to homeowners but protecting tenants by not touching the standard deduction. Since I would largely eliminate the standard deduction and thus obtain additional financing for rate reductions, I would keep the bottom-line tax liability of almost all lower-middle-income groups fairly close to the starting point. If forced to allow some deductions for property taxes, I would try to eliminate second residences and perhaps amounts over $1,000. The advent of revenue sharing may be useful in dealing with the objections of state and local governments to difficulties caused by such changes in deductibility.

The interest deduction presents the most troublesome difficulties. Due's proposal to allow personal and investment interest of $3,600 beyond property income is too generous because personal interest is really an expense of consumption. I would disallow interest that is not a business expense or an expense of producing income. Under present law home mortgage interest has been found not to be for the purpose of carrying tax-exempt securities, so arguably the corollary would be true that home mortgage interest would not be an expense of carrying one's interest-producing savings account.

Some economists argue that any loan, even if it is for a home mortgage or to finance consumption, enables the borrower to maintain his property productive of income. I find this argument difficult to answer. In addition, complete disallowance of a deduction for home mortgage interest, even where there is a small amount of property income, would favor wealthy taxpayers with high property income who can borrow against securities to finance a home purchase. This argument can be made regarding a disallowance of any home mortgage interest, but it would be less persuasive if the total reform package taxed capital gains fully and eliminated other preferences of high-income taxpayers. If it were necessary as a fallback, a certain amount of home mortgage interest on a principal residence could be allowed in excess of property income, but $3,600 is far too high.

As indicated above, I would cut out the standard deduction, except for a vanishing low-income allowance to prevent taxing the very poor on the first dollars of income. As Due points out, the only justification for the standard deduction is to provide some simplification. Except for employee business expenses, the simplification proposed above through the elimination of most itemized deductions ought to do the job. Some complication would still exist because taxpayers would have to itemize union dues, uniforms, tools, and the like.

Due dismisses out of hand the alternative of a floor on all itemized deductions. While it is a second choice to the program outlined above, it has more merit than he concedes. The 1963 proposal was presented basically as a device to raise revenue for tax cuts. A 5 percent floor provided no real simplification because it would not have shifted too many itemizers. It also did not affect the standard deduction, so it tilted against the perceived "good guys." It did not provide enough rate reduction to be attractive.

A floor of, say, 15 percent of itemized deductions, with abolition of the standard deduction save for a low-income allowance, would be different. The rate reductions and simplification effect would be substantial. The rationale is that personal deductions that do not have the same theoretical underpinning as business expenses may be claimed where in toto they constitute a significantly higher than normal portion of income. On balance, however, I am against this approach because it would retain the recordkeeping complications around the margin where it cuts in and is hard to explain.

As to the less important deductions, I would not expand the education deduction as Due proposes. As he points out, there are combined personal and income-producing aspects to this expenditure. Moving in the direction of allowing greater deductibility requires a higher burden of proof than is now available that educational outlays are current costs of producing income. There is too much of a capital and personal nature in educational expenditure to warrant relief.

I would like to eliminate the political contribution deduction. It is not fair to generalize from personal experience, but in raising funds for three local political campaigns since 1973, I do not believe a single contribution I have seen was induced by deductibility. The amount of deduction for high-income givers is too small to make a difference, and the amount of subsidy for middle-income givers is too small to be as efficient as a matching grant program.

The travel and entertainment expense area remains troublesome. Aside from the most exotic abuses, I do not believe the 1962 legislation seriously curbed expense account living on most taxpayers' travel and entertainment deductions. I would not accept Due's $1,000 a year limit on the deduction of expenses of attending foreign conventions. Such a proposal would distract from the more important ones. Moreover, to the extent that convention expenses are business related, it is too stringent.

To conclude, an income tax reform program should strive for a significantly broadened tax base that would permit a radically lower rate scale and provide greater simplification. Without major changes in personal deductions, I doubt that the revenue will be available to accomplish major tax reform. Reform in this area is needed not only on its merits, but also as a catalyst to upper bracket reform.

Comments by Charles E. McLure, Jr.

Following the time-honored tradition of discussants, I shall comment on omissions and points with which I disagree rather than on the many points in John Due's fine paper with which I do agree.

I was pleased to see the discussion of the crucial question of deductions versus tax credits. There is an unfortunate but pervasive tendency to prefer credits because they increase the progressivity of the income tax. I believe that in some instances tax relief should logically take the form of tax credits and in others, the form of deductions. While one may be willing to sacrifice logic in the design of tax policy on the altar of increased progressivity, he should recognize what he is doing and note that horizontal equity may be sacrificed as well.

Due notes two types of deductions: those needed to refine the definition of income and those that deliberately favor specific consumption expenditures. To these I would add (as he does implicitly) an intermediate type of deduction—adjustments to economic income required to reflect further differences in ability to pay, the most important of which is the deduction for medical expenses.

For the first purpose, deductions are clearly the preferable approach. It makes no sense to allow credits rather than deductions for the cost of earning income. As Due states, "The deductions that are essentially costs of earning an income cannot be appropriately judged on this basis [progressivity], any more than business deductions can be."[20] Moreover, Due is quite right in noting that the conversion of the deduction for child-care expense to a tax credit in 1976 was inappropriate. Whether the relief should be limited is less clear.

Similar reasoning applies to such items as medical expenses that reduce ability to pay at a given level of income. If ability to pay begins only after medical expenses have been met, a deduction should be allowed, even though the relief in terms of tax savings depends on the marginal tax rate of the taxpayer. If one argues instead that the government should provide partial medical insurance through the personal income tax, the tax credit makes sense and the deduction does not, since the fraction of medical expenses met by the government should be the same for all. But in this case any excess of credits over tax liability should be refunded. (Whether excess deductions should be refundable at some marginal tax rate is discussed further below.) I prefer the former rationale, but whichever is chosen, the policy should match the rationale. In either event a floor below which no relief is granted seems sensible. The two rationales also lead to different results in the case of casualty losses— reduction in ability to pay (negative income) implies a deduction, but partial federal insurance implies a credit (with refunds).

The same line of reasoning also supports the use of deductions for personal exemptions, and not credits, as the appropriate method of allowing for basic necessities and family size. That is, a certain allowance should be made in arriving at the amount of income that measures ability to pay, regardless of how far above the minimum tax-free income the family's income happens to be. The result is less progressive than the result with tax credits would be, but the deduction is logically consistent with the basic reason for allowing relief. In this sense the per capita credit allowed under the 1975 law and extended under the 1976 law is a step (although only a small one) in the wrong direction.

It is farfetched to regard charitable contributions as reducing ability to pay and therefore as being justifiable deductions, except in societies where such contributions are not voluntary. A more reason-

20. See p. 60 of this volume.

able rationale for tax relief for contributions is the "public-goods," or "externalities," argument—the government should encourage contributions to organizations engaged in activities that it might otherwise have to undertake. This rationale implies tax credits rather than deductions, since the degree of the publicness of various activities does not depend on the marginal tax rates of donors. (And so, for that matter, does relief for the costs of education based on "external benefit" grounds. Deduction is required only if educational expenses are regarded as costs of earning income.) Thus rather than placing a floor under contributions, I would prefer to see the deduction replaced with a credit. Note, in addition, that there is no case for the allocation of tax credits corresponding to that for the allocation of deductions on the basis of the rationale for tax credits presented here (for medical expenses and educational expenses, as well as for charitable contributions).

Replacing the charitable deduction with a tax credit costing the same amount of revenue would alter both the distribution of tax benefits among taxpayers and patterns of support in ways that some might not approve. But there is no reason to limit the credit to one rate. The American Cancer Society and the National Rifle Association, for example, might be granted different credit rates. Allowing different credits for different classes of institutions would raise difficult political questions, but that may be preferable to the all-or-nothing decision made under today's law.

Neither tax credits nor deductions should be allowed for state and local taxes. First, most state and local taxes can be thought of as being fairly closely related to benefits received; certainly the "layer-cake" model of fiscal federalism tells us that state and local governments should use benefit-type taxes. There is not much more reason to allow deductions or credit for such taxes than for private purchases of apples or oranges. Second, states can prevent total income tax rates from exceeding 100 percent simply by allowing deduction of the federal tax. This would be perfectly sensible because the federal income tax (1) does reduce the capacity to pay state income tax, and (2) is an instrument of redistribution rather than merely a benefit tax. Third, allowing relief for only the state income tax (or the part in excess of 2 percent of income) would discriminate against taxpayers living in states with sales taxes and would artificially encourage the use of the income tax, especially at progressive rates. Besides being inequitable, such a result is undesirable because it involves unwarranted federal interference in state fiscal decisions in a way that runs directly counter to the lesson of the layer-cake model that income redistribution should be primarily a federal function and is inappropriate for state and local governments. Finally, if relief is to be allowed for state and local taxes, it seems better on distributional and other grounds to allow it as a tax credit rather than as a deduction.

Due's discussion of the real estate tax raises a number of issues. First, the case for deductibility may depend on whether the incidence of the tax is viewed from the national or local perspective. The national perspective, which I prefer for this purpose, leads to the conclusion that the tax is borne by landlords, not by tenants. Second, even though tenants do not deduct property taxes, landlords—who are generally in higher marginal tax brackets—do. Thus the discrimination between renters and homeowners is not caused by the property tax deduction; it is the result of the exclusion of gross imputed income on owner-occupied housing. Third, I do not share Due's fear that nondeductibility of property taxes would raise resistance to property tax increases and be detrimental to local financing of education. It is not obvious to me that the property tax is a good local tax, and I would not greatly mourn its demise. Beyond that, education, like welfare, should be financed more heavily at the federal level, and local governments should rely more heavily on taxes related more directly to benefits. The latter should not be deductible, as Due notes.

The deduction for interest is also related to the treatment of the homeowner. The problem is that gross rental income is excluded from income for tax purposes, not that mortgage interest is deductible. Given that virtually every owner-occupied house in the nation is assessed for property tax purposes, it is not clear why assessment for income tax purposes is generally thought to be impractical. A more reasonable conclusion might be that federal-local cooperation could improve both the income and the property taxes.

It might be argued that for social reasons the tax preference for housing should not be eliminated. But perhaps such a preference should be available for all housing and not just for owner-occupied housing. The choice depends on equity considerations and whether "housing" or "owner-occupied housing" is thought worthy of public support. In either event the tax relief should not depend on the marginal tax rate of the taxpayer; that is, a credit would be preferable to a deduction. Unfortunately, there seems to be no administratively feasible way of allowing a credit for owner-occupants rather than a deduction. As a second-best alternative perhaps renters might be allowed to take either a deduction or a credit for rent, the latter to be calculated at the bottom tax rate (14 percent). Such a provision would help to equalize the treatment of tenants and owners, something Due's proposed limitation on interest expense would not do, since it would affect few families.

Another issue is whether credits and deductions should be made to vanish as income rises, as the earned-income credit does, for example. In cases where deductions are justified (that is, to improve the definition of income and to refine income to a measure of ability to pay), there is no reason why the amount of the deductions should be discounted as income rises, though the equity argument against discounting may not seem to be very strong, either. Similar arguments seem applicable to credits. But the effects the provisions for vanishing have on marginal tax rates should not be overlooked. The earned-income credit has the potentially salutary effect of reducing the effective marginal tax rate on earnings up to $4,000 by 10 percent. But between $4,000 and $8,000—the range over which the credit is phased out—the effective marginal tax rate is *increased* by 10 percent to roughly 30–35 percent if only the employee's contribution to social security is counted and to about 35–40 percent if the employer's contribution is also counted. Those who designed this feature probably did not want to achieve either the startling discontinuities in marginal tax rates (a jump of 20 percent at $4,000 and a fall of as much as 10 percent at $8,000) or the very high marginal rates in the $4,000–$8,000 range implied by the vanishing credit; they simply wanted to avoid giving the earned-income relief to all families with earned income. But the discontinuities and the incentive effects are certainly there, whether intended or not. They should serve as a warning against a proliferation of other vanishing deductions and credits: taking away a credit or a deduction as income rises is algebraically and economically equivalent to imposing a tax on the incremental income. At the very least an effort should be made to take account of payroll and income tax rates and the ranges over which (and rates at which) food stamps and other public assistance decline as income rises so as to avoid excessively high marginal tax rates.

Several points deserve to be made about the standard deduction. First, its character changed considerably in 1969 with the advent of the low-income allowance. The standard deduction has gone from being primarily a way of avoiding the need for most families to itemize deductions to being primarily low-income relief. Whereas the standard deduction and the personal exemptions now do fairly well in freeing poverty-level families from income tax, this was not the case before 1969. It is unclear whether Due would want to revert to the pre-1969 system by allowing a standard deduction of 10 percent (or less) of adjusted gross income and by eliminating the low-income allowance, or would simply use 10 percent of the amount of adjusted gross income above the low-income allowance (perhaps with a ceiling). Given the importance of the low-income allowance, one hopes he means the latter.

Second, the standard deduction has quite different effects in states with and without income taxes—at least in states that have substantially different levels of expenditures on state and local services. A healthy family in Texas that rents or owns its own home outright would generally be unlikely to itemize deductions, even at fairly high income levels. In New York, the reverse is true. A corollary of this is that beyond a certain point paying off one's mortgage in some states results in the saving of 100 percent interest dollars. Similarly, the deductions for contributions, medical expenses, and so on, cease to be effective in reducing taxes and thus—as with renters and the poor —are worth nothing.

My final point relates to an issue that was long a matter of concern to Professor Harold Groves but of little concern to the U.S. Congress: what to do about unused deductions and credits. The public goods arguments for the credit for charitable contributions and the insurance argument for a credit for medical expenses and casualty losses suggest that credits should be refundable if they exceed tax liabilities. One could also argue that excess deductions should be refundable (at some arbitrary marginal tax rate), or at least carried forward indefinitely. This could be especially important for medical expenses viewed as a reduction of taxpaying capacity, for the standard deduction and personal exemptions, and for educational expenses. Whereas indefinite carry-forward provides a rough measure of averaging, providing refunds can be seen as the germ of a negative income tax. A full-blown negative income tax could be achieved from such a modest start by increasing the personal exemption or low-income allowance and by providing nonproportional rates on negative taxable income.

CHAPTER THREE

Employee Benefits and Transfer Payments

EMIL M. SUNLEY, JR.

COMPREHENSIVE income taxation requires the elimination of exclusions and deductions that now erode tax revenues. This paper focuses on the major exclusions, namely, employee benefits and transfer payments, that benefit large numbers of taxpayers.[1] The elimination of these exclusions would be strongly resisted by affected taxpayers. Yet eliminating them and reducing marginal tax rates would yield substantial gains. Horizontal equity—the equal treatment of equals—would be improved, and the incentives to work, to save, and to take risks would be increased. The overall progressivity of the income tax could be maintained if the marginal rates were cut so that each income class would still pay the same average amount of tax.

Taxing employee benefits and transfer payments would not simplify the tax law. It must be recognized that an income tax that taxes employee benefits and transfer payments is more complex than one that does not. It is possible, however, to tax them so that taxpayers

1. The additional exemption for taxpayers aged sixty-five and over and interest on life insurance savings are two exclusions that affect large numbers of taxpayers and that each reduce federal revenues by at least $1 billion a year. These exclusions and a number of less important ones that primarily benefit low- and middle-income families are not considered in this chapter.

would be faced with little additional complexity. Employers could furnish each employee with a statement of his benefits. The government could furnish similar information about transfer payments. Taxable employee benefits and transfer payments would be made subject to withholding.

Employee benefits and transfer payments would be regarded as income under a comprehensive definition of income. The major issue is how they should be taxed, and this essentially is a question of whether one wants to tax the value of a right to receive a benefit when that right accrues or to tax the benefit if and when received. The answer to this question affects both when taxes are paid and by whom. For most insurance programs I conclude that it is the value of the right to receive benefits that should be taxed. For tax-transfer programs it is the benefits themselves that should be taxed. The benefits, however, should be taxed in the case of insurance programs, such as unemployment insurance, that provide benefits that are essentially wage replacement. To do so would improve equity and reduce the adverse incentive effects of these programs.

Employee Benefits

The principal employee benefits are retirement; health, disability, and life insurance plans; and workmen's compensation. Employer contributions to these plans increased from 3.9 percent of wages and salaries in 1955 to 9.6 percent in 1975, as shown in table 3-1. Benefits paid increased from 3.0 percent to 8.4 percent of wages and salaries between 1955 and 1975. Whether measured by employer contributions or benefits paid, tax-favored employee benefits have increased in importance as a portion of total employee compensation.[2]

The tax law encourages the substitution of tax-free employee benefits for wages and salaries. It may cost an employer a dollar to provide a tax-free benefit that an employee values at only 85 cents. An employee in a tax bracket above 15 percent, however, would prefer the dollar of employee benefit to a dollar of wages that would be taxed, leaving less than 85 cents after tax.

The tax-free status of employee benefits leads not only to a misallocation but also to inequities. Tax exemption is worth more the

2. The Social Security Administration prepares annual statistics on employee benefit plans. See Alfred M. Skolnik, "Twenty-five Years of Employee-Benefit Plans," *Social Security Bulletin,* vol. 39 (September 1976), pp. 3–21.

higher the employee's tax bracket. For an employee in the 14 percent tax bracket, a dollar of exempt employee benefits is worth only 14 cents, but for an employee in the 30 percent tax bracket, it is worth 30 cents.

Not all employee benefits are tax-favored. For example, vacation pay and year-end bonuses are taxable income to employees.[3]

In addition to the major employee benefits listed above, employees also receive tax-favored fringe benefits such as subsidized cafeterias, free parking, company cars, employee discounts, and the like. These fringe benefits may serve the business purpose of the employer, but they also involve an important component of personal consumption. Taxing these benefits raises difficult questions of valuation and administrative feasibility.

Private Pension Plans

Employer contributions to private pension (and profit-sharing) plans that meet certain participation, vesting, and funding rules are tax deductible when paid out, even though they are not considered current income to the employees.[4] Earnings on the pension trusts are also not taxed currently. Benefits paid by pension plans are considered taxable income, but beneficiaries are permitted to recover tax free any contributions they made to the pension plan.

The present tax treatment of private pensions permits tax deferral on both employer contributions and the earnings on those contributions. If one looks through the veil of the pension fund and considers the employer contribution as income to the employee, the present treatment is equivalent to exempting from taxation the earnings on the amount of money that would ordinarily be available after tax, assuming that the employee remains in the same tax rate bracket.[5]

3. Vacation pay is tax-favored to the extent that employers are able to deduct its cost on an accrual basis as it is earned. Employees, being on a cash basis, include vacation pay in income only as it is used.

4. Only private pensions are discussed here, but the same considerations are involved in determining the appropriate treatment of profit-sharing plans under a comprehensive income tax.

5. This equivalence can be seen as follows: Assume t is the employee's marginal tax rate, and r is the annual rate of earning on the pension fund. If the employer contributes $1,000 to the fund, then after n years the fund will have grown to $1,000$(1 + r)^n$. When the funds are paid out, both the employer contribution and the earnings are taxable. The income after tax is therefore $1,000(1 - t)(1 + r)^n$. But this is the same amount of after-tax income the employee would have if he had paid tax on the $1,000 and then had invested the after-tax proceeds, $1,000(1 - t)$, in a tax-exempt account at rate r for n years.

Table 3-1. Employer Contributions for Major Social Insurance Programs and Employee Benefits as a Percentage of Wages and Salaries, Selected Years, 1955–75

Amounts in millions of dollars

	1955		1960		1965		1970		1975	
Contribution or benefit program	Amount	Percent of wages and salaries	Amount	Percent of wages and salaries	Amount	Percent of wages and salaries	Amount	Percent of wages and salaries	Amount	Percent of wages and salaries
Employer contributions										
Pension and profit sharing	3,377	1.6	4,866	1.8	7,646	2.1	12,972	2.4	28,449	3.5
Federal civilian employees' retirement	144	*	838	0.3	1,146	0.3	2,104	0.4	4,457	0.6
State and local employees' retirement	985	0.5	1,775	0.7	2,525	0.7	4,921	0.9	9,303	1.2
Group health insurance[a]	1,706	0.8	3,374	1.2	5,890	1.6	11,801	2.2	22,270	2.8
Group life insurance	561	0.3	1,080	0.4	1,651	0.5	2,848	0.5	4,015	0.5
Workmen's compensation[b]	1,467	0.7	1,942	0.7	2,747	0.8	4,568	0.8	8,358	1.0
Cash sickness compensation[c]	5	*	7	*	9	*	28	*	32	*
Supplemental unemployment	51	*	120	*	121	*	130	*	172	*
Total employer contributions	8,296	3.9	14,002	5.1	21,735	6.0	39,372	7.2	77,056	9.6

Benefits paid

Pension and profit sharing	850	0.4	1,720	0.6	3,520	1.0	7,360	1.3	12,930[d]	1.7[d]
Federal civilian employees retirement	453	0.2	938	0.3	1,516	0.4	3,024	0.6	7,725	1.0
Military retirement	466	0.2	757	0.3	1,507	0.4	3,162	0.6	6,827	0.8
State and local employees retirement	760	0.4	1,372	0.5	2,137	0.6	3,898	0.7	7,526	0.9
Group health insurance[a]	2,210	1.0	4,332	1.6	7,572	2.1	14,459	2.6	23,023[d]	3.0[d]
Group life insurance	608	0.3	1,065	0.4	1,642	0.5	2,639	0.5	3,359[d]	0.4[d]
Workmen's compensation[b]	1,015	0.5	1,416	0.5	1,947	0.5	3,121	0.6	5,347[e]	0.7
Cash sickness compensation[c]	63	*	138	0.1	261	0.1	398	0.1	517	0.1
Supplemental unemployment	0	0.0	91	*	62	*	125	*	400[d]	0.1[d]
Total benefits paid	6,425	3.0	11,829	4.3	20,164	5.6	38,186	7.0	67,654	8.4

Sources: U.S. Bureau of Economic Analysis, *The National Income and Product Accounts of the United States, 1929–74: Statistical Tables* (Government Printing Office, 1977); and *Survey of Current Business*, vol. 56 (July 1976), tables 1.13, 3.11, 3.12, and 6.13 in each of these two sources.

a. Includes most group disability insurance.
b. Includes government social insurance funds and private plans.
c. State and local temporary disability insurance.
d. For 1974.
e. Government payments data for 1975 combined with 1974 data for payments from private funds.
* Less than 0.05 percent.

Since a tax-exempt rate of return is clearly worth more the higher the employee's marginal tax rate, the present treatment of pension income favors high-income employees.[6]

The accrual of pension rights would be considered income under the Haig-Simons definition of income. Employees each year would include in income the year-to-year increase in the present value of expected future retirement benefits. (This would also be the appropriate amount for each firm to deduct annually.) To avoid taxing employees on hypothetical benefits they might never obtain, future pension benefits would be included in income only to the extent that the employee is fully vested. Including only vested benefits, however, might discourage liberal vesting rules, unless such rules were required of all qualified pension plans. Furthermore, in the year an employee first vests, he may have a significant increase in income. Presumably this increase could be handled by income averaging.[7]

At the time of retirement the worker would have paid taxes on an amount equal to the present value of the expected future benefits. After retirement the benefits paid would represent both a return of capital and earnings on that capital. Given the uncertainty about just how long benefits will be paid out, the annuity rule would be an appropriate way to separate the return of capital from the return on capital. Under this rule a worker would exclude a fraction of his benefits each year. This fraction would be determined by the pension fund at the time of retirement, and it would be equal to the ratio of the present value of his expected future benefits to the undiscounted value of his expected future benefits. Workers who die early (and their spouses if there is a survivor benefit) would not fully recover their investment tax free. Workers (and their spouses) who live longer than expected would more than recover their investment tax

6. It might be noted that pension fund investments are even better investments than tax-exempt municipals, because the return on municipals is lower than the return on taxable securities of equal risk. Tax deferral of both employer contributions and the earnings permits employees to earn a tax-exempt return equal to the before-tax return on taxable securities on the amount of money that would ordinarily be available after tax.

7. Government pensions are not required to meet the vesting standards of the Employee Retirement Income Security Act of 1974. Military pensions generally do not vest until twenty years of service. Thus military servicemen would have a substantial increase in income the year their pension first vests. It must be recognized, however, that the net worth of servicemen takes a big jump the year their pensions vest.

free. Assuming that appropriate mortality tables are used, workers on the average would just recover their investment.[8]

A reasonable approximation for taxing each employee's year-to-year increase in the present value of expected future retirement benefits would be to tax him on any employee contributions and on his allocable share of both employer contributions to and earnings on pension trust funds. Businesses would continue to deduct contributions paid to pension trust funds. This would generally ensure that the amounts deductible by businesses would be recognized currently as income by employees.[9] Taxing employees on contributions and earnings would differ somewhat from taxing the year-to-year increase in expected future benefits, particularly in the case of unfunded past-service benefits, which would be taxable to employees only as they are funded.

Allocating employer contributions and fund earnings to employees would involve certain difficulties. Some would even argue that there is no fair way for making the required allocation. If actuaries, however, can estimate future pension liabilities, they can surely allocate the present value of accrued future liabilities among employees. Employer contributions for any one year might then be allocated to employees based on the difference between the present value of accrued future benefits and the amount of contributions and earnings previously allocated to each employee. Each year's earnings on pension trust funds would be allocated to employees, based on the amount of contributions and earnings previously allocated to each employee. The Internal Revenue Service should be able to develop simplified rules for allocating employer contributions. For pension plans not integrated with social security, it is possible that employer contributions could be allocated on the basis of the amount of wages and sal-

8. The annuity rule may be said to give a preference to annuity income. If it were known that a worker and his spouse would receive benefits for a specific term, say fifteen years, then the pension investment could be amortized. In the early years most of the benefits paid would represent earnings on the investment, and in the later years most of the benefits would represent a return of the capital. This would be similar to the amortization of a level-payment mortgage; in the early years most of the payment represents interest. The simpler annuity rule described above is reasonable when it is uncertain just how long the pension will pay out. In effect it permits the government and the beneficiary to share in mortality gains and losses.

9. To the extent that employers make contributions to fund the future benefits of unvested workers, these contributions would be deductible currently even though not taxable to employees until their pension rights have vested.

aries paid each worker.[10] For plans that are integrated, however, employer contributions could not be allocated in proportion to wages and salaries. Instead, higher-paid workers would be allocated a larger share of the contributions.

Although it would be possible to allocate pension fund earnings to employees, one would not want to do this as part of a comprehensive income tax for several reasons. First, if only realized earnings were allocated, pension funds would have an incentive not to realize gains and to invest in assets that do not yield current ordinary income. If instead, accrued earnings were allocated, this component of income would fluctuate widely from year to year depending on the ups and downs of the stock market. Moreover, the tax system should not treat the accrued capital gains of pension trust funds less favorably than the accrued capital gains of individual investors. A final difficulty with taxing the earnings currently is that the workers would not actually be receiving the income and they might have difficulty finding the funds to pay tax on income they have not received.[11] The pension trust funds could withhold taxes on fund earnings at a flat rate. This would mitigate the problem but not completely solve it.

The considerations above lead me to conclude that employer contributions to pension funds (but not the earnings of the funds) should be taxed currently to vested employees. These contributions would be amortized once an employee began to receive benefits.[12] This scheme would permit employees to continue to defer taxation on pension fund earnings—a tax benefit that in itself would be worth more the higher an employee's marginal tax rate. If the tax system, however, did not provide some form of lifetime averaging, the advantage of tax deferral on pension fund earnings might be partly or fully offset to the extent that contributions would be taxed at a higher rate during an employee's working life and that the capital recovery of those contributions would save taxes at a lower marginal tax rate after the employee retired.

10. Employer contributions to fund past-service benefits might be allocated only to employees who qualify for these benefits. Most plans, however, liberalize benefits from time to time, creating new past-service benefits. Rough justice might be adequately served if contributions to fund past-service benefits were allocated to all workers.

11. This is not a major problem with respect to employer contributions allocated to an employee since the employer could increase withholding out of wages and salaries.

12. The three-year rule for recovering previously taxed contributions would be repealed.

Taxing employer contributions would continue to provide an incentive for companies to increase current funding of pension plans. The greater the funding, the greater the proportion of benefits that are paid from earnings and the smaller the proportion from past or current contributions. Since the earnings are tax-favored, increased funding increases the tax benefits from a pension plan.

There are a number of difficulties with taxing only vested employees on pension plan contributions. First, even after passage of the Employee Retirement Income Security Act of 1974, most employees are not vested. Many of the unvested employees will become vested, but until they do, no contributions would be allocated to them. Second, there are degrees of vesting. Under some pension plans a vested employee may have a right to receive a benefit only if he lives until age sixty-five. Under other plans, however, if a vested employee should die before reaching retirement age, a payment is made to his estate or beneficiary. An employee covered by the second type of plan is in some ways more vested than employees covered by the first type of plan.

Special rules would have to be provided for when a vested employee left a firm and withdrew his own pension contributions. He no longer would have vested benefits under the plan.[13] Presumably he would be able to take a deduction for the amount of any employer contributions previously included in his income. A special downside averaging rule would probably be required for cases where an employee has a very large deduction relative to his current income. In addition, the estate of a worker who dies without receiving any benefits might be permitted an income tax deduction for any previously taxed employer contributions.

Because government pension plans are not required to meet the funding standards of the Employee Retirement Income Security Act, some state and local pension plans are on a pay-as-you-go basis and many plans are underfunded. State and local employees covered by unfunded plans would have no employer contributions to include in income, even though they might have the same increase in accrued future pension benefits as employees covered by private plans. A solution to this problem would be to impute income to state and local employees covered by plans not meeting the funding standards of the act.

13. For example, the U.S. civil service retirement system is funded by employee and government contributions. When an employee leaves the government he can withdraw his own contributions but not the government contributions.

The imputation could be based on the amount of employer contributions that would have been made if the plan had met the act's standards.[14]

If employees are taxed currently on employer contributions to pension plans, the deductibility of payments to Keogh retirement plans for the self-employed and individual retirement accounts could be eliminated. Earnings on these special accounts would continue to be tax deferred until the funds were withdrawn.

At the end of the Ford administration the Treasury Department outlined an alternative approach to taxing pensions. Under this scheme both employer and employee contributions would be deductible. Benefits would be taxed when received. In addition, the earnings of pension plans would be included currently in the income of those employees having assigned rights to earnings as they accrued. Otherwise, the earnings would be included in the income of the employer.[15] Assuming that the earnings, benefits, and contributions would all be taxed at the same tax rate, the Treasury proposal is equivalent to taxing employees currently on pension plan contributions and earnings.[16] The Treasury scheme would eliminate any incentive for employers to increase the funding of pension benefits, and it might provide a disincentive because to the extent that pension plan earnings are included in the income of the employer they would be taxed more heavily than if they were included in the income of employees.

Sick Pay and Certain Disability Pensions

The Tax Reform Act of 1976 replaced the sick pay exclusion with an exclusion of up to $5,200 a year for retirees under age 65 who are permanently and totally disabled. The exclusion is reduced dollar for dollar as adjusted gross income (including disability income) exceeds $15,000. The bill continues the exemption for Veterans Administra-

14. A good case can be made for requiring state and local governments to meet the same funding standards as those required of private pension plans. This, however, is outside the scope of this paper.

15. See U.S. Department of the Treasury, *Blueprints for Basic Tax Reform* (Government Printing Office, 1977), pp. 56–58. This study was released after the Brookings conference on comprehensive income taxation.

16. Assume t is the tax rate and r is the annual rate of earnings on the pension fund. If both contributions and earnings were taxed currently, a $1,000 contribution would have grown to $(1-t)(\$1,000)(1+(1-t)r)^n$ after n years. This is the same result that would occur if earnings were taxed currently and benefits were fully taxed with no recognition of the tax previously paid on the earnings.

tion disability pensions or an equivalent amount paid by the Department of Defense.[17] Ordinary sick pay is now fully taxable.

The special exclusion or exemption of disability pensions is inappropriate under a comprehensive income tax. Disability pensions should be treated like other pensions. Retirees would use the annuity rule to recover their pension investments tax free. The treatment proposed here for disability pensions would differ from that proposed later for disability insurance benefits.[18] It is important, however, that disability pensions be treated the same as normal retirement pensions. Otherwise, important tax consequences would ride on whether an employee who retired, say at age fifty-eight, had done so because of a disability or had simply elected a normal early retirement. It is generally undesirable to have major tax consequences hang on small differences in facts and circumstances.

Group Term Life Insurance

Under present law employer payments for group term life insurance premiums for coverage up to $50,000 per employee are not taxable to the employee. Life insurance proceeds also are not taxed. Thus the value of employer-provided group life insurance (up to the $50,000 limit) is never subject to tax. Employees, however, are required to include in income the cost of group life insurance in excess of $50,000 of such insurance.

Under a comprehensive income tax employees would be subject to tax on employer payments for group life insurance (and also on employer payments for accidental death and travel insurance). If an employer provides death benefits directly, the employees would be imputed income equal to what it would cost the employer to provide the coverage through an insurance company. Death benefits then would not be taxed when paid. The amount included in income would depend on the amount of coverage and the employee's age and sex. The Internal Revenue Service could provide tables for determining the value of $1,000 of group term life insurance. This approach, which is similar to that recommended for health insurance, recognizes that the economic benefit for the employee is the coverage itself

17. The exclusion for noncombat-related disability pensions is eliminated for those who joined the armed forces after September 24, 1975.

18. In the case of disability insurance it is proposed that employer contributions not be taxed to the employee. Instead, all benefits paid would be taxable.

and not the eventual proceeds. Its treatment of employer-provided coverage is similar to the present tax treatment of insurance purchased separately by individuals.

The alternative to taxing the premiums is to tax the actual benefits when paid. This treats a family in which an insured person has died as having more taxpaying ability than a similar family in which an uninsured person has died. Most families, however, view the death of a wage earner as an economic loss and do not consider death benefits a source of additional income that increases taxpaying ability.

Group Health Insurance

Group health insurance is the leading employee benefit after pensions. Under a comprehensive income tax either the employer payments for insurance could be allocated to the employees or the benefits received under the plans could be considered taxable income. An employee covered by medical insurance has a right of considerable value even though he may file no claims for benefits. I believe that this right is the appropriate basis for taxation, and allocating employer payments to the employees would provide an adequate proxy for the value of this right. The allocation probably should depend on age, marital status, and number of covered dependents.

Some might argue that benefits actually received should be taxed instead of taxing the right to receive benefits. An employee who receives benefits is better off than an employee without insurance who incurs similar medical bills, and for this reason one may want to tax benefits received. An employee who receives benefits, however, is not better off than another covered employee who does not receive benefits. Both employees have coverage, and the employee who receives benefits is in effect only reimbursed for the medical expenses he incurred. A second reason advanced for taxing benefits is that it would ensure that medical services are not a free good at the margin. The insurance plans themselves, however, can limit the overutilization of medical services induced by insurance coverage by requiring coinsurance for those services that are largely voluntary.

Workmen's Compensation

All states and the District of Columbia have enacted workmen's compensation laws to provide benefits in the case of work-related injuries or death. In addition, federal laws cover maritime workers

Table 3-2. Benefits Paid under Workmen's Compensation, 1972

Type of payment	Amount (millions of dollars)	Percent of total
Medical and hospitalization	1,230	30.5
Disability	2,339	58.1
Survivor	460	11.4
Total	4,029	100.0

Source: Alfred M. Skolnik and Daniel N. Price, "Workmen's Compensation under Scrutiny," *Social Security Bulletin*, vol. 37 (October 1974), p. 9.

(other than seamen) and federal government employees. Benefits paid under workmen's compensation include medical services, wage replacement for disabled workers, and death and survivor benefits, as shown in table 3-2. Thus workmen's compensation combines elements of three kinds of insurance—health, unemployment, and life.

Employer contributions for workmen's compensation, whether made to a private insurance company or to a state insurance fund, are deductible when made. Large companies that are permitted to self-insure deduct benefit payments when made. Neither employer payments nor benefits are taxable under the individual income tax.

There is no easy answer to the question of how workmen's compensation should be treated under a comprehensive income tax. To the extent that this program is similar to group health and group life insurance, the economic benefit is the insurance coverage itself, and one would want to tax employees on employer payments to fund these benefits. For this portion of the program the benefit payments would not be taxable.[19] The disability payments, however, replace wages that would have been taxed. If these payments are not taxed, there may be adverse labor market effects.[20]

On the basis of benefits paid shown in table 3-2, about 40 percent of employer workmen's compensation payments are for medical and

19. In the case of survivor benefits, one might want to compute the expected present value of future benefits and then, using the annuity rule, to treat a portion of the benefits as being a return of capital and the remaining portion as earnings on that capital. The earnings would be taxable income to the survivors. This would ensure that survivors who receive periodic payments would be treated about the same as survivors who receive lump-sum payments.

20. The adverse effects are likely to be most severe in the case of temporary total disability payments (about half of all disability payments) that end when a worker returns to work. Permanent disability payments generally are not reduced if a worker becomes employed.

survivor benefits, and employer contributions to support these benefits would be taxable to employees.[21] The other 60 percent fund disability benefits that would be taxable to beneficiaries. The exact allocation might vary from state to state depending on each state's workmen's compensation program. It might also vary between industries.

Disability Insurance

In addition to workmen's compensation, many employees are covered by employer-financed group disability insurance. Five states—California, Hawaii, New Jersey, New York, and Rhode Island—have laws requiring temporary disability insurance. Railroad workers are protected under a federal act.[22] Disability insurance generally protects workers from loss of income during periods of temporary or permanent disability. The injuries or illness giving rise to the disability need not be job related. Benefits may be reduced by amounts received under social security and workmen's compensation. They may be paid only for a limited period of time or may end at retirement age when workers begin to receive retirement benefits.

Since disability benefits replace wages that otherwise would have been taxed, the benefits would be taxed and not the payments required to provide the insurance coverage.[23] Thus the tax treatment for these benefits would be the same as that proposed for disability benefits under workmen's compensation and social security. Moreover, these benefits would be treated the same as paid sick leave, which currently is taxable to employees when paid.

Disability coverage is often provided as part of a health insurance package. In such cases, employer premiums to finance medical services would have to be separated from the premiums for disability benefits. The premiums for medical services would be considered taxable income to all covered employees. The premiums for disability benefits would not be taxable to the beneficiaries.

21. For companies that self-insure, each employee would be taxable on his share of the payments made for medical and survivor benefits.

22. In the national income accounts most disability insurance is included in group health insurance. However, the state programs of California, New Jersey, New York, and Rhode Island use a state trust fund and are classified under "cash sickness benefits." For a description of temporary disability insurance programs, see Daniel N. Price, "Cash Benefits for Short-Term Sickness, 1948–74," *Social Security Bulletin,* vol. 39 (July 1976), pp. 22–34.

23. Under a comprehensive tax, any employee payments for disability insurance should be excluded from the tax base.

Supplemental Unemployment Benefits

The auto, steel, rubber, and other industries subject to high cyclical unemployment have established supplemental unemployment benefit plans. These plans provide additional unemployment benefits to covered workers who become unemployed. Under the present law these plans are treated the same as employer-financed pension plans: payments by employers into a trust are tax deductible, and earnings on the trust funds are not taxed as they accrue. Benefits are taxable to the employee when they are paid.

Supplemental unemployment is privately financed unemployment insurance. It should be taxed the same as the government unemployment insurance program. It is argued later that for the government program it is the benefits that should be taxed, because if they are not, the unemployment insurance program might have a significant adverse impact on the level of unemployment. Thus I would conclude that the benefits paid under supplemental unemployment should continue to be taxed when paid.

Retaining the present treatment of supplemental unemployment would permit employers to continue to deduct payments to the plans when made, even though employees may not have to recognize income for a number of years. This timing difference is less serious for supplemental unemployment where the timing difference is likely to be only a year or two than for private pensions where current employer payments may fund benefits to be paid many years in the future. The timing difference, however, could be eliminated by denying a deduction for employer payments into the fund. Under this scheme any earnings of the fund would be treated as gross income to the firm, and payments from the fund to beneficiaries would be the deductible expense. Beneficiaries would then be taxed at the same time that firms claim a tax deduction.

Group Prepaid Legal Services

The Tax Reform Act of 1976 established a new tax-favored employee benefit. Under the act employees may exclude from income amounts contributed by an employer to a qualified group legal services plan as well as the value of any legal services received under the plan. Employer payments to the plan are tax deductible.[24]

24. The Tax Reform Act of 1976 provides that the special tax treatment of group legal services will apply only to tax years 1977–81.

Under a comprehensive income tax, group prepaid legal services would be treated like most other employee benefits that are insurance programs. Thus each employee would be taxed on his share of the amount contributed by the employer to the group legal services plan. An employee's share might reasonably depend on age, marital status, and number of dependents.

Some would argue, however, that it would be better to tax the value of any legal services received so that they would not be priced at the margin like a free good. Instead, it would cost an employee something to sue his neighbor, divorce his wife, or revise his will. Deductibles and coinsurance could also ensure that legal services are not a free good.

Fringe Benefits

The employee benefits discussed up to now are included in the national income accounts as part of the compensation of employees. What are generally known as fringe benefits—the company car, subsidized meals, and so on—generally are not included in the compensation of employees.[25] Instead, the cost of providing these benefits are treated as part of purchased materials and services. These fringe benefits, however, do involve an important consumption component. This suggests that employees who receive them should be required to include them, or at least some portion of them, in income for tax purposes.

It must be recognized that no clear line separates compensation from conditions of employment. Almost everyone would agree that employees do not receive compensation just because they work in air-conditioned offices. When employers provide saunas, squash courts, and offices with all the creature comforts, then these superior work conditions begin to look very similar to compensation. At the extreme, most people would agree that chauffeur-driven automobiles, $50 martini lunches, monthly cocktail parties, and personal flights on the company plane have a very high consumption component that should be taxed as compensation if administratively feasible.

Present law draws a distinction between compensation and conditions of work in the case of meals and lodging furnished by an employer. Employees may exclude from gross income the value of meals

25. One exception is meals furnished to restaurant employees. These meals are included in wages and salaries and are valued at cost.

and lodging furnished them on their employer's business premises for his convenience. In the case of lodging, an employee must be required to accept such lodging as a condition of his employment.[26] Employer-provided meals and lodging obviously affect the attractiveness of a job. Many would argue that the present exclusion is too generous. For example, Goode suggests that where meals and lodging are significant, they should be included in income, conservatively valued to allow for the lack of free choice.[27]

Clearly a basic problem in taxing fringe benefits is valuation. Consider a salesperson at Neiman-Marcus who receives a 40 percent discount on goods purchased at the store. This discount is undoubtedly of considerable value, but just how valuable is very difficult to determine. It clearly is not worth 40 percent of the fair market value of the goods purchased with the discount, because without the discount the employee might have purchased the same goods at Sears for 20 percent less than the cost at Neiman-Marcus. Thus the discount may only be worth 20 percent to the employee. The basic valuation problem was recognized by Henry Simons:

We are asked to measure the relative incomes of an ordinary officer serving with his troops and a *Flügeladjutant* to the sovereign. Both receive the same nominal pay; but the latter receives quarters in the palace, food at the royal table, servants, and horses for sport. He accompanies the prince to theater and opera, and, in general, lives royally at no expense to himself and is able to save generously from his salary. But suppose, as one possible complication, that the *Flügeladjutant* detests opera and hunting.[28]

The Treasury Department in 1975 released a discussion draft of proposed regulations relating to the taxation of fringe benefits. If adopted, they would tend to codify present practices.[29] In developing

26. A separate section (107) of the Internal Revenue Code exempts the rental value of parsonages from taxation, including any rental allowance paid to a minister as part of his compensation. Thus ministers are not required to meet the general test for excluding lodging.

27. Richard Goode, *The Individual Income Tax*, rev. ed. (Brookings Institution, 1976), p. 117.

28. Henry C. Simons, *Personal Income Taxation: The Definition of Income as a Problem of Fiscal Policy* (University of Chicago Press, 1938), p. 53.

29. Several days after the Brookings conference the *Wall Street Journal* (December 16, 1976) reported that the Treasury was considering taxing employees' discounts, including travel discounts received by airline employees. The public outcry from affected employees led Secretary William E. Simon to announce that such a

the draft the Treasury concluded that only fringe benefits that threaten the integrity of the basic tax system should be taxed.[30] Taxable benefits would be valued at their fair market value. The proposed regulations, however, would not tax the travel passes of airline employees and travel agents, merchandise discounts of store employees, free parking, payment of bar association dues by a law firm, or periodic social functions of a firm. These regulations have been criticized for being too generous.[31] Obviously, in this instance no simple line separates compensation from conditions of work. Whatever line is drawn in the tax law must be somewhat arbitrary; in drawing it consideration should be given to the importance of the fringe benefit, the ease in valuing it, and the problems of recordkeeping.

The elements of reform of the taxation of employee benefits are brought together in table 3-3. If the full package were implemented, federal revenues would increase by $19.8 billion in 1977. This would permit a reduction in marginal tax rates of about 12 percent across the board. The major share of the increase is due to taxing contributions to pension and group health plans. The revenue increase from the reform package is distributed by comprehensive income classes in table 3-4. The tax increases would be substantial in most income ranges.

Transfer Programs

The major transfer programs are social security and railroad retirement, Medicare, unemployment insurance, veterans' benefits, supplemental security income, aid for dependent children, and food stamps. Payments under the transfer programs listed in table 3-5 increased from 4.4 percent of personal income in 1955 to 11.5 percent in 1975. All payments under these programs are exempt from the individual income tax.

---

change was no longer under active consideration. ("Fringe Benefit Taxation No Longer to Be Considered," *Department of the Treasury News*, December 17, 1976.) He also withdrew the discussion draft pertaining to taxing employee discounts. This incident illustrates the difficulty of getting political support for comprehensive tax reform.

30. "Summary and Explanation of Discussion Draft of Proposed Regulations on Fringe Benefits," *Department of the Treasury News*, September 3, 1975, p. 11.

31. "Federal Income Taxation of Employee Fringe Benefits," *Harvard Law Review*, vol. 89 (April 1976), pp. 1141–73.

Table 3-3. Revenue Effect of Reform of Taxation of Employee Benefits under the Individual Income Tax, 1977
Billions of dollars

Benefit and reform provision	Amount of revenue
Pension and profit-sharing plans Tax vested employees on employer contributions attributable to them. Tax benefits in excess of amortized contributions.	9.4
Sick pay and certain disability pensions Repeal sick pay provisions. Treat disability pensions like other pensions.	*
Group term life insurance Tax employees on employer premiums attributable to them.	1.3
Group health insurance Tax employees on employer premiums attributable to them.	6.6
Workmen's compensation Tax disability benefits when paid. Tax employees on employer premiums for medical and survivor benefits.	1.4
Disability insurance Tax benefits when paid. Permit employees to exclude any employee contributions from income.	0.3
Supplemental unemployment Tax benefits when paid.	*
Group prepaid legal services Tax employees on employer premiums attributable to them.	*
Total[a]	19.8

Source: Brookings MERGE File.
a. The revenue gain from the package is greater than the sum of the individual estimates because as the tax base is expanded taxpayers are pushed into higher tax rate brackets.
* Less than 0.05.

Social security and railroad retirement are financed by both employer and employee contributions. Unemployment insurance is financed only by employer payments, and the medical insurance part of Medicare only by personal contributions (matched by general revenues). These four programs have important insurance elements, and what the appropriate tax treatment of them should be under a comprehensive income tax depends on considerations very similar to those relevant to the decision on what the appropriate treatment of employee benefits should be. The remaining transfer programs are financed entirely by general revenues, and they represent pure government transfers. As a general rule these transfers should be included in income by the recipients. For practical reasons, however,

Table 3-4. Revenue Effect of Reform of Taxation of Employee Benefits under the Individual Income Tax, by Comprehensive Income Class, 1977

Comprehensive income class (*thousands of dollars*)	*Effect of reform*[a]	
	Revenue increase (*millions of dollars*)	Tax increase (*percent*)
Less than 2.5	0	0.0
2.5–5	87	79.0
5–10	701	15.3
10–15	1,552	12.2
15–20	2,480	12.9
20–25	3,004	14.0
25–30	2,673	13.9
30–50	5,399	14.4
50–100	2,617	12.5
100–200	827	6.7
200 and over	434	2.7
All classes	19,774	12.1

Source: Brookings MERGE File.
a. See table 3-3 for the reform provisions.

transfer payments that are subject to a stringent means test might be excluded from the tax base of the individual income tax.

Social Security

Old age, survivors, disability, and health insurance, generally known as social security, is financed by contributions by employers, employees, and the self-employed and by earnings on the accumulated trust funds. The system is essentially on a pay-as-you-go basis, with accumulated trust funds equal to less than one year's benefits. Under present law employer contributions are deductible by firms. Contributions by employees and the self-employed (but not the employer contributions) are included in the base of the individual income tax. All benefits paid under social security are tax exempt.

The social security system involves elements of a pure insurance system and of a welfare or a tax-transfer system, and this makes the appropriate treatment of social security under a comprehensive income tax particularly troublesome. If social security is viewed primarily as a tax-transfer system, one would want to tax all benefits when received, with no tax recognition for either employer or employee contributions. In addition, one would permit employees to exclude from the tax base both employer and employee contributions on the grounds that these contributions are not buying the employees any vested rights. Thus they are not income. The contributions are essentially a tax, and unless they are excluded one ends up with a tax on a tax.[32] Excluding employee contributions and taxing all social security benefits, including medical benefits, would reduce federal revenues by $2.7 billion.

Social security can also be viewed as insurance against certain events—retirement, disability, death, or illness. Viewed this way, one would want to tax social security similarly to privately financed insurance for the same events. Thus employees would include in income both employer and employee contributions (and the self-employed would include in income their contributions). Beneficiaries of retirement, disability, and survivor payments would recover tax free any previous contributions (both employer and employee) attributable to the benefits by amortizing them over their remaining life expectancy. Medical and death benefits would not be taxable.

A strict application of the Haig-Simons concept would require workers to include in income the year-to-year increase in the present value of expected future social security benefits. For the Social Security Administration to calculate this annually for every worker would be virtually impossible, since future benefits depend on a worker's marital status, number of dependents, his earnings record, and the earnings record of his spouse. Furthermore, when a worker's marital status changes either through death or divorce, the present value of his expected future benefits could increase or decrease dramatically, causing a large year-to-year change in income from social security coverage. For a social security system that is on a pay-as-you-go basis, however, employer and employee contributions are equal to the present value of expected future benefits if the future benefits are discounted by the rate of growth of real wages plus the rate of growth of the labor force.[33] Thus attributing contributions to current workers would, on the average, approximate attributing the present value of expected future benefits to these workers. This approach would attribute too little income to workers favored by the benefit formulas—for

32. There is considerable agreement among economists that employees pay both the employer and employee tax under social security. In the national income and product accounts, employer contributions are included as a component of compensation of employees.

33. This is a steady-state condition. If the economy is not in steady state, pay-as-you-go financing will lead to redistribution among age cohorts.

Table 3-5. Contributions for Major Social Insurance Programs and Government Transfer Payments to Persons, Selected Years, 1955–75
Amounts in millions of dollars

	1955		1960		1965		1970		1975	
Contributor and program	Amount	Percent of personal income	Amount	Percent of personal income	Amount	Percent of personal income	Amount	Percent of personal income	Amount	Percent of personal income
Employer contributions										
Social security	2,825	0.9	5,632	1.4	8,330	1.6	16,381	2.0	30,504	2.4
Hospital insurance	...	...	...	...	...	...	2,371	0.3	5,611	0.4
Unemployment insurance[a]	1,550	0.5	2,808	0.7	3,783	0.7	3,475	0.4	6,909	0.6
Railroad retirement	308	0.1	297	0.1	326	0.1	517	0.1	1,108	0.1
Total	4,683	1.5	8,737	2.2	12,439	2.3	22,744	2.8	44,132	3.5
Personal contributions										
Social security	3,123	1.0	6,331	1.6	9,351	1.7	20,690	2.6	39,609	3.2
Supplementary medical insurance (Medicare)	...	0.1	...	0.1	...	0.1	1,091	0.1	1,908	0.2
Railroad retirement	308	0.1	297	0.1	326	0.1	437	0.1	364	*
Total	3,431	1.1	6,628	1.7	9,677	1.8	22,218	2.8	41,881	3.4

Transfer payments to persons

Social security	4,915	1.6	11,130	2.8	18,067	3.4	31,380	3.9	65,852	5.3
Hospital and supplementary medical insurance	...	...	...	...	...	...	7,075	0.9	15,531	1.2
Unemployment insurance[a]	1,516	0.5	2,996	0.7	2,299	0.4	3,986	0.5	16,631	1.3
Railroad retirement	566	0.2	949	0.2	1,140	0.2	1,745	0.2	3,275	0.3
Veterans' benefits	3,733	1.2	3,828	1.0	4,259	0.8	6,788	0.8	13,408	1.1
Food stamp benefits	...	...	...	...	45	*	1,103	0.1	4,599	0.4
Black-lung benefits	...	...	...	...	...	...	110	*	959	0.1
Supplemental security income[b]	...	...	...	...	...	...	...	...	5,919[b]	0.5[b]
Aid to families with dependent children	613	0.2	991	0.2	1,650	0.3	4,823	0.6	9,186	0.7
Other categorical public assistance	1,670	0.5	1,947	0.5	2,098	0.4	2,953	0.4	[c]	[c]
General assistance	212	0.1	322	0.1	259	*	618	0.1	1,139	0.1
Other[d]	410	0.1	584	0.1	1,256	0.2	3,360	0.4	6,915	0.6
Total	13,635	4.4	22,747	5.7	31,073	5.8	63,941	8.0	143,414	11.5

Sources: U.S. Bureau of Economic Analysis, *The National Income and Product Accounts of the United States, 1929–74: Statistical Tables* (GPO, 1977); and *Survey of Current Business*, vol. 56 (July 1976), tables 1.9, 3.11, and 3.12 in each of the two sources.

a. Includes state unemployment insurance, federal unemployment tax, and railroad unemployment insurance.

b. Includes both federal and state supplemental security income payments formerly listed under other categorical public assistance programs.

c. Replaced by supplemental security income program.

d. Includes both state and federal payments. Largely consists of educational assistance, veterans' bonuses, etc. In 1975 included $50 payment to recipients of social security, railroad retirement, and supplemental security income, as provided by the Tax Reduction Act of 1975.

* Less than 0.05.

example, low-paid married workers with nonworking spouses—and too much to those not favored.

Another problem with taxing contributions is that the workers who are paying social security taxes to finance hospital insurance generally do not become eligible to receive benefits until they reach age sixty-five or are disabled. Thus to a large extent current workers would be taxed for both employer and employee contributions for hospital insurance, even though they do not currently benefit from the program. The alternatives would be to tax benefits when received, to attribute the contributions to individuals who are currently eligible to receive benefits, or to tax neither the contributions nor the benefits. The first of these alternatives must be rejected, since the economic benefit from hospital insurance is the coverage itself and not the benefits received. Attributing the contributions to the aged and the disabled would be a better solution, but in most people's view it would be a very harsh treatment. Retirement and disability benefits would have to be adjusted upward to ensure that the aged and disabled could pay the increased income taxes. Taxing neither the contributions nor the benefits would exclude an important source of income from taxation altogether. I conclude, but not very strongly, that current workers should be taxed on both employer and employee contributions to finance hospital insurance. In effect, current workers can be viewed as prepaying the tax on the insurance coverage they will receive when they become sixty-five or older or when they become disabled.

Taxing benefits (other than medical and death) but permitting tax-free recovery of employer and employee contributions that previously have been taxed would lead to what many retirees would view as an anomalous result: the proportion of benefits included in income would be highest for relatively low-paid workers who are favored by the benefit formulas. This would be particularly true if recovery were permitted only for contributions not offset by the earned-income tax credit. It would, of course, be an appropriate result, given the income concept underlying a comprehensive income tax, but it would appear inequitable to many retirees.[34]

To simplify as much as possible the tax treatment of social security, all workers might be required to include in income both employer and employee contributions for social security, even though younger

34. Goode, *Individual Income Tax*, p. 105.

workers with less than forty quarters of covered employment are not "vested" for retirement benefits. Most workers will become vested for social security benefits, and only a small inequity would be caused by taxing all workers on both employer and employee contributions.[35]

Taxing social security benefits (other than medical and death) would remove the major justification for the tax credit for the elderly.[36] Repeal of this credit would improve equity and simplify the tax law for taxpayers aged sixty-five and over.

Taxing social security benefits, with appropriate recovery of employer and employee contributions that previously have been taxed, would increase federal revenue by $4.6 billion. Repealing the tax credit for the elderly would increase revenue by an additional $0.8 billion. These tax increases could be used to reduce marginal tax rates and expand the low-income allowance so that the overall progressivity of the income tax would not be reduced.

Railroad Retirement

The Railroad Retirement Act of 1974 integrated railroad retirement and social security by establishing a two-tier structure of retirement benefits. The first tier of benefits is similar to social security, and it is financed by employer and employee contributions at the same tax rate as that for social security. The second tier of benefits is similar to a private pension, and it is entirely financed by employer contributions.[37] Employer contributions are not included in the base of the individual income tax. All railroad retirement benefits except supplemental annuities are tax exempt.

Under a comprehensive income tax, railroad retirement should be

35. Workers over the age of sixty-five who are ineligible for retirement benefits could receive a refund for any employer and employee contributions made into the social security trust fund in their behalf.

36. This was formerly called the retirement income tax credit but was renamed in the Tax Reform Act of 1976, which limited the credit to people aged sixty-five and over. The tax benefits under this credit are reduced to the extent the taxpayer receives social security benefits. Thus this credit provides a tax break for the elderly who do not benefit from tax-exempt social security benefits. If social security is made taxable, the major justification for the tax credit for the elderly disappears.

37. In addition to the two tiers of benefits, employees and spouses who had vested rights to both railroad retirement and social security benefits at the end of 1974 are entitled to an additional benefit known as the "dual benefit windfall." This windfall component, which is financed by general revenues, preserves an employee's rights to dual benefits earned before 1975.

treated the same as social security and private pensions. This means that employer contributions should be taxable to employees. Retired or disabled beneficiaries would be permitted to recover the previously taxed contributions over their remaining life expectancy. Benefits in excess of recovery of contributions would be fully taxable.

Unemployment Compensation

Unemployment benefits paid under the federal-state program, the railroad program, or the Trade Act of 1974 are based on the worker's past wages during a base period. Benefits are reduced if the worker is partially unemployed, but they are not reduced if the claimant has unearned income or if the spouse has income.[38] Under present law, benefits are not taxable, nor are employer unemployment contributions taxable to the employees.

Unemployment benefits (and not employer contributions) would be made taxable under a comprehensive income tax both to improve tax equity and to reduce the disincentive effect the benefits may have on employment. The exclusion of unemployment compensation, like all exclusions from gross income, provides a tax benefit that increases with the worker's marginal tax rate. For some workers this exclusion provides no tax benefit because the worker would be nontaxable even if the unemployment compensation were included in income. The largest benefit from tax exemption goes to the unemployed who have other sources of income, or who have a spouse with substantial income, or who earned high salaries during part of the year and were unemployed for the rest of the year. It is estimated that in 1974 almost 40 percent of the tax savings from excluding unemployment compensation went to families with an adjusted gross income (AGI) of more than $15,000. Only 22 percent went to families with an AGI of less than $7,000.[39] In addition, because unemployment compensation is tax exempt, the replacement rate on the amount of income lost due to unemployment varies arbitrarily. If two workers have the same earnings history during the base period, the worker with more income

38. Benefits under the Trade Act of 1974 are also reduced by the amount of unemployment compensation received.

39. In contrast, 93 percent of the tax savings from the exclusion of public assistance, which is subject to a stringent means test, goes to families with an AGI of less than $7,000. See U.S. Senate, Committee on the Budget, *Tax Expenditures: Compendium of Background Material on Individual Provisions,* 94 Cong. 2 sess. (GPO, 1976), pp. 110, 113.

from other sources would receive a higher replacement rate on lost after-tax income.

Even if the exclusion of unemployment compensation were found to be equitable, these benefits should be made taxable to reduce the disincentive effects of this program. Feldstein has found that on the average, unemployment benefits replace more than 60 percent of lost after-tax income. For women the replacement rates are nearly 80 percent.[40] These high replacement rates very likely have an adverse impact on the frequency and duration of unemployment.[41] Taxing unemployment compensation cannot eliminate the adverse incentive effects of the program, but it can reduce them. It would also ensure that a larger share of the benefits go to low-income families.

Black-Lung Benefits

Special benefits are paid to coal miners who are totally disabled due to pneumoconiosis (black-lung disease) and to survivors of coal miners whose deaths were due to this disease. Benefits are reduced by the amount of the miner's excess earnings under the social security retirement test and by the amount of workmen's compensation payments, unemployment compensation, or state disability payments received because of the miner's disability. Benefits are not reduced on account of social security benefits, unearned income, or the income of the spouse.

Since the black-lung program does not have a stringent means test, benefits should be considered taxable income. Most beneficiaries who receive only black-lung payments would remain nontaxable after this change in the law. Eighty percent of the beneficiaries, however, also receive social security benefits. Taxing both social security and black-

40. Feldstein takes into account federal and state income taxes and social security taxes. See Martin Feldstein, "Unemployment Compensation: Adverse Incentives and Distributional Anomalies," *National Tax Journal*, vol. 27 (June 1974), pp. 231–44.

41. Suppose unemployment compensation had no effect on the frequency of unemployment but increased the average period of unemployment by two weeks. I suspect that many people would consider this to be an estimate on the lower side. If the average duration of unemployment, however, had been reduced in 1975 from 14.1 weeks to 12.1 weeks, the overall unemployment rate would have been reduced from 8.5 percent to 7.3 percent. Marston has concluded that unemployment insurance tends to lengthen the period of unemployment but not enough to outweigh the positive aspects of this income support program. See Stephen T. Marston, "The Impact of Unemployment Insurance on Job Search," *Brookings Papers on Economic Activity, 1:1975*, pp. 13–48.

lung benefits would make some black-lung beneficiaries taxable. Taxing black-lung benefits would be treating disabled coal miners in the same way as that proposed for disability insurance beneficiaries.

Veterans' Benefits

All veterans' benefits are exempt from the income tax. The major benefits are compensation for service-connected disabilities, compensation to survivors of veterans for service-connected deaths, pensions for veterans with nonservice connected disabilities, pensions for widows and children of veterans, and education or GI benefits.[42]

Payments to veterans with service-connected disabilities are related to the average impairment of earning capacity in civil occupations and are not subject to an income test. Thus they are not related to the amount of other income the veteran or his spouse may have.[43] Pensions for veterans with nonservice connected disabilities are subject to an income test, but not a very stringent one. Most important, the earned income of the spouse is excluded. Pensions for the widows and children of these veterans are also subject to an income test. The income limits, however, are set sufficiently high that many widows would be taxable on these benefits if they were included in income. Education payments under the GI bill vary with the number of dependents and the type of program, but they are not subject to an income test.

The exclusion of veterans' benefits is worth more the higher the recipient's marginal tax rate. The equity of the tax system would be improved if these benefits and all other transfer payments not subject to a stringent means test were made taxable. The personal exemption and the low-income allowance can ensure that poor individuals and families are not subject to the income tax.

Means-Tested Transfer Programs

Supplemental security income, aid to families with dependent children, and general assistance are means-tested cash transfer programs. The benefits paid under these programs are reduced depending on the amount of other income or wealth the beneficiary or other members

---

42. Unemployment benefits for ex-servicemen are considered under the section on unemployment benefits.

43. The income of parents is considered in determining their eligibility as dependents.

of his family may have. Because of these stringent income and asset tests, federal revenues would increase by only $100 million if public assistance payments were made subject to tax.[44]

Although benefits under programs with stringent means tests are presumably set to meet certain target levels of disposable income, they should not be taxable to beneficiaries. The income test in effect often subjects benefits to tax rates of 50 to 100 percent, depending on the amount of earned or unearned income the family has. Moreover, one probably would not want to tax means-tested cash transfer programs unless the benefits provided under the various in-kind transfer programs such as low-rent public housing, the school lunch program, and food stamps, were included in the tax base. Taxing in-kind benefits, however, raises important valuation problems.[45] For example, beneficiaries receiving food stamps with a bonus value of $100 do not value these stamps as much as they would value $100 in cash. Requiring food stamp beneficiaries to include the bonus value in income would overvalue the "income." Finally, if means-tested transfer payments were included in the income tax base, the benefit levels would have to be increased if the programs were going to provide the same levels of disposable income for the needy. This would involve taxing Peter to pay Peter.

The strongest case for taxing transfer payments, including those under means-tested programs, has been made by Pechman.[46] If transfer payments are not taxed, beneficiaries often have a higher exempt level of income than other families have whose income is from taxable sources alone. Horizontal equity, therefore, requires that these benefits be taxed. Taxing means-tested benefit payments would not hurt the really needy, because they would remain nontaxable, given the level of the personal exemption and the low-income allowance. If the exempt levels of income are thought to be set too low, they should be increased for everyone, not just for those receiving transfer payments.

44. *Special Analyses, Budget of the United States Government, Fiscal Year 1978,* p. 129.

45. The valuation problems of in-kind benefits also apply in the case of most employee benefits. I believe, however, that the value of employee benefits and their costs are sufficiently close that the problem is not serious. If employee benefits are overvalued for taxation, the compensation package can be altered.

46. Joseph A. Pechman, "What Would a Comprehensive Individual Income Tax Yield?" in *Tax Revision Compendium,* Submitted to the House Committee on Ways and Means (GPO, 1959), vol. 1, pp. 260–61.

In addition, taxing means-tested transfer payments would help to reduce some of the overlap in the various transfer programs, but it must be recognized that this would be only a very poor substitute for comprehensive welfare reform.

I would conclude that means-tested transfer programs should be excluded from the base of a comprehensive income tax unless integration of the negative and positive taxes is achieved. A line has to be drawn somewhere, and it seems to me that it would be better to draw the line between transfer programs with stringent means tests and other transfer programs than between transfer programs that provide cash benefits and those that provide in-kind benefits. To include in income in-kind benefits provided low-income families would involve such serious valuation problems that it is uncertain whether their inclusion would increase or decrease equity. A comprehensive income tax cannot substitute for the reform of overlapping welfare programs. Taxing means-tested benefits would add little to federal revenues but would increase the complexity of the tax laws.

Reform Package

The increase in federal revenue for 1977 from taxing transfer programs without a stringent means test is $22.7 billion, as shown in table 3-6. More than two-thirds of the total is the result of taxing social security benefits and contributions, with the latter raising the larger revenue. These increases are distributed by income class in table 3-7, where it is evident that the omission of transfer payments from the tax base has benefited low-income groups the most; the tax bill of the $2,500–$5,000 comprehensive income class would be increased by more than 300 percent by the taxation of transfers. Rate reductions to compensate for the additional revenue raised would have to be heavily concentrated in the lower brackets, and if it were desired to keep most transfer recipients off the tax rolls, an increase in the personal exemption or the low-income allowance would be necessary as well.

Conclusion

Taxing employees on employer payments for various types of insurance probably is viewed by Congress and the general public as too esoteric for general acceptance. Taxing transfer payments is viewed

Table 3-6. Revenue Effect of Reform of Taxation of Transfer Payments under the Individual Income Tax
Billions of dollars

Transfer payment and provision	Amount of revenue
Social security	
Tax employer contributions	10.8
Tax benefits other than health and death with capital recovery of previous contributions	4.6
Unemployment compensation	
Tax benefits when paid	3.1
Black-lung benefits	
Tax benefits when paid	*
Veterans' benefits	
Tax benefits when paid	2.1
Benefits for the elderly	
Repeal tax credit for the elderly	0.8
Total[a]	22.7

Source: The Brookings MERGE File.
a. The revenue gain from the package is greater than the sum of the individual estimates because as the tax base is expanded taxpayers are pushed into higher tax rate brackets.
* Less than 0.05.

Table 3-7. Revenue Effect of Reform of Taxation of Transfer Payments under the Individual Income Tax, by Comprehensive Income Class, 1977

Comprehensive income class (*thousands of dollars*)	*Effect of reform*[a]	
	Revenue increase (*millions of dollars*)	*Tax increase* (*percent*)
Less than 2.5	0	0.0
2.5–5	353	321.7
5–10	3,003	65.7
10–15	3,726	29.2
15–20	3,961	20.6
20–25	3,559	16.6
25–30	2,620	13.7
30–50	3,910	10.4
50–100	1,248	6.0
100–200	193	1.6
200 and over	97	0.6
All classes	22,670	13.8

Source: Brookings MERGE File.
a. See table 3-6 for the reform provisions.

as inequitable. Most of the beneficiaries of the transfer payment programs are in a deplorable state. They are in poor health, unemployed, or disabled. Politically, it would be very difficult to tax these people, even if the personal exemption and the low-income allowance were raised. It even would be politically difficult to increase the tax on the aged, whose only misfortune is that they have lived long enough to reach retirement age. Reform of the tax treatment of employee benefits and transfer payments cannot be sold as simplification of tax administration and compliance, though it would simplify tax planning.

Yet a strong case can be made for eliminating the exclusion of employee benefits and transfer payments. These exclusions are worth more the higher the family's tax rate bracket, and much of the tax savings from these exclusions go to middle- and upper-income families. This is particularly true of all employee benefits and transfer payments that are not subject to a stringent means test. If the exclusions were eliminated, horizontal and vertical equity would be improved, and marginal tax rates could be reduced. This would increase the incentives to work, to save, and to take risks.

Comments by Gerard M. Brannon

First, a comment on Emil Sunley's opening argument in favor of the comprehensive tax base. The argument is that repealing tax expenditures will benefit the nation by permitting a reduction in the marginal tax rates. I agree, even without the word "tax" in front of "expenditure." Many direct expenditures should be repealed, and this would also permit us to lower tax rates. The analogy suggests that a thoroughgoing expenditure analysis might throw a different light on the priorities for reform.

Consider the exclusion of social security income benefits, which is an expenditure program for the aged, a constituency numerous enough to demand some expenditures. The relevant issue for Congress is the comparison between this and other programs for the aged. Sunley says only that tax benefits for the aged benefit rich old people more than poor old people. This charge is not exactly devastating when the tax expenditure is considered along with other expenditures for the aged. Since Congress does a great deal through other expenditures for old people who are poor, it is arguable that a comprehensive program for the aged requires that old age assistance and the welfare element in social security be supplemented by transfers to some old people above the poverty levels.

An analysis along these lines would still conclude that the exclusion of social security benefits from the income tax base is bad policy. On the other hand, a proposal advanced by the Treasury Department in the 1960s to substitute a phased-out tax credit for the present tax benefits is attractive. I mention this only to point out that emphasizing the word "tax" in tax expenditure leads one to focus exclusively on tax subsidies. Emphasizing the word "expenditure" leads to a different sort of analysis than that initiated by Sunley.

I now turn to a discussion of Sunley's paper on its own terms. Table 3-8 is my effort to reproduce his recommendations in terms of several principles.

Principle 1 is the one that present law applies to commercial annuities. No deduction is allowed for investments in annuities (except for the individual retirement annuity and Keogh plans), but annuitants are taxed on income above cost. Sunley would also tax employees on employers' contributions, including amounts paid into social security, since taxability of the employer contribution to the employee is equivalent to nondeductibility. Contributions would only be taxed when they vest; social security is presumed to vest immediately and interest on pension reserves would remain tax free.

Like Sunley, I am uncomfortable with some details—the determination of employee shares, the vesting rule, the nontaxation of interest, and the treatment of the welfare component of social security under this annuity rule. On balance, however, I agree with the theory of Principle 1.

Principle 2 is that if the employer-paid plan provides for non-income benefits, that is, if it provides death benefits or medical expense benefits, the employee should still be taxed on the employer contribution, but there should be no tax on the proceeds. I find this broadly satisfactory even though some tax literature holds that insurance premiums should be deducted and benefits should be taxed in full. Again, like Sunley, I am uncomfortable about the absence of tax on interest on insurance reserves.

Principle 3, which applies current tax to current benefits (unemployment insurance), does not tax employees on employers' contributions. The principle also applies to plans that involve highly

Table 3-8. Principles Applying to Taxation of Employee Benefits and Transfer Payments

Principle	Case	Rule	Application	Exception
1	Plan providing future income-type benefits	Tax employees on employers' contribution; tax beneficiaries on benefits (with deduction for contribution)	Pension and public employee retirement plans; social security retirement, disability, and survivor benefits	Defer tax on employee until vested; assume vesting in social security
2	Plan providing payments for future or present special costs	Tax employees on employers' contribution; do not tax beneficiary	Group term life insurance; group accident and health insurance; workmen's compensation (excluding disability income); Medicare; social security death benefit; group prepaid legal insurance	
3	Plan providing income-type benefits that are either current or highly contingent	Do not tax employees on employers' contribution; tax payment to beneficiary	Unemployment compensation; supplementary unemployment benefits; workmen's compensation (disability income only); disability insurance	
4	Fringe benefits that are not part of a formal plan	Tax when practical to do so	Certain meals and lodging, company discounts, etc.	
5	Contingent government payments (generally not related to employment)	Tax beneficiary unless program is under stringent means test	Welfare payments (nontaxable); veterans' benefits and black-lung benefits (taxable)	Revise if good negative income tax is adopted

contingent benefits. Under the unemployment insurance, disability, and supplementary unemployment benefits plans, a reserve is built up, but Principle 1 is not applied, because it is too difficult to allocate contributions to potential beneficiaries.

Principle 4 is a cry of desperation in the face of many different kinds of fringe benefits ranging from business lunches to company discounts. I judge that Sunley would be tougher than present law, but sorting out all these things would take another conference.

Under Principle 5, Sunley comes out against taxing welfare payments. Again, tax purists differ on the issue, but I side with Sunley. If welfare is calculated with reference to disposable income, the imposition of a tax should lead to a modification of the welfare payment, so little is gained. If there were a comprehensive negative income tax, other receipts would be taken into account in fixing the basic allowance, so income tax is an unnecessary complication. It seems cleaner to design the welfare payment for what it is desired to be *net* and to leave income tax out of the picture.

Principle 5, however, makes veterans' benefits and black-lung benefits taxable on the grounds that they are only loosely means-tested. This produces a peculiar benefit structure. A part of the understanding with draftees was that they would become eligible for benefits in the future if they were "near poor." Other people qualify for welfare only if they are really poor. If a veteran is really poor, some of his distinctive military-related benefit is lost because of the way the welfare formula takes account of other income. Sunley seems to be on solid ground when he says that the benefit given to a near-poor veteran who is subject to tax should be subject to some tax offset by analogy to the welfare offset applied to a benefit to a veteran who is really poor (and nontaxable).

In general, I find Sunley's principles to be reasonable, if less than perfect. I am disturbed, however, that he does not mention transition problems. Most of these plans represent decisions made under one set of game rules, and changing the rules in mid-pension would create a host of problems. Many of the problems may be trivial, but they are the types of problems that taxpayer representatives talk about at great length before congressional committees. Some of the transition problems are interesting theoretically. Under Medicare, for example, the real windfall comes to the currently retired who never paid a Medicare tax or only did so for a few years. The burden of Medicare is on young workers, the only group that pays more tax under the Sunley reforms.

Finally, to round out the discussion I would like to suggest a different and more flexible approach to many of the employee benefit plans discussed by Sunley. This would be an excise or withholding tax imposed on the employer when the deduction is claimed or when interest is earned on the reserves under the plan. Some calculations that I have done suggest that a 20 percent excise tax rate would be close to the current rate for the overwhelming portion of beneficiaries. (Where identifiable executive-type fringe benefits are concerned, I would tax them to the employee when practical.) On insurance-type plans (unemployment, disability, or pension), I would give a tax credit to the beneficiary when the benefit is paid.

This approach has both drawbacks and advantages when compared with Sunley's plan. There is some inelegance in using an arbitrary rate for the present tax. On the other hand, it is practical to tax the interest under an excise-withholding tax. The excise tax could be extended to a large group of noninsurance fringe benefits that would be too messy to handle as taxable to the beneficiary. The excise tax approach would bypass a host of problems that would be involved in the current allocation of insurance or pension plan contributions to particular employees. It also would avoid the vesting problem. An excise-withholding tax would make it possible to incorporate Principle 3 into Principle 1.

Finally, the excise tax approach has flexibility. It could be introduced at a low rate and gradually increased. If my earlier strictures about the political consequences of these issues are correct, even an excise tax that was gradually increased to only 10 percent might be a tax in the hand that would be better than Sunley in the bush.

Comments by John K. McNulty

It is hard to disagree with Emil Sunley's main thesis that in principle the exclusions for employee benefits and transfer payments ought to be narrowed or repealed altogether. The result of the more comprehensive tax base thus obtained could be better equity, lower tax rates, and greater efficiency. (I think that he has in mind either lowering tax rates across the board, or perhaps even "degressing" the rates, that is, making them less progressive.) At a number of points, he shows that equity and efficiency considerations, which elsewhere often conflict, both favor repeal of the exclusions for employee benefits and transfer payments. Perhaps the effect on savings and investment, as distinguished from expenditures and consumption, would have to be analyzed and estimated further to put to rest fears about lost incentives to save and an overall bias in the income tax system against saving.

Sunley mentions that his proposals would not simplify the system, although he states that the taxpayer alone would not face a much more complex world. I would like to suggest that in fact his reforms might simplify the system a good deal if the concern is not just about simplifying the tax law but also about the cost of administration and the behavior of taxpayers in complying with, or avoiding, taxes. Reform along these lines might reduce taxpayer efforts—now so common—to change taxable compensation into tax-free or tax-favored forms of compensation, or "noncompensation." The end result may be a simpler structure of compensation and lower transaction costs in the world at large, in the form of compliance, avoidance, and administrative, legislative, and judicial costs.

The question then boils down to *how* these benefit and transfer items are to be taxed, and in particular, *when* they are to be taxed. The answer to these questions will in part determine *who* pays the taxes. This part of Sunley's analysis obviously leads the reader onto the right track.

Sunley distinguishes insurance programs from what he calls tax transfer programs; the benefits of the latter, he says, should be taxed when received. Fair enough. But one question is whether he has used that principle throughout his paper completely. Perhaps that principle could be tested, particularly if applied to social security, which has elements of both an insurance program and a tax transfer program. Can his approach be applied here? Or does the distinction break down? He leaves me somewhat unconvinced.

How to define the categories of insurance, as differentiated from tax transfer programs, may prove to be a haunting and stubborn problem. The paper does not dwell on this definitional problem or establish that these two categories are exhaustive—or sufficient to the task. Social security is only one illustration of the mixed character of categorical programs with which Sunley's principle must contend.

I am less sure of his recommendation for the tax treatment of insurance programs. Sunley proposes that the value of the *right to receive* the benefit should be taxed as it accrues, although he admits a vesting problem and distinguishes between vested and unvested benefits. He adds that even in the case of insurance programs, if the benefits are essentially wage replacements, they should be taxed as received rather than as the right to receive them accrues. This would improve equity and reduce the adverse incentive effects of such insurance programs.

Particularly in connection with programs whose benefits Sunley recommends be taxed as they accrue, liquidity problems appear prominent. He mentions the possibility of increased withholding, but I think there may be more serious liquidity problems if the right to receive the benefit is to be taxed on an accrual basis and if taxpayers are forced to pay the tax at a time when they have not yet received the benefits (and the possibility exists that they will never receive them).

One of Sunley's reasons for advocating the change to a comprehensive base is to lower or level the rates. This appeals to me because I am convinced that the complexity of the taxpayer's and tax-planner's worlds is caused in large part by the nonuniform and nominally steeply progressive tax rate schedules. If the rate of tax could be made uniform on all forms of income, and with an identical (proportional) rate, so much would be gained in simplicity and in reduced transaction costs that it might be well worth the price paid in progressivity. Incentives for much taxpayer maneuvering (such as income-shifting from high-bracket taxpayers to lower ones, from high-bracket years to lower ones, from ordinary income to capital gains or other preferred categories) and governmental policing would be removed by these basic structural changes. Furthermore, progressivity would not necessarily be reduced despite the proportional, uniform rate schedule. The use of a credit income tax and a comprehensive tax base, for example, could result in as much or more progressivity than is actually obtained in the present system in which the marginal income tax rates are (nominally) steeply graduated.

Sunley helpfully emphasizes that an exclusion is the counterpart of a deduction. In discussing exclusions he looks in the direction of counterparts on the deduction side, such as Keogh or individual retirement annuity plans, that ought to be changed to parallel changes on the exclusion side (for employee benefits). I believe it follows that if there are two counterpart allowances, one should not lightly be repealed unless the other is also repealed. To put it more generally, if a given allowance is one taxpayer's equivalent of another taxpayer's allowance in a different form, or the same form of a different allowance, then perhaps both should remain if both cannot be abolished. At some points, Sunley seems to agree.

To the same effect, I would also mention that with respect to welfare payments and employee benefits, a counterpart exists in the form of the present exclusion for gifts and bequests, which may be much like welfare for students and other notably poor but deserving human beings. Can one exclusion be repealed while the other remains?

A hard look should also be taken at the provision (section 83) in the Internal Revenue Code that has to do with property given as compensation by an employer to an employee, to determine whether and how it bears, or could be brought to bear, directly or by analogy on benefits or transfers or their counterparts.

It is worth adding a little more about the difficulty of separating the consumption element of business costs, particularly in the fringe benefit area. This is perhaps the toughest nut to crack. The problem, of course, is in part a valuation problem. If fair market value of some of those fringe benefits is used, there is a likelihood of overtaxation of the recipient because their "actual" value to the recipient is less, even if he or she elects to consume them, since their marginal cost to the employee lies below fair market value. On the other hand, if the employer's cost is used, there is a danger of undertaxation inasmuch as value to the employee often will exceed such cost. Sunley does not seem to solve this problem, to my way of thinking.

A somewhat related problem is that of using "proxies" for valuation purposes. For example, is it a reasonable approximation for taxing each employee on his year-to-year increase in present value of expected future benefits to tax each employee on his own and his employer's contributions and (possibly) earnings on pension trust funds, as Sunley suggests? He leaves me unpersuaded.

Sunley helpfully points out that it would be unsound economic or tax policy to have voluntary benefits, such as health care, costless at the margin because of the moral hazard problem—which is to say that vast and inefficient overconsumption can be expected if qualified persons can obtain such benefits at no apparent cost to themselves.

He also makes the point that an exclusion should be continued in the case of transfers that are subject to a stringent means test. The question is whether he has proven his case. My own feeling is that it would be better to include all the transfer payments in income and let the income tax exemptions or standard deductions or credits or other allowances take care of the problem of subsistence. But Sunley makes powerful arguments to the contrary, to the effect that it may be wasteful to both include them and then just take them out again with no net change. A question arises whether the desired rate of tax would apply if all benefits were included in the (positive) income tax base; if the present benefits are viewed as tax expenditures, one may not want those (or any) positive rates to apply. Or perhaps different rates should apply to earned and to investment income, especially during retirement years.

Sunley argues that the more comprehensive tax base would affect incentives to save, to work, and to take risks. It may not be immediately apparent why that is true, but evidently his point has to do more with the extent to which rates will be lowered. Though the analysis is generally correct, the actual effect would appear to depend on whether the slope of the rates has actually become more gradual or not. Moreover, an interreactive effect of changes in the employee benefit and transfer payment rules with changes elsewhere would have to be expected.

A most important observation about Sunley's paper is that he has worked in such a terribly tough area—one that is fraught with administrative difficulties, problems of valuation and timing, and ability to pay tax. Nevertheless, he shows that a comprehensive tax base approach—a much more comprehensive tax base—can be attained without undue complexity, and perhaps, as I have suggested, with some gain in simplification. He has worked out many (though not all) of the problems and has shown them to be less intractable than we might have thought.

Altogether, Sunley has shown the way to a more equitable and fiscally efficient tax base in an area where Congress and the Treasury Department either have feared to tread or have retreated in the face of organized taxpayer objections and in the name of administrative feasibility. His efforts have produced sound analytical approaches to tough problems and will make it harder for theorists and policymakers alike to duck the issues in future tax reform efforts.

CHAPTER FOUR

Capital Gains and Losses

JAMES W. WETZLER*

THE TREATMENT of capital gains and losses has been one of the
most controversial issues of federal tax policy, having been changed
by Congress in no fewer than ten separate revenue bills. The lack of
any consensus on the subject is suggested by the fact that while the
Tax Reform Act of 1976 contains a significant increase in the income
tax on many capital gains, both the Ford administration and a sizable
minority in Congress supported a large capital gains tax reduction
during the writing of that act.

Controversy over taxing capital gains is not an American idiosyn-
crasy. France has recently enacted a limited capital gains tax that will
stand as a monument to tax complexity. Among the strange provisions of the new French law are preferential treatment for gains on
vineyards that produce vintage wine (but not those producing *vin
ordinaire*) and more favorable treatment of gains on inherited property than of gains on assets accumulated from saving.

The first section of this paper describes the several ways in which
the present tax treatment of capital gains and losses differs from a
comprehensive income tax base. The second discusses what administratively feasible method would most closely approximate full taxa-

* I wish to thank Peter Davis for making the estimates of the revenue effect of
full taxation of capital gains and Robert P. Strauss, Emil M. Sunley, Jr., and Joseph
A. Pechman for their helpful suggestions.

115

tion of capital gains and losses. This is followed by a summary of the effects of such a program on federal revenues and the distribution of the tax burden. The final sections compare the present law with full taxation of capital gains in terms of complexity, horizontal equity, and economic efficiency.

Present Tax Treatment of Capital Gains and Losses

There are four principal legislated differences between the current tax treatment of capital gains and what would occur under a comprehensive tax base: (1) the exclusion and alternative rate, (2) deferral, (3) the limited step-up in basis at death, and (4) the limits on the deduction of capital losses. A fifth unlegislated deviation from a comprehensive tax base is the underreporting of capital gains by taxpayers.

Exclusion and Alternative Rate

Individuals may exclude from taxable income 50 percent of their "net capital gains," defined as the excess of net long-term capital gains over net short-term capital losses. They may also elect to have the first $50,000 of net capital gains taxed at an alternative rate of 25 percent, a choice that is advantageous only to taxpayers whose marginal tax bracket exceeds 50 percent.[1] After 1977 the holding period

1. The exclusion and alternative rate have a long legislative history. Between 1913 and 1921 capital gains were fully included in taxable income, although appreciation that accrued before March 1, 1913, was exempt from income tax. In 1921 Congress enacted an alternative capital gains rate of 12.5 percent, which was half the 25 percent top rate on ordinary income that prevailed through the latter part of the 1920s. By 1934, however, the top rate on ordinary income had risen to 56 percent, and for taxpayers in the upper brackets the 12.5 percent alternative rate was a much larger tax preference for capital gains than had been intended in 1921. Congress therefore repealed the alternative rate in 1934 and enacted a sliding scale under which the inclusion proportion declined from 100 percent for short-term capital gains to 30 percent for gains on capital assets held more than ten years. The resultant lock-in effect created much dissatisfaction, and the present combination of exclusion and alternative rate began to evolve in the Revenue Act of 1938, which contained an alternative rate of 15 percent, a 33⅓ percent exclusion for gains on capital assets held between eighteen months and two years, and a 50 percent exclusion for gains on capital assets held more than two years. In 1942 Congress raised the alternative rate to 25 percent and made the exclusion 50 percent for all long-term gains. The Tax Reform Act of 1969 put a $50,000 cap on the amount of net capital gains eligible for the alternative rate.

defining long-term capital gains and losses will be one year.[2] There would be no such exclusion or alternative rate under a comprehensive income tax base.

The Treasury recaptures almost 15 percent of the revenue lost from the exclusion and the alternative rate because the excluded half of net capital gains is treated as a tax preference under the minimum tax.[3] In addition, excluded capital gains reduce the amount of earned income eligible for the 50 percent maximum tax rate.[4] These provisions reduce the effective exclusion from 50 percent to an average of about 43 percent.[5]

Deferral

Taxpayers must report a capital gain or loss when the underlying asset is sold (that is, on realization). A comprehensive income tax base would recognize the gain or loss as the appreciation occurs (that is, on accrual). Such tax deferral from the time of accrual to the time of realization has several consequences. First, taxpayers with accrued gains can receive income by investing the deferred tax; in effect tax deferral provides them an interest-free loan from the government.

2. Since 1921 there has always been a distinction between short-term and long-term capital gains based on the holding period of the underlying assets, with short-term gains fully included in taxable income. This holding period was two years between 1921 and 1934, one year between 1934 and 1938, eighteen months between 1938 and 1942, and six months between 1942 and 1976. The Tax Reform Act of 1976 raised the holding period defining short-term capital gains to nine months for assets sold in 1977 and to one year for assets sold after 1977. There are some exceptions to this rule.

3. The minimum tax, which is added to the regular income tax, equals 15 percent of the sum of eleven tax preferences, reduced by either $10,000 or half the individual's regular tax liability, whichever is greater. The minimum tax was enacted in 1969 and was significantly increased in the Tax Reform Act of 1976.

4. It is possible for the marginal tax rate on a long-term capital gain to approach 49.125 percent. This is the sum of a 35 percent regular tax, a regular tax increase on earned income equal to 20 percent of half the gain, and a 4.125 percent minimum tax (15 percent of the difference between half the gain and half the 45 percent increase in the regular tax).

5. Because it has a flat rate and a deduction for half the regular income taxes, the minimum tax reduces the effective exclusion by a larger percentage for taxpayers in low regular income tax brackets than for those in high brackets. For someone in the 70 percent bracket who pays the minimum tax and does not elect the alternative rate, the marginal tax rate on long-term capital gains is 39.88 percent and the effective exclusion is 43 percent. For someone in the 40 percent bracket who pays the minimum tax, the marginal tax rate for long-term capital gains is 26 percent and the effective exclusion is only 35 percent.

(Taxpayers with capital losses, however, must postpone their tax saving from deducting the loss.) Second, because a taxpayer frequently can decide when to realize an accrued capital gain or loss, he can reduce his taxes by realizing gains in years when his marginal tax rate is relatively low and realizing losses when his marginal tax rate is high. This option provides a form of income averaging that is unavailable for ordinary income. Third, gains that have accrued over several years are taxed in one year at progressive rates, a practice that can lead to a higher overall tax burden than would taxing them on accrual.

The interest-free loan from deferral can be almost as large a tax preference as the much more controversial exclusion. For example, if the holding period is ten years, the interest rate is 8 percent, the marginal tax rate is 30 percent, and the asset price has risen arithmetically, the interest-free loan from deferral is equivalent to an exclusion of one-third of the included part of the gain. Because the value of deferral rises with interest rates, moreover, it has been growing in significance in recent years as interest rates have risen. The recently enacted rule that requires carry-over of basis at death will make deferral still more important.

Step-up in Basis at Death

When there is a gift of appreciated property, the donor does not report the gain, and the recipient of the gift carries over the donor's cost or other basis, adjusted upward for the gift tax attributable to the appreciation.[6] As a result of the Tax Reform Act of 1976, carry-over of basis is now the general rule for bequests of appreciated property as well. (Under prior law, the basis of appreciated property held at death was stepped up to its fair market value at time of death.)

Under certain exceptions, however, there will still be a limited step-up in basis at death, and to this extent appreciation during the decedent's lifetime will permanently escape income tax. The new law contains a step-up in basis for appreciation occurring before December 31, 1976. In addition, the heirs of each decedent will get a step-up in basis as long as the overall basis in the estate is less than $60,000.

6. A capital gain is computed by subtracting the taxpayer's "basis" from the selling price. Generally the basis equals the cost of purchasing the asset; however, the cost is adjusted for various reasons, such as the downward adjustment for depreciation taken on the asset or the upward adjustment for gift tax.

These exceptions to carry-over of basis would not exist under a comprehensive income tax base.

Limits on the Deduction of Capital Losses

With a comprehensive income tax base, capital losses would be fully deductible as they accrued. The present law, however, recognizes capital losses on realization and contains several limits on deducting them. While individuals may deduct capital losses against capital gains, they may deduct capital losses against only $3,000 of ordinary income each year and must reduce long-term capital losses by 50 percent when deducting them against ordinary income.[7] (Capital losses not deducted in the current year may be carried forward until death.)

When someone gives away an asset on which there is an accrued loss, the recipient of the gift must use as his basis the asset's value at the time of the gift. This step-down in basis means that the recipient may not deduct the donor's loss when he sells the asset. The usual carry-over of basis applies, however, when someone bequeaths an asset on which there is a loss, so that heirs may deduct the decedent's accrued losses.

Capital Gains and Losses in a Comprehensive Income Tax Base

A comprehensive income tax base would require the repeal of the exclusion and alternative rate. To permit greater deduction of capital losses, there would be repeal of the $3,000 limit on the amount of ordinary income against which capital losses can be deducted, the 50 percent reduction of long-term capital losses when they are deducted against ordinary income, and the step-down in basis for gifts of assets on which there are accrued losses. Moreover, a comprehensive tax base would require repealing the $60,000 minimum basis that is imputed to each estate and the grandfather clause exempting pre-1977 appreciation from carry-over of basis at death. None of these changes presents a serious administrative problem.

7. There have been numerous changes over the years in the rules for the deduction of losses, ranging from no deduction at all to full deduction against ordinary income. Most recently the Tax Reform Act of 1976 raised the amount of ordinary income against which capital losses may be deducted from $1,000 to $2,000 in 1977 and $3,000 thereafter.

It is more difficult to decide on an administratively feasible method of limiting deferral. Completely eliminating deferral means taxing on accrual, which must be ruled out because it would be extraordinarily difficult to value nonmarketable assets every year in order to measure the accrued gain or loss. In addition, accrual taxation would impose a tax at a time when the taxpayer does not necessarily have any cash; thus there would have to be liberal extensions of time for payment, and it would be desirable to have long loss carry-backs and liberal income-averaging provisions to prevent the imposition of a tax in cases of transitory fluctuations in asset values.

There are two more promising ways to limit deferral: constructive realization of gains and losses on assets transferred at death or by gift, and the imposition of an interest charge for the deferral privilege. Of these, an appropriate deferral charge would probably more closely approximate accrual taxation, although the two ways are not mutually exclusive.

Under constructive realization, appreciation on assets transferred by gift or bequest would be included in income, either in the donor's income tax return for the year of the gift or in the decedent's final income tax return. For bequests of appreciated assets, the income tax liability would be a debt of the estate and hence deductible under the estate tax.

The principal administrative advantage of constructive realization over accrual taxation is that taxpayers subject to the gift and estate tax must already value their assets, so that in these cases there is no additional administrative burden in valuing them for the income tax. For assets owned by taxpayers whose wealth is below the filing requirement for the gift and estate tax, constructive realization does require a separate valuation, but making such a valuation once in a lifetime is not an onerous administrative burden. An exemption for gifts and estates below certain sizes would reduce the administrative burden still further.[8]

Constructive realization would approximate accrual taxation more closely than present law does by putting a limit on the time period during which someone could defer tax on an accrued gain; however, its results would often differ significantly from those of accrual taxation. Constructive realization would do nothing to reduce the benefit

8. The 1968 tax reform program of the Treasury Department included constructive realization, as did the 1963 tax reform proposals of President Kennedy.

from deferral during the period before an asset is transferred, which could be many decades. In many cases, constructive realization at death will impose a smaller tax than accrual taxation because a taxpayer's marginal income tax rate in the year of his death will often be lower than his marginal rate during the period in which his capital gains accrued; many people with high taxable incomes during their lifetimes have low taxable incomes in the year they die because they die early in the year, have high medical expense deductions, or have low earnings in their last year. In other cases, however, constructive realization at death would be harsher than accrual taxation because taxing a lifetime accumulation of unrealized gains in one year would exacerbate the "bunching effect" of taxing several years' income in a single year at progressive tax rates. This last problem could be mitigated with more liberal income averaging.

The principal congressional objection to constructive realization has been that it would impose an income tax at a time when the taxpayer or his estate does not necessarily have the cash needed to pay the tax. Thus it would either induce forced sales of assets or would require long extensions of time for payment of the tax.

The second way to reduce the advantage of deferral would be to keep the present rule for carry-over of basis at death or upon making a gift, modified to include all assets, and to impose an interest charge for deferral based on the holding period of the asset.[9] There could also be a deferral credit for capital losses. The taxpayer would compute the charge or credit from a table based on the actual interest rates that prevailed during the years in which he held the asset and computed under certain arbitrary assumptions concerning the rate at which the asset price rose or fell during the holding period.

This deferral charge approach would have two advantages over constructive realization. A deferral charge would reduce the advantage from deferral over the entire holding period, rather than just terminate deferral at the time of death or the making of a gift. The deferral charge would also avoid the major administrative problems of constructive realization: the need to value assets not subject to the transfer tax and the need for extensions of time for payment of tax.

The deferral charge, however, would still differ from accrual taxa-

9. This is recommended in Roger Brinner and Alicia Munnell, "Taxation of Capital Gains: Inflation and Other Problems," Federal Reserve Bank of Boston, *New England Economic Review,* September-October 1974, pp. 3–21.

tion in several ways. Only by accident would the actual gain accrue in whatever manner must be assumed in computing the deferral charge.[10] In addition, since the deferral charge retains carry-over of basis, the gain on a transferred asset would be taxed at the marginal tax rate of the recipient of the gift or bequest, not that of the transferrer. Finally, the precisely appropriate deferral charge would vary nonlinearly with the marginal tax rate, and some shortcut formula would be needed.

There are several ways to compute such a deferral charge; as an illustration, one possible method is given in the appendix to this chapter. For a holding period of ten years and an interest rate of 8 percent, the deferral charge on a $1 gain under this shortcut formula would be 10 cents; it would be 25 cents for a holding period of twenty years.

Revenue and Distributional Effects

Full taxation of capital gains and losses would produce substantial revenues for the federal government, and most of these additional taxes would be paid by families with high incomes. Table 4-1 presents a first-order estimate of the revenue effect of full taxation of capital gains from the Treasury Tax Model.[11] The estimate assumes no change in behavior in response to the tax change. Repealing the exclusion and alternative rate, introducing a deferral charge based on table 4-3 in the appendix (with an 8 percent interest rate), and eliminating the $3,000 limit on the deduction of capital losses against ordinary income would raise $11.9 billion at 1976 income levels. Over half of this revenue would come from taxpayers with incomes over

10. The Tax Reform Act of 1976, however, created a precedent for assuming an arithmetic rate of appreciation. For nonmarketable assets, the amount of pre-1977 appreciation, which is exempt from the new rule requiring carry-over of basis at death, is determined by prorating the entire gain uniformly over the holding period.

11. The Treasury Tax Model is a sample of 50,000 tax returns for 1973 that has been extrapolated to 1976 income levels. Imputations made to the model adjust for changes in the law since 1973. The imputations assume an increase in long-term realizations as a result of the increase in the holding period to one year. They also assume that the rule for carry-over of basis in the Tax Reform Act of 1976 is fully effective, which also increases the amount of capital gains subject to tax. Because of this last assumption, the estimate overstates the actual revenue effect in the next several decades by gradually decreasing amounts (initially $1.1 billion), but it should give a reliable picture of the situation after the "fresh start" in the carry-over-of-basis rule is eroded by the passage of time.

Table 4-1. Revenue Effect of Full Taxation of Capital Gains and Losses, by Income Class, 1976 Income Levels
Millions of dollars

Income class[a] (thousands of dollars)	Repeal of 50 percent capital gains exclusion and alternative rate[b]	Introduction of deferral charge for capital gains and credit for capital losses[c]	Unlimited deduction of capital losses against ordinary income	Total
Less than 0	0	−193	−279	−472
0–5	9	36	−44	−1
5–10	99	85	−207	−23
10–15	173	274	−116	331
15–20	279	309	−108	480
20–30	528	483	−233	778
30–50	1,075	816	−202	1,689
50–100	1,866	1,215	−253	2,828
100 and over	4,271	2,177	−179	6,269
Total	8,299	5,201	−1,620	11,880

Source: U.S. Department of the Treasury, Treasury Tax Model. For additional imputations made to the model, see text note 11. Figures are rounded.

a. Income is defined as adjusted gross income plus the excluded part of capital gains minus capital losses not deducted in arriving at adjusted gross income.

b. Data also reflect repeal of the 50 percent reduction in long-term capital losses deducted against ordinary income.

c. The deferral charge and credit are computed from table 4-3, using an interest rate of 8 percent.

$100,000.[12] If such changes were in effect, it would be possible to reduce the top rate bracket to 39 percent without any net revenue loss from taxpayers with incomes over $100,000. Alternatively, there could be approximately a 9 percent reduction in the entire tax rate schedule without any overall revenue loss.[13]

The first-order revenue estimate, however, probably overstates the progressivity of full taxation of capital gains. After any increase in tax rates on capital gains, investors would sell assets on which they expect to receive capital gains and buy other assets; this would increase the before-tax rate of return on the assets on which investors expect to

12. Income is defined as adjusted gross income plus the excluded part of capital gains minus capital losses not deducted in arriving at adjusted gross income.

13. Another difference between the present system and a comprehensive income tax base is underreporting by taxpayers. Unpublished data collected by the IRS for 1969 estimate underreporting of capital gains at 12.5 percent, with a standard deviation of 3.75 percent. This estimate comes from the Taxpayer Compliance Measurement Program, under which the IRS carefully audits a sample of taxpayers to estimate compliance with the tax laws.

receive capital gains and would reduce the before-tax rate of return on other assets. This market response to the tax change would shift some of the tax burden from recipients of capital gains to other owners of wealth. In addition to the extent that higher capital gains taxes reduced capital accumulation, labor productivity and real wage rates would decline, which would shift some of the tax burden to labor. Both of these shifts in the tax burden would reduce the progressivity of the tax change. Such market responses are examined in greater detail in the section below on economic efficiency.

The first-order revenue estimate for repealing the exclusion, the alternative rate, and the 50 percent reduction in long-term capital losses deducted against ordinary income is $8.3 billion, 51 percent of which would come from taxpayers with incomes over $100,000. These changes could finance a reduction in the top bracket rate to 46 percent, with no net revenue loss to taxpayers with incomes over $100,000. (Repealing the alternative rate by itself would produce only about $100 million, since most eligible taxpayers now forgo the alternative rate in order to elect income averaging.)

These revenue estimates assume no change in realizations in response to the change in the law. This is a reasonable assumption if repeal of the exclusion and the alternative rate were accompanied by a deferral charge. Otherwise, the first-order revenue estimate would overstate the actual revenue gain and probably its progressivity as well, since people would respond to the higher capital gains tax by reducing realizations and high-income people would have more flexibility and more incentive to do this than others.

The additional revenue from a deferral charge and credit, using the table in the appendix with an 8 percent interest rate, would be $5.2 billion, 42 percent of which would come from taxpayers with incomes over $100,000. The use of a lower interest rate in computing the deferral charge would reduce this revenue gain, as would the use of a formula that assumed exponential appreciation rather than arithmetic appreciation. The deferral charge would be less progressive than repeal of the exclusion and alternative rate because it would not depend on the taxpayer's marginal tax rate, while the exclusion and alternative rate are worth more to taxpayers in high brackets than to those in lower brackets. The deferral charge would increase realizations, but this effect is not considered in the first-order revenue estimate.

Eliminating the $3,000 limit on the amount of ordinary income against which capital losses may be offset would reduce revenues by $1.6 billion.

Complexity

The complexity of the present income tax is perhaps its most widely criticized feature. Tax simplification itself, however, is a complicated goal. For the average taxpayer, tax simplification means simplifying the tax forms and instructions, reducing the amount of recordkeeping needed for tax purposes, and reducing the number of tax considerations that he must take into account in making economic and other decisions. For tax lawyers and accountants and for the Internal Revenue Service (IRS), tax simplification also means reducing the amount of costly litigation. For legislators, simplification means making the tax law itself sufficiently accessible to enable them to analyze its impact and decide whether and how to change it.

Tax Forms

Repealing the exclusion and alternative rate would permit a substantial simplification of the tax forms. The new Schedule D of Form 1040, on which an individual calculates his net short-term or net long-term capital gain or loss, stretches to twenty-nine lines on two pages. Repealing the exclusion and the alternative rate would enable the IRS to reduce Schedule D to only nine lines.

With repeal of the exclusion, the IRS could also eliminate the new Form 4798, which is four pages long and deals solely with carry-overs of pre-1970 capital losses.[14] Repealing the alternative tax would enable the IRS to delete half of the thirty-four lines on Form 4726, which deals with the maximum tax on personal service income. The number of people who must file the two-page minimum tax form would also decline significantly if the exclusion and alternative rate were repealed.

A deferral charge and credit, however, would add a good deal of complexity to Schedule D. Taxpayers would have to compute the holding period for each transaction subject to the deferral charge, refer to a table to get the deferral charge per dollar of gain for each

14. Pre-1970 capital losses need not be reduced by 50 percent when they are deducted against ordinary income, a result of the transitional rule adopted in the Tax Reform Act of 1969.

such transaction, multiply by the gain to get the deferral charge per transaction, and then sum up to get the overall deferral charge. This complexity is an important objection to the deferral charge.

Recordkeeping

Repealing the exclusion and alternative rate would not increase the records that taxpayers must keep for tax purposes. The deferral charge, however, would require exact knowledge of the holding period, which is now unnecessary after the first year. Unlimited deduction of capital losses against ordinary income would simplify recordkeeping by allowing taxpayers to use up their capital loss carry-overs faster, thereby reducing the need for the taxpayer to remember his carry-over from year to year.

It is not clear whether carry-over of basis at death involves more difficult recordkeeping than either constructive realization or a step-up in basis. Under carry-over of basis, the heir must determine the decedent's basis, which in some cases will undoubtedly be difficult or even impossible. Under both constructive realization and step-up in basis, however, the heir would have to know the exact asset value at time of death; this would present a problem for assets (especially nonmarketable ones) in estates whose gross value is below the filing requirement for the gift and estate tax and that therefore need not be valued for the transfer tax. These estates contain well over half of the total personal wealth of those who die in any one year.

Economic Decisions by Taxpayers

A significant simplification that would result from full taxation of capital gains and losses is the elimination of a whole series of tax considerations that must now be taken into account in making investment decisions. A rational investor must now consider not only the underlying rate of return to be expected from an investment but also whether that return is likely to be in the form of ordinary income or a capital gain. Similarly, a taxpayer with an accrued gain or loss must take into account the tax consequences of realizing his gain or loss in a particular year, consequences that would be much less important if there were a deferral charge and credit and unlimited deduction of capital losses against ordinary income. Without the deferral charge, however, repeal of the exclusion and alternative rate would increase the impact of tax considerations on the realization decision.

Tax Law

Full taxation of capital gains and losses would permit a simplification of the tax law itself. This would reduce the amount of litigation and would make the law more easily accessible to legislators and other policymakers.

Repeal of the exclusion and alternative rate would make unnecessary many provisions of the tax law that are specifically intended to limit the scope of the capital gains exclusion. The sections that would become deadwood include the "recapture" rules for depreciation and intangible drilling costs, which require certain gains to be treated as ordinary income (sections 1245, 1250, and 1254 of the Internal Revenue Code); the special rules for collapsible corporations (section 341); and the distinction between short-term and long-term capital gains based on the holding period (section 1223).

If there were also a repeal of the $3,000 limit on the deduction of capital losses against ordinary income, there would no longer be any need for a definition of a "capital asset" (section 1221), for the special rules concerning short sales and income from buying and writing options (sections 1233 and 1234), and for the rules for so-called section 1231 gains and losses.[15]

The major issue in simplifying the Internal Revenue Code and the related rulings and regulations is deferral. Much of the code attempts to specify exactly when a gain or loss must be recognized, and complex rules permit nonrecognition for certain corporate reorganizations, involuntary conversions, like-kind exchanges, and so forth. Another large subchapter of the code is needed to distinguish between taxable dividend distributions to corporate shareholders and nontaxable distributions. All these distinctions would be much less important if there were no tax advantage to deferring tax on a capital gain and no exclusion or alternative rate. Unfortunately, this would require accrual taxation, which is at least as complex.

Summary

Repeal of the exclusion and alternative rate would clearly represent simplifications of the tax system. So would unlimited deduction

15. When a taxpayer has a loss under section 1231, which deals with certain business-related gains and losses, he may deduct it in full against ordinary income, but a gain is considered a capital gain.

of capital losses against ordinary income. All of the three possible methods of dealing with capital gains at death are complex, but their relative complexity is unclear. The deferral charge appears to be the only part of full taxation of capital gains and losses that clearly complicates the tax system.

Horizontal Equity

A widely held goal of tax policy is horizontal equity—that taxpayers in similar economic circumstances should pay the same amount of tax. While other interpretations can be justified, the assumption in this paper is that taxpayers in similar economic circumstances have the same real income.

Full taxation of capital gains, as outlined above, might be a departure from horizontal equity for two reasons: inflation and the bunching of income. This section analyzes these two objections to full taxation of capital gains and also considers in greater detail the inequity under present law affecting taxpayers with net capital losses.

Inflation

One argument against increasing capital gains taxes is that part or all of capital gains merely reflects inflation and therefore is not real income. For example, if a person bought an asset for $10,000 in 1955 and sold it in 1975 for $20,000, he had no real income from the sale because the price level doubled in that twenty-year period. The purchasing power represented by the sales price was no greater than that represented by the purchase price. Under the present law, however, he must report a gain of $10,000 and include $5,000 in taxable income.

While the problem of correctly defining income in an inflationary economy is perhaps most easily understood in the case of an illusory capital gain, the same issue arises with all types of income from capital and with debt. If the owner of a savings account receives interest of $5 on a $100 balance during a year in which the price level has risen by 5 percent, he too has received no increase in real income; the interest merely offsets the decline in the real value of his account. Under the law, he must still include $5 in taxable income; unlike the recipient of an illusory capital gain, he gets no deferral and no exclusion.

A complete program of adjusting the definition of income for inflation would require four adjustments. First, taxpayers would increase the basis of capital assets by the rate of inflation to exclude from tax all purely illusory gains. Second, owners of savings accounts and similar assets would deduct the loss resulting from the decline in the real value of their accounts due to inflation. Third, businesses would be allowed to adjust their basis upward by the rate of inflation in computing depreciation deductions and inventory profits. Fourth, debtors would report income whenever inflation reduced the real value of their indebtedness. From the standpoint of horizontal equity, much can be said for such indexing for inflation; however, it is not clear that greater horizontal equity would be achieved by making an inflation adjustment for some types of income from capital and not for others.[16]

If there is to be an inflation adjustment for only certain types of income from capital, an alternative approach to making such an adjustment for capital gains, either precisely with a basis adjustment or haphazardly with tax preferences, is to use whatever revenue is available to make the appropriate inflation adjustment for interest from savings accounts. Unlike capital gains, interest income now receives no tax preference (neither an exclusion nor deferral), and interest rates on savings accounts often cannot rise in response to expected inflation because of legislated ceilings on these rates (which are, in effect, a tax on such income). Interest income from savings accounts is also much less highly concentrated than capital gains.[17]

Moreover, even if one accepts the proposition that there should be an inflation adjustment for capital gains but not for the less highly concentrated types of income from capital for which the inflation

16. Under certain conditions, a horizontally equitable adjustment for inflation can be achieved simply by indexing the basis of depreciable assets and making no other adjustments. Market interest rates would then rise by enough to compensate investors for the additional tax burden caused by inflation. This will occur if borrowers and lenders have the same marginal tax rates, inflation is fully anticipated, and interest rates are determined by market forces. On this point, see Martin Feldstein, Jerry Green, and Eytan Sheshinski, "Inflation and Taxes in a Growing Economy with Debt and Equity Finance," Discussion Paper 481 (Harvard Institute for Economic Research, June 1976; processed). These conditions do not hold in the U.S. economy today, so that horizontal equity requires indexing for all forms of income from capital and for debt.

17. In 1975 taxpayers with adjusted gross incomes of over $50,000 received 40 percent of net capital gains and 13 percent of interest income.

issue is more serious, the exclusion, the alternative rate, and deferral do not very closely approximate the tax reduction justified by inflation.[18] The appropriate inflation adjustment is to increase the basis of capital assets by the rate of inflation, not to exclude a fraction of the gain, defer the tax on the gain, or tax it at a preferential rate.

No simple way exists to approximate an inflation adjustment with an exclusion equal to a percentage of the gain, even if the exclusion percentage is varied according to the holding period, as under proposals for a sliding scale. While during a period of inflation the absolute amount of the illusory part of a capital gain rises as the holding period lengthens, the absolute size of the real part of the gain is likely to rise with the holding period as well. There is no reason why the fraction of the total capital gain that is illusory should rise with the holding period; therefore, if the goal is merely to exclude illusory gains, there is no reason for the inclusion percentage to fall as the holding period lengthens. Similarly, the tax benefit from deferral, which rises with the holding period, does not approximate an inflation adjustment.

Bunching

Taxing capital gains on a realization basis rather than on an accrual basis can be a disadvantage to particular taxpayers, since gains that have accrued over several years are taxed in a single year at progressive rates. This bunching of the gain can result in a larger tax burden than would taxation on accrual, especially for taxpayers who realize gains only occasionally.

For example, consider a married couple whose ordinary taxable income (under the pre-1977 definition) has been $20,000 a year for forty years and who realize a capital gain of $100,000 on an asset held for forty years. While there are cases in which the bunching effect is greater, this case is typical of the once-in-a-lifetime capital gain that has been of concern to legislators.[19]

Under present law this couple would pay a regular income tax of $23,000 and a minimum tax on the excluded part of the capital gain

18. The inadequacies of an exclusion as an inflation adjustment are fully discussed in Roger Brinner, "Inflation, Deferral and the Neutral Taxation of Capital Gains," *National Tax Journal*, vol. 26 (December 1973), pp. 565–73; and P. A. Diamond, "Inflation and the Comprehensive Tax Base," *Journal of Public Economics*, vol. 4 (August 1975), pp. 227–44.

19. It can be shown that the bunching effect is positively related to the length of the holding period, the size of the gain, and the steepness of the tax rate schedule.

of $5,775, a total tax burden of $28,775 (including a tax saving of $4,200 from income averaging).[20] If the exclusion were repealed, the tax would rise to $45,560 (including an $11,840 tax saving from income averaging).

To illustrate the bunching effect, assume that the taxpayer could prorate the entire gain over the holding period into forty increments of $2,500 and pay tax on the entire $100,000 gain at the tax rate applicable to the next $2,500 of income (in this case 32 percent). Under such a rule, which completely eliminates the bunching effect, tax liability for the year the gain is realized would be $36,200. Thus the present exclusion overcompensates for the bunching effect by $7,425 ($36,200 minus $28,775); but without any exclusion or alternative rate, the tax penalty from bunching would be $9,360 ($45,560 minus $36,200). Even in this extreme case of bunching, the exclusion comes only slightly closer to the horizontally equitable result than would repeal of the exclusion.

The bunching effect, moreover, cannot justify the exclusion and alternative rate as long as capital gains continue to receive tax deferral. The once-in-a-lifetime gains on assets with long holding periods are precisely the gains that receive the largest benefits from deferral. In the example above, with repeal of the exclusion, the married couple would receive after-tax income of $82,869 over the forty-year holding period by investing the deferred tax on its accrued gain at 8 percent. This benefit from deferral would be over eight times as large as the penalty from bunching.

Three ways to alleviate the bunching problem if there is full inclusion of capital gains are to reduce the steepness of the rate schedule, to prorate the gain, and to expand income averaging.

The horizontal inequity from bunching would be reduced to the extent that full taxation of capital gains would be accompanied by a tax rate reduction that reduced the steepness of the rate schedule.[21] If such a rate cut were designed to be distributionally neutral, for

20. Under present law, to the extent that taxable income exceeds 120 percent of the average of the prior four years, a taxpayer may in effect prorate that excess over the entire five-year period. The excess is called "averageable" income, and if it exceeds $3,000, the taxpayer may elect to pay five times the regular tax on one-fifth of the averageable income. A taxpayer may not elect income averaging if he elects either the alternative capital gains rate or the 50 percent maximum rate on personal service income. Capital gains were made eligible for income averaging in 1969.

21. The steepness of a rate schedule is the first derivative of the marginal tax rate with respect to taxable income.

example, there would be a significant reduction in both the steepness of the rate schedule and the tax penalty from bunching.

Under proration, taxpayers would divide the gain by the holding period to get a prorated gain and would pay tax on the entire gain at the rate applicable only to the prorated gain. This would eliminate any bunching effect. Proration, however, presents several serious problems. It would require a major complication of the tax forms. In addition, the interaction of proration with such other provisions as income averaging and the maximum tax on personal service income would be so complex that the use of these provisions would have to be denied to anyone who elected proration. Such an election would add complexity to the tax system because many taxpayers would compute their tax three ways to see how best to minimize their tax burden.[22]

Under the third possibility (expanding the income-averaging system), without a 50 percent exclusion or alternative rate but with a nine-year base period for income averaging, the tax liability in the illustration used above would be $42,200. This would reduce the tax penalty from the bunching effect in this case to $6,000. The extra base period could be limited to taxpayers with relatively large capital gains on assets with long holding periods.

Unfair Treatment of Taxpayers with Net Capital Losses

The present method of taxing capital gains and losses is unfair to taxpayers who have net capital losses. First, because the losses are deductible only upon realization, the tax saving from deducting the loss is postponed from the time of accrual to the time of realization— in effect an interest-free loan from the taxpayer to the government. (The penalty here is not precisely symmetrical to the tax benefit that taxpayers with net capital gains receive from deferral. Because taxpayers with losses can still decide when to realize their loss, they can do so in a year in which their marginal tax rate is unusually high.) Second, taxpayers may deduct capital losses against up to only

---

22. The other objection to proration is that it can raise the marginal tax rate on ordinary income above 100 percent in certain cases. Consider a married taxpayer with taxable income, other than capital gains, of $19,900. The marginal tax rate applying to a $4,000 capital gain prorated over a forty-year holding period would be 28 percent. If taxable income were increased by $100, however, the marginal rate on the gain would rise to 32 percent, so that the incremental tax resulting from the additional $100 of ordinary income would be $188, a marginal tax rate of 188 percent.

$3,000 of ordinary income each year and must exclude 50 percent of long-term capital losses when doing so. Finally, losses on capital assets that are given away to other people cannot be deducted by either the donor or the recipient.

Despite this unfairness, as long as there is a tax preference for capital gains, there will have to be harsh treatment of people with capital losses to prevent widespread tax avoidance. The 50 percent exclusion for net long-term capital gains necessitates the 50 percent reduction of net long-term capital losses when they are deducted against ordinary income (which was enacted in the Tax Reform Act of 1969); otherwise, people would simply realize gains and losses in alternate years, excluding half their gains and deducting all their losses up to the $3,000 limit. Furthermore, the limit on the deduction of capital losses against ordinary income provides a limit to the advantage of deferral on capital gains for taxpayers with both gains and losses. If there were an unlimited deduction of capital losses against ordinary income without a deferral charge for capital gains, people would realize their capital losses quickly, claiming deductions against ordinary income, and would defer realization of their capital gains.[23]

An important contribution to horizontal equity that would result from full taxation of capital gains, including a deferral charge, is that it would greatly reduce the potential for tax avoidance that has required the harsh treatment of people with net capital losses. Eliminating the exclusion and alternative rate would permit the repeal of the 50 percent reduction of net capital losses that are deducted against ordinary income. A deferral charge for capital gains and credit for capital losses would permit the repeal of the $3,000 limit on the deduction of capital losses against ordinary income by greatly reducing the incentive for quickly realizing capital losses and postponing the realization of capital gains (although there would still be the possi-

23. Even under present law, the average holding period for assets on which losses are realized is much shorter than the holding period for assets on which gains are realized. Preliminary tabulations from the 1973 IRS study on transactions in capital assets, made available by the Treasury Department, indicate that 26 percent of capital losses are short term, compared with 8 percent of capital gains, and that the average holding period for long-term losses is only two years, compared with about nine years for capital gains. It is not clear to what extent the shorter average holding period for capital losses has resulted from the general rise in the prices of assets, which means that there is a smaller probability of a loss on an asset with a long holding period, or from the investors' response to the tax incentive for early realization of losses and postponement of gains.

bility of realizing gains in years when the tax bracket is relatively low and losses in years when it is relatively high). These would be important steps toward horizontal equity.[24] The step-down in basis for gifts of depreciated assets would still probably be necessary to prevent the transfer of these assets to people with higher marginal tax rates than the person who incurred the loss.

Summary

Repealing the 50 percent exclusion and alternative rate would be consistent with horizontal equity. These provisions do not very closely approximate the adjustments that would be needed to exclude only the illusory capital gains that result from inflation, and in any case it is not clear that horizontal equity is served by making such an inflation adjustment for capital gains but not for other forms of income or loss from capital, or for debt. Nor can the exclusion and alternative rate be justified by the bunching effect. The exclusion far overcompensates for bunching, even in extreme cases of bunching, and there are other feasible ways of alleviating the bunching effect in such cases—expanding income averaging and reducing the steepness of the rate schedules. Furthermore, as long as there is deferral, its benefits will far outweigh the tax penalty from bunching, even in the cases where the bunching effect is significant.

A deferral charge for capital gains and credit for capital losses would also promote greater horizontal equity. It would reduce the favorable tax treatment of capital gains relative to other types of income. It would also eliminate much of the potential for tax avoidance that has made it necessary to limit the deduction of capital losses against ordinary income. Like the exclusion and alternative rate, deferral is a poor adjustment for inflation, and it far overcompensates for the bunching effect.

Economic Efficiency

Most taxes lead to economic inefficiency and in that sense impose an excess burden. Defenders of the current tax preferences for capital

24. A more modest step to provide relief to taxpayers with capital losses would be a carry-back of capital losses to prior years, thus enabling people to deduct capital losses against capital gains of prior years. Under present law, when capital losses precede capital gains, they can be carried forward and deducted against the subsequent gains; but when gains precede losses, the losses cannot be carried back and deducted against the prior gains. An objection to the capital loss carry-back is the complexity of recomputing tax liability for prior years.

gains frequently argue that the excess burden of an increase in the tax on capital gains would be larger than that of the other taxes that could be reduced if there were higher taxation of capital gains. The three sources of economic inefficiency most often cited in reference to the capital gains tax are its lock-in effect, its effect on savings, and its effect on the allocation of capital. This section is an analysis of these three possible excess burdens.

The Lock-In Effect

The lock-in effect of capital gains taxation refers to its tendency to cause investors to postpone sales of appreciated assets. There are four reasons why there is such an incentive under present law. First, when realization is postponed, an investor gets the use of the deferred tax, or in effect receives an interest-free loan from the government. Second, if his wealth is less than $60,000 or if the unrealized appreciation occurred before 1977, the investor's heirs will benefit from the step-up in basis at death if the investor dies before realizing the gain. Third, if a person believes that his marginal tax rate will decline in the future or that he will transfer his appreciated asset to someone with a lower marginal tax rate, he has a tax incentive to postpone realizing his capital gain.[25] Fourth, if the marginal tax rate on a capital gain declines with the holding period, as is now the case with the distinction between short-term and long-term capital gains and as would also be true under the sliding-scale proposal, there is an additional incentive to defer realization.

THE LOCK-IN INCENTIVE UNDER FULL TAXATION
OF CAPITAL GAINS

It is possible to derive theoretical results about how the incentive to defer realization of gains on appreciated assets would change as a result of moving toward full taxation of capital gains. A useful way to measure the incentive to postpone realizing an accrued capital gain is to determine by how much the expected rate of return of an alternative asset would have to exceed the expected rate of return of the appreciated asset in order to induce an investor who is trying to maximize his wealth to sell the appreciated asset and purchase the alterna-

25. The reverse is also true: if a person expects the marginal tax rate applying to his gain to be higher in the future, he has an incentive to realize the gain immediately. Thus talk of increasing tax rates on capital gains promotes "unlocking," while talk of reducing the rate aggravates the lock-in effect.

tive asset.[26] If there is carry-over of basis at death and if the marginal tax rate applying to the gain is not expected to change, this lock-in incentive is strictly proportional to the marginal tax rate on the gain.[27] Thus repealing the exclusion and the alternative rate would increase the lock-in effect.

For example, consider an investor in the 70 percent tax bracket who owns asset that yields 8 percent before taxes and on which there is an unrealized gain equal to 40 percent of the selling price. Under present law he will unlock his gain only if the rate of return on an alternative asset exceeds 9.52 percent.[28] With repeal of the exclusion, the required rate of return would rise to 11.11 percent; however, if the top bracket rate were also lowered to 50 percent, the required rate of return would rise only to 10.00 percent. Thus the rate reduction in the upper brackets that could accompany the repeal of the exclusion and alternative rate would offset most of the additional lock-in effect.

Unfortunately, very little is known about the extent to which investors respond to such incentives. There is evidence that investors respond to the strong incentive in the law to postpone the realization of a short-term gain until after it has become a long-term gain.[29] The data on individual transactions in capital assets for both 1962 and 1973, when a long-term capital gain was a gain on an asset held for more than six months, indicate greater realizations of gains in the seventh month than in any other single month. But the evidence is inconclusive on the existence of a significant lock-in effect after a gain has become long term.[30]

26. See Charles C. Holt and John P. Shelton, "The Lock-in Effect of the Capital Gains Tax," *National Tax Journal,* vol. 15 (December 1962), pp. 337–52.

27. If r is the rate of return on the appreciated asset, r^* is the required rate of return on the alternative asset, m is the ratio of the appreciation to the selling price, and t_g is the marginal tax rate on the capital gain, an investor trying to maximize his wealth will unlock his capital gain and buy the alternative asset only if $r^* - r > r^* m t_g$.

28. This calculation assumes that the taxpayer is subject to the minimum tax and does not elect the alternative tax rate (perhaps because he elected income averaging).

29. See J. Eric Fredland, John A. Gray, and Emil M. Sunley, Jr., "The Six-Month Holding Period for Capital Gains: An Empirical Analysis of Its Effect on the Timing of Gains," *National Tax Journal,* vol. 21 (December 1968), pp. 467–78.

30. See Lawrence H. Seltzer, *The Nature and Tax Treatment of Capital Gains and Losses* (National Bureau of Economic Research, 1951), chap. 6; Harley H. Hinrichs, "An Empirical Measure of Investors' Responsiveness to Differentials in Capital Gains Tax Rates Among Income Groups," *National Tax Journal,* vol. 16

Theoretically it is not clear whether carry-over of basis at death creates a larger lock-in effect than did the step-up in basis. A step-up in basis reduces the amount of unrealized gains that would be subject to tax if realized, but it increases the lock-in incentive for each dollar of unrealized gains by creating the possibility that all income tax on the gain can be avoided if the taxpayer dies before realizing the gain.[31] For younger taxpayers, whose mortality rate is low and whose wealth is more likely to consist of inherited property, eliminating the remaining step-up in basis at death would increase the lock-in effect; but the opposite would be true for older taxpayers.[32]

Reducing or eliminating the benefits from deferral with a deferral charge based on the holding period would clearly reduce the lock-in incentive relative to present law. For example, if there were a deferral charge based on the formula derived in the appendix to this chapter, the additional deferral charge that would result from deferring tax for one year on a capital gain on an asset that has been held nine years would be 1 percent of the gain. This would reduce the rate of return

---

(September 1963), pp. 224–29; and Gerard M. Brannon, *The Effect of Tax Deductibility on the Level of Charitable Contributions and Variations on the Theme; The Lock-In Problem for Capital Gains: An Analysis of the 1970–71 Experience; Buildings and the Income Tax* (Fund for Public Policy Research, 1974). Seltzer and Brannon analyzed changes in realizations in time periods during which marginal tax rates on capital gains changed; both concluded that there was a significant lock-in effect for people with high marginal tax rates. (Seltzer also concluded that an important lock-in effect was limited to those groups.) The difficulty with such time-series studies is that realizations have been notoriously hard to predict, and it is impossible to isolate the effects of tax changes without a reliable model of what else determines realizations. Hinrichs noted that the ratio of short-term to long-term capital gains is higher in the lower tax brackets and concluded that this is evidence of a greater unwillingness of people in high brackets to realize short-term capital gains. His data, however, do not say anything about the lock-in effect once a gain has become long term.

31. If t_i is the marginal tax rate on ordinary income and p is the probability of dying in the upcoming year, the rational investor will unlock his gain only if $r^* - r > \frac{pmt_g}{1 - t_i} + r^*mt_g$. The first term on the right-hand side is the pretax equivalent of the expected value of the tax saving from the step-up in basis at death; the second term is the value of deferral for one year.

32. Replacing carry-over of basis with constructive realization at death or upon making a gift would reduce the lock-in effect by reducing the amount of unrealized gains subject to tax. Under constructive realization the same amount of unrealized gains would be potentially subject to tax as with a step-up in basis at death; but like carry-over of basis and unlike the step-up in basis, constructive realization would not retain any incentive to postpone realization in the hope of permanently escaping income tax on the gain.

on an alternative asset needed to cause a rational investor to unlock a capital gain.[33] In the previous example of an appreciated asset yielding 8 percent, with such a deferral charge and the repeal of the exclusion and alternative rate, the required rate of return needed to induce unlocking would be 9.26 percent with a 70 percent marginal tax rate and 9.00 percent with a 50 percent marginal tax rate.[34] These are smaller incentives for deferring realization than under present law. A deferral charge would also permit a larger rate reduction, which would further reduce the lock-in incentive.

EFFECTS OF LIMITS ON LOSS DEDUCTIONS

The $3,000 limit on the deduction of capital losses against ordinary income and the recognition of losses on realization rather than accrual also influence the timing of transactions, leading to so-called tax-loss selling at the end of each year. When a taxpayer has an unrealized capital loss on an asset and realizes a capital gain during a year, he has an incentive to realize his loss during the year in which he has the taxable gain, since he cannot be sure he will have other capital gains in the future against which to deduct his capital loss. The incentive is still greater if the loss is long term and the gain is short term.

To the extent that capital losses are deductible against either ordinary income or capital gains, taxing these losses on realization rather than on accrual creates an incentive for early realization similar to the lock-in effect for capital gains (but in the opposite direction). Like the lock-in effect on gains, this incentive for premature selling could be reduced with a deferral credit for losses similar to the deferral charge for gains and with unlimited deduction of capital losses against ordinary income.

ECONOMIC SIGNIFICANCE OF THE LOCK-IN EFFECT

Any lock-in effect may make the economy less efficient for three reasons. First, by inhibiting transfers of assets, the lock-in effect will reduce the productivity of the stock of capital to the extent that it con-

33. If d is the additional deferral charge resulting from deferral for one additional year, under carry-over of basis a rational investor will unlock a gain and buy an alternative asset only if $r^* - r > r^* m t_g - \dfrac{d}{1 - t_i}$.

34. The reason why the deferral charge does not completely eliminate the lock-in effect is that it assumes steady appreciation over the holding period, rather than the actual pattern of appreciation.

sists of assets whose productivity depends on the specific identity of the owner. Second, the lock-in effect may interfere with the efficient allocation of new investments across firms and industries. Third, it may reduce the well-being of households by inducing them to arrange their portfolios of assets in ways that they consider less desirable than the portfolios they would have chosen in the absence of a capital gains tax.

The productivity of some assets (mainly tangible assets but also some intangible assets like patents) depends on the specific identity of their owner. Owner-occupied homes clearly belong in this category, since tastes differ and any particular home will please some people more than others. Another example is the assets of a business that would run more efficiently if it were managed by an owner with certain specific skills. A third example is real estate whose best use is to be developed in connection with adjacent land.

In these cases a lock-in effect can prevent an asset from being transferred to the owner for whom the asset would be most productive. This would create an excess burden. Unfortunately, there is little evidence on how large this category of assets is and by how much their productivity would be increased by eliminating the lock-in effect. For example, a locked-in landowner can often enter into a long-term lease with a developer, or an owner of a business can often hire a manager with the skills needed to manage the business. For most plant and equipment, moreover, productivity is clearly unrelated to the specific identity of the owner. The productivity of the assets owned by General Motors (GM), for example, is unrelated to the specific identity of GM's shareholders and would be unaffected by their being locked into their shareholdings by the tax on their capital gains.

The second possible source of inefficiency from the lock-in effect is that it makes the allocation of new investment across firms and industries less efficient by reducing the cost of capital for firms whose owners are locked into their shareholdings. The significance of this distortion will depend not only on the strength of the lock-in effect itself, but also on the degree to which participants in asset markets consider different assets to be substitutes for one another. For example, suppose that there are unrealized gains on International Business Machines (IBM) stock but not on GM stock and that an increase in the capital gains tax would cause some IBM shareholders to refrain from selling their stock. That IBM's shareholders are locked in does not necessarily mean that the stock price of IBM would rise relative to that of GM and reduce IBM's cost of equity capital. As long as a large enough group of investors will sell IBM and buy GM in response to any increase in the relative price of IBM that does not reflect a change in the underlying values of the two companies, IBM's relative price and cost of capital will not be changed by the lock-in effect.[35] Investors probably consider a wide range of assets to be quite good substitutes for one another, including most corporate stocks, so the lock-in effect need not significantly change the allocation of investment within this class.[36]

The third potential economic inefficiency caused by the lock-in effect is that it will discourage households from rearranging their portfolios of assets, forcing them to assume more risk than necessary. Suppose that both IBM and GM have appreciated so that the lock-in effect applies equally to the shareholders of both companies. There will not be a misallocation of capital between the two corporations; but it is still possible that the locked-in IBM shareholders would prefer to diversify their portfolios by buying some GM stock, and the same may be true of GM shareholders. In this case the lock-in effect will cause both IBM and GM shareholders to assume risks that they would have preferred to reduce through diversification. This would be an excess burden from the lock-in effect.

SUMMARY

The lock-in effect is a potential source of excess burden from the present tax on capital gains that would be aggravated by repealing the exclusion or the alternative rate. Little empirical evidence, however, exists on the magnitude of the lock-in effect under present law or the amount of economic harm that results. In any case a program of repealing the exclusion and reducing the top bracket rate to 50 percent would result in only a modest increase in the lock-in incentive in the high tax brackets relative to present law. A deferral charge based on the holding period of an asset would reduce the lock-in incentive below that in present law.

35. This would be a case where IBM and GM stock were "perfect substitutes" for one another.

36. Even when assets are not perfect substitutes, the lock-in effect will cause a misallocation of investment only to the extent that it differs from one asset to another. If both GM and IBM have appreciated equally, the effect on stock prices of any tendency of IBM's shareholders to hold IBM stock will be offset by an opposite tendency among GM's shareholders.

Effect on Saving

If full taxation of capital gains reduced the rate of saving, there could be an excess burden when the economy is at full employment.[37] While the federal government could offset any reduction in private saving by increasing the government surplus, in that case the revenue from increased capital gains taxation could not be used to finance general tax reductions or additional government expenditures.

The two principal sources of private saving in the U.S. economy are saving by individuals (personal saving) and earnings retention by corporations (corporate saving), both of which may be influenced by changes in capital gains taxation.

PERSONAL SAVING

There are four routes by which a change in capital gains taxation may affect personal saving: its effect on income, its effect on wealth, its effect on the rate of return received by savers, and through the lock-in effect.

It is widely agreed among economists that a decline in income will cause a person to reduce his saving and that the reduction in saving per dollar of reduced income (the marginal propensity to save) will be larger for a transitory change in income than for a permanent change. Capital gains probably contain a larger transitory component than ordinary income, in which case a shift in the tax burden from ordinary income to capital gains would reduce saving.[38] Little is known about the magnitude of this effect, and the empirical studies of whether there is a larger marginal propensity to save out of capital gains than out of ordinary income are inconclusive.[39]

37. Because it taxes income from capital, the United States probably has less than the optimal amount of investment. In periods of full employment, the amount of investment is limited by the amount of saving; therefore a reduction in saving at full employment would lead to a further reduction in investment and could be an excess burden.

38. Like ordinary income, however, the bulk of capital gains is predictable income. See Martin J. Bailey, "Capital Gains and Income Taxation," in Arnold C. Harberger and Martin J. Bailey, eds., *The Taxation of Income from Capital* (Brookings Institution, 1969), pp. 11–49.

39. See Kul B. Bhatia, "Capital Gains and the Aggregate Consumption Function," *American Economic Review,* vol. 62 (December 1972), pp. 866–79. Depending on the precise specification of his regression equations, Bhatia finds marginal propensities to save out of realized capital gains anywhere from zero to one.

Increasing the tax on capital gains should also cause declines in the prices of assets on which investors expect capital gains, especially land and corporate stock. This will be partly offset by price increases for other assets. Any decline in the wealth of households would cause people to increase their saving for a period of time until they had rebuilt their stock of wealth.[40]

Increased taxation of capital gains would also reduce the rate of return to savers, unless there are fully offsetting tax reductions on income from capital. The most common view among economists is that personal saving is not very sensitive to changes in the rate of return, in which case any reduction in the rate of return will not significantly affect saving.[41] In a recent study, however, Michael Boskin has questioned the consensus view.[42] If Boskin's results are correct, full taxation of capital gains would reduce saving significantly unless there were fully offsetting tax reductions on income from capital. (Since most income in the upper brackets is income from capital, an increase in the tax on capital gains that is accompanied by rate cuts in the upper brackets would have a relatively small effect on the overall after-tax rate of return.)

Finally, any lock-in effect will increase saving by discouraging some sales of assets when the seller would have consumed part of the proceeds.

CORPORATE SAVING

There is now a significant tax incentive for corporate saving, since dividends are ordinary income while retained earnings are subject to the individual income tax only to the extent that they lead to capital gains. This tax incentive is probably one cause of the high rates

40. For a recent estimate of the magnitude of the "wealth effect," particularly in relation to capital gains, see Irwin Friend and Charles Lieberman, "Short-Run Asset Effects on Household Saving and Consumption: The Cross-Section Evidence," *American Economic Review*, vol. 65 (September 1975), pp. 624–33.

41. The 1970s, for example, have had relatively high rates of personal saving even though the real after-tax rate of return to savers has been close to zero. In Japan the real rate of return for many financial assets is relatively low because of the high rate of inflation, but the Japanese savings rate is the highest in the world. See Henry C. Wallich and Mable I. Wallich, "Banking and Finance," in Hugh Patrick and Henry Rosovsky, eds., *Asia's New Giant: How the Japanese Economy Works* (Brookings Institution, 1976), pp. 256–78.

42. See Michael J. Boskin, "Taxation, Saving and the Rate of Interest," OTA paper 11 (U.S. Treasury Department, Office of Tax Analysis, 1976; processed). He estimates an elasticity of saving with respect to the real after-tax rate of return of 0.4 (p. 33).

of earnings retention by U.S. corporations.[43] Full taxation of capital gains would eliminate the incentive for earnings retention and would reduce corporate saving, possibly by a significant amount. There is evidence, however, that changes in corporate saving are largely offset by opposite changes in personal saving, in which case the net effect on total private saving would be small.[44]

SUMMARY

Full taxation of capital gains could affect private saving in several ways, but it is very uncertain how large the effect might be. A tax rate reduction in the upper brackets would mitigate some of these impacts. It may be wise to put full taxation of capital gains and any offsetting tax cuts into effect during an economic downturn, when a reduction in private saving and a corresponding increase in consumption would benefit the economy. Alternatively, full taxation could be phased in so that any effect on saving could be monitored and offset by the appropriate budget policies.

Effect on Allocation of Capital

One goal of tax policy, often honored largely in the breach, is that the tax system should be neutral between different types of investment. Considered by itself the tax preference for capital gains patently violates neutrality; however, some of the distortions caused by the capital gains preference offset distortions elsewhere in the tax system and to that extent contribute to neutrality.

Corporate stock and land are the two principal types of assets for which capital gains are a significant part of the expected rate of return, and the tax preference for capital gains encourages people to purchase these assets.[45] A second, more general issue is the extent to

43. This is the view presented in John A. Brittain, *Corporate Dividend Policy* (Brookings Institution, 1966), p. 196; and in M. S. Feldstein, "Corporate Taxation and Dividend Behaviour," *Review of Economic Studies*, vol. 37 (January 1970), pp. 69–70. (Feldstein's study relates to British corporations.) Japan, however, has an extremely high rate of corporate saving without as strong a tax bias toward retained earnings as there is in the U.S. tax structure.

44. Feldstein has estimated that a reduction in corporate saving of $1 and a corresponding increase in dividend payout would reduce private saving by only 25 cents. See Martin S. Feldstein "Tax Incentives, Corporate Saving, and Capital Accumulation in the United States," *Journal of Public Economics*, vol. 2 (April 1973), p. 170.

45. Several kinds of ordinary income are treated in the tax law as capital gains, including income from the cutting of timber, coal and iron ore royalties, income

which the present tax treatment of capital gains and losses encourages risk-taking by investors relative to a comprehensive tax base. One common argument for a tax preference for capital gains is that it is needed to encourage the appropriate amount of investment in risky enterprises.

CAPITAL GAINS ON CORPORATE STOCK

Investors act as if they expect common stock prices to appreciate. Since the late 1950s the dividend yield of common stocks has consistently been lower than the interest rate on corporate bonds, which can only be plausibly explained by widespread expectations of capital gains on stocks. Preferential tax treatment of capital gains therefore encourages people to purchase common stock, and this probably increases stock prices and reduces the cost of new equity capital to corporations. To this extent, it partly offsets the increase in the cost of new equity capital that results from the corporate income tax.

Preferential tax treatment of capital gains, however, is an extremely inefficient and inequitable way to offset the distortions caused by the corporate income tax because it offsets a much larger proportion of the double taxation of corporate-source income for shareholders in high tax brackets than for those in low tax brackets. This is demonstrated in table 4-2, which shows the after-tax income that results from $1 of pretax earnings in different tax brackets both with and without the 50 percent capital gains exclusion (assuming a dividend payout of 50 percent of earnings). The difference in the tax burden between corporate and noncorporate income measures the double taxation of corporate-source income, and the table shows the percentage reduction in double taxation that results from the 50 percent exclusion in different tax brackets. The exclusion offsets only 7.6 percent of double taxation for someone in the 14 percent bracket, but it offsets 31 percent of double taxation in the 40 percent bracket and 46 percent in the 50 percent bracket. In the 70 percent bracket the exclusion more than compensates for double taxation.

Because the exclusion offsets a larger fraction of double taxation in some brackets than in others, market responses offset some of the incentive effect of the tax preference. Any increase in stock prices re-

---

from certain livestock, and gains on the sale of patents by an inventor or someone who buys a patent from an inventor. I do not consider the effects of these specific tax expenditures on the allocation of capital.

Table 4-2. Illustration of Effect of 100 Percent and 50 Percent Taxation of Capital Gains on Corporate and Noncorporate After-Tax Earnings[a]
Income in dollars

Marginal individual tax rate on ordinary income (percent)	Income after corporate and individual income taxes resulting from $1 of pretax earnings						Reduction in double taxation from 50 percent exclusion (percent)
	100 percent inclusion of capital gains			50 percent inclusion of capital gains			
	Corporate earnings	Noncorporate earnings	Difference —extent of double taxation	Corporate earnings	Noncorporate earnings	Difference —extent of double taxation	
14	0.559	0.860	0.301	0.582	0.860	0.278	7.6
40	0.390	0.600	0.210	0.455	0.600	0.145	31.0
50	0.325	0.500	0.175	0.406	0.500	0.094	46.3
70	0.195	0.300	0.105	0.309	0.300	−0.009	108.6

a. Assuming a dividend payout ratio of 0.5 and an effective corporate tax rate of 35 percent. Retained earnings are assumed to result in realized capital gains in the year the income is earned.

sulting from stock purchases by high-bracket shareholders in response to the capital gains exclusion causes sales of stock by investors who receive little or no benefit from the exclusion, such as tax-exempt institutions or shareholders in low tax brackets. These offset some of the allocative effect of the stock purchases by high-bracket shareholders.

An alternative way to deal with double taxation is to integrate the individual and corporate income taxes. Integration for all corporate income would make the tax system neutral between corporate and noncorporate investment for all shareholders. It would be both a more efficient and a more equitable way of achieving this goal than a tax preference for capital gains would be.

A rate reduction in the upper brackets (where most dividend income is received) would significantly reduce double taxation, thereby offsetting the increase in double taxation of corporate income resulting from repealing the capital gains exclusion. Table 4-2 shows that the after-tax income resulting from $1 of corporate-source income for a person in the 70 percent bracket would fall from 30.9 cents under present law to 19.5 cents if there were no exclusion, but it would rise to 32.5 cents if there were both no exclusion and a 50 percent top bracket rate.

The tax preferences for capital gains also encourage earnings retention by corporations, since dividends are taxed as ordinary income and retained earnings are exempt from the individual income tax except insofar as they lead to capital gains. This tax incentive for retention may increase private saving, as discussed above, but it leads to a distortion in the allocation of capital by reducing the relative cost of capital to those firms that already have high earnings. This is a distortion that does not offset distortions elsewhere in the economy. It is probably a major cause of corporate mergers and takeovers.

CAPITAL GAINS ON LAND

Another asset on which capital gains are a predictable source of income is land, since the quantities of labor and capital grow, while the amount of land is essentially fixed. Preferential tax treatment for capital gains encourages the purchase of land and raises its price.[46]

46. Two special provisions eliminate most of the tax on gains from the sale of a taxpayer's principal residence. The tax on such gains is deferred if the proceeds of the sale are reinvested in a new principal residence. If a person over 65 sells his

If the tax preference for capital gains in land were the same for all investors, it would cause land prices to rise to the point where the after-tax rate of return from investment in land would be the same as for other assets (that is, the tax preference would be fully capitalized in higher land prices).

The capital gains exclusion, however, provides a stronger incentive for higher-bracket investors than for lower-bracket ones.[47] It causes land prices to rise only to the point where the tax preference is fully capitalized for a middle-bracket taxpayer. As a result, for high-bracket taxpayers the exclusion raises the after-tax rate of return from investment in land, thus encouraging these people to own land. For investors in lower tax brackets, however, the tax benefit from the exclusion is insufficient to compensate them for the increase in the price of land, so that the exclusion discourages ownership of land.

The present tax treatment of owner-occupied homes provides a strong incentive for home ownership. The capital gains exclusion and alternative rate serve to augment this incentive for households in upper tax brackets and to offset it for those in lower brackets.

EFFECT ON RISK-TAKING

The tax preference for capital gains can be viewed as an incentive to make risky investments, since in many such cases the profits from successful risk-taking can be taken as long-term capital gains. The owner of a successful new business or of a productive oil well, for example, can realize capital gains by selling the asset involved. In addition, the reduction in the cost of equity capital resulting from the capital gains preferences encourages businesses to engage in risky activities, like research and development or exploratory drilling for oil and gas, since equity capital reduces the risk associated with the financial structure of a business. These considerations have suggested to many people that the tax preferences for capital gains are needed to offset a tendency of the tax structure to discourage risk-taking.

Economists have been able to derive theoretical results about when an income tax will discourage risk-taking. It can be shown that if the

principal residence, a fraction of the gain equal to $35,000 divided by the sales price is exempt from tax, and the rest of the gain is eligible for the exclusion and alternative rate.

47. In the 14 percent bracket the exclusion raises the after-tax return on an asset yielding income in the form of long-term capital gains by 8.1 percent; in the 70 percent bracket the increase is 116.7 percent.

losses from unsuccessful risk-taking are fully deductible, the imposition of a proportional income tax will increase risk-taking. If losses are not deductible, however, the imposition of an income tax will reduce risk-taking.[48]

Unfortunately, the conclusion that income taxation with full loss offset increases risk-taking is not directly transferable to a progressive tax system, since progression may result in the profits from successful risk-taking being taxed at rates higher than those at which the losses from unsuccessful risk-taking are deductible. It strongly suggests, however, that liberalizing the deduction of losses is at least as effective a stimulus to risk-taking as tax preferences for capital gains. This would also be a more efficient way to encourage risk-taking, since only a small fraction of aggregate capital gains results from successful risk-taking, while most capital losses by definition result from unsuccessful risk-taking. The repeal of the capital gains exclusion and alternative rate alone would probably reduce investment in risky assets, but there is no reason to think that a complete package that included unlimited deductibility of capital losses against ordinary income would discourage risk-taking relative to a situation where there was no income tax at all.[49]

The risky asset that is perhaps the object of greatest concern in the debate over capital gains taxation is equity in new businesses—venture capital.[50] Successful investments in new businesses lead to capital gains, sometimes extraordinarily large ones, and the capital gains

48. See Evsey D. Domar and Richard A. Musgrave, "Proportional Income Taxation and Risk-Taking," *Quarterly Journal of Economics*, vol. 58 (May 1944), pp. 388–422; and J. E. Stiglitz, "The Effects of Income, Wealth and Capital Gains Taxation on Risk-Taking," *Quarterly Journal of Economics*, vol. 83 (May 1969), pp. 263–83.

49. Allowing full deduction of capital losses against ordinary income does not ensure that a taxpayer will have enough ordinary income against which to deduct them. The tax law tries to deal with this problem through net operating loss carrybacks and carry-overs, which permit averaging of income and losses over several years. (The Tax Reform Act of 1976 extended the net operating loss carry-over period from five years to seven years.) Under current law capital losses deducted against ordinary income cannot be carried back or forward under the averaging provisions for net operating losses; and it would be appropriate to change this rule if there were a deferral charge and full deduction of capital losses against ordinary income.

50. Under current law a limited amount of losses resulting from equity investment in certain small business corporations is considered ordinary loss and is deductible against ordinary income.

preferences probably increase the flow of venture capital. Losses on such investments, however, are much more common than gains, which suggests that more liberal deduction of capital losses would be at least as effective in stimulating venture capital as the preferences for capital gains.[51]

SUMMARY

Full taxation of capital gains would have several desirable effects on the allocation of capital. It would eliminate the misallocation resulting from the current tax incentive for earnings retention and would reduce land prices. If accompanied by full deduction of losses, it would not discourage risk-taking. The undesirable allocative effect of full taxation would be that it would aggravate the bias against corporate investment financed by new issues of stock; however, integrating the corporate and individual income taxes or reducing tax rates in the top brackets are alternative solutions to this problem.

Conclusion

Between 1942 and 1969 the tax treatment of capital gains and losses underwent relatively little change. Recently, however, the trend has been toward reducing the tax preference for capital gains and cutting tax rates in the upper brackets. The Revenue Act of 1964 lowered the top bracket rate from 91 percent to 70 percent. The Tax Reform Act of 1969 increased the effective capital gains tax in the upper brackets by imposing the minimum tax and by limiting the alternative rate, and it reduced the maximum marginal tax rate on income from personal services to 50 percent. The Tax Reform Act of 1976 significantly increased the tax on many capital gains by requir-

51. Hans Stoll and Anthony Curley analyzed new small issues of stock in 1957, 1959, and 1963 and concluded that the rate of return on such stocks was lower than for the overall stock market. Sixty-four percent of the offerings studied performed less well than the market averages, and less than 3 percent showed a rate of return exceeding 20 percent. Craig Simmons performed a similar analysis for new issues in 1971. By October 1973, 85 percent were selling at or below the offering price, and only 8 percent had appreciated by more than 50 percent. See Hans R. Stoll and Anthony J. Curley, "Small Business and the New Issues Market for Equities," *Journal of Financial and Quantitative Analysis,* vol. 5 (September 1970), pp. 309–22; and Craig A. Simmons, "Immediate, Short, and Longer Run Performance of New Issues" (Rodney L. White Center for Financial Research, University of Pennsylvania, n.d.; processed).

ing carry-over of basis at death in most cases, lengthening the holding period defining long-term capital gains, and greatly increasing the minimum tax. There appears to be no decisive argument against a continuation of this trend, since there are ways to avoid the ill effects commonly associated with higher taxes on capital gains.

Complete Program of Full Taxation

An administratively feasible way to treat capital gains in a comprehensive income base would be to repeal the exclusion and alternative rate, eliminate what remains of the step-up in basis at death, permit full deduction of capital losses against ordinary income, and introduce a deferral charge based on the holding period to offset the benefits derived from deferring tax on a capital gain until the gain is realized.

This program could increase tax revenues by as much as $12 billion a year, thus permitting a significant tax rate reduction, including a cut in the top bracket rate to 50 percent or below for all income. Of this amount, 53 percent would come from taxpayers whose incomes exceed $100,000.

Repealing the 50 percent exclusion and alternative rate would be a major simplification of the tax law and forms. Full deduction of capital losses against ordinary income would permit further simplification of the tax law itself. The deferral charge, however, would be a significant complication of the tax form.

Full taxation of capital gains and losses would markedly reduce the disparities in the tax burdens of similarly situated taxpayers, eliminating the undertaxation of those with net capital gains and the overtaxation of those with net capital losses. This conclusion that full taxation of capital gains is consistent with horizontal equity is not altered by taking into account the bunching of income when capital gains are realized or the fact that some part of capital gains results only from inflation. The bunching problem could be reduced by expanding income averaging and reducing the steepness of the rate schedules. The current preferences for capital gains are only a very crude adjustment for inflation; and even an exact inflation adjustment for capital gains may not promote equity when there is no such adjustment for debt or less highly concentrated types of income from capital.

Full taxation of capital gains would have several effects on economic efficiency. Whatever inefficiency is caused by the lock-in effect —and it is not clear that this is significant—would be reduced by a deferral charge but increased by repeal of the exclusion and alternative rate. Full taxation of capital gains would probably reduce the rate of private saving, but it is difficult to estimate by how much. It would have some beneficial effects on the allocation of capital, mainly by reducing the existing bias toward corporations that already have earnings to retain. With full deduction of losses, a comprehensive income base would probably not create a tax bias against risk-taking relative to the present law. The principal adverse allocative effect of full taxation of capital gains is that it would remove the counterweight to the distortion caused by the corporate income tax, but integrating the corporate and individual income taxes is a more equitable and efficient way to achieve this goal. Any adverse effects of full taxation of capital gains on saving, the lock-in effect, and the double taxation of corporate income would be greatly reduced, if not eliminated, by the tax rate reductions, especially in the upper brackets, that could accompany higher capital gains taxation. Any adverse impact on private saving could be offset by government saving.

Fifty Percent Exclusion and Alternative Rate

Limiting change to repealing the exclusion and alternative rate would avoid the complexity associated with a deferral charge and would retain most of the advantages of the complete program of full taxation. It would leave in place the significant tax preference for capital gains that results from deferral, and the retention of deferral would greatly weaken the argument that higher taxes on capital gains would be unfair because of the bunching effect and inflation.

Repealing the exclusion and alternative rate would increase the lock-in effect, but it is not clear that this would lead to significant inefficiency. It is probably more important that repeal of the exclusion and alternative rate by itself would tend to discourage risk-taking by investors.

Unlimited Deduction of Capital Losses against Ordinary Income

Permitting unlimited deduction of capital losses against ordinary income, along with repealing the exclusion and alternative rate, would eliminate the current unfairness to taxpayers with net capital losses and would be a significant stimulus to risk-taking by investors. Unless accompanied by a deferral charge, however, unlimited deduction of capital losses against ordinary income would increase the tax advantage from deferral by enabling investors to realize their capital losses quickly and to deduct them against ordinary income, while deferring realization of their capital gains.

Appendix: Illustrative Calculation of Appropriate Deferral Charge

This appendix presents one way to compute an interest charge that approximately compensates for the interest-free loan provided by deferral of tax on capital gains from the date the appreciation occurs to the date the gain is realized, that is, taxation on realization rather than on accrual. The taxpayer would compute a deferral charge or credit on each capital gain or loss from a table based on his holding period. The table would be derived from a formula that calculates the benefit from the interest-free loan resulting from deferral, under the assumption that the gain accrued arithmetically over the holding period.

Assume that a taxpayer has a capital gain of $1 on an asset he has held for n years. He has a marginal tax rate of t, and the interest rate is r. Assume also that the $1 gain has accrued arithmetically over the holding period, so that the gain accruing in each year was $1/n$ and the tax on the gain from that year would have been t/n under accrual taxation.

The gain accruing in year x receives deferral for $n - x$ years. The compound interest on a $1 loan for this period would be $[e^{r(n-x)} - 1]$ before taxes and $[e^{r(1-t)(n-x)} - 1]$ after taxes (since the interest would have been deductible). Thus the interest charge for deferral of the tax on the gain accruing in year x is

$$\frac{t}{n}[e^{r(1-t)(n-x)} - 1].$$

If D is the deferral charge for the entire $1 gain, then

$$D = \int_{x=0}^{n} \frac{t}{n}[e^{r(1-t)(n-x)} - 1]dx.$$

Integrating and rearranging terms, the result is

$$D = \frac{t[e^{rn(1-t)} - 1 - rn(1-t)]}{rn(1-t)}.$$

It would be difficult for the taxpayer to do this calculation pre-

Table 4-3. Deferral Charge or Credit per Dollar of Capital Gain or Loss, by Selected Interest Rates and Holding Periods

Holding period (years)	Interest rate (percent)		
	4	6	8
1	0.00	0.01	0.01
2	0.01	0.01	0.02
3	0.01	0.02	0.03
4	0.02	0.03	0.04
5	0.02	0.03	0.05
6	0.03	0.04	0.06
7	0.03	0.05	0.07
8	0.04	0.06	0.08
9	0.04	0.06	0.09
10	0.05	0.07	0.10
15	0.07	0.12	0.17
20	0.10	0.17	0.25
25	0.13	0.23	0.35
30	0.17	0.30	0.48

Source: Calculated from the formula $D = \dfrac{t[e^{rn(1-t)}-1-rn(1-t)]}{rn(1-t)}$, where the marginal tax rate, t, is 0.3, r is the interest rate, and n is the holding period.

cisely, since he would have to know his precise marginal tax rate. A shortcut would be to assume the same value of t for all taxpayers; for example, to assume $t = 0.3$.[52]

Because the deductibility of interest is taken into account in deriving the formula under which the deferral charge is computed, the deferral charge itself would not be deductible. It would be possible to compute a formula for a deferral charge using the before-tax interest rate and to make the deferral charge deductible, but this formula would be a less accurate approximation because the correct deferral charge would be more sensitive to the marginal tax rate.

Table 4-3 shows the deferral charge or credit per dollar of gain or loss under the shortcut formula derived above with various interest rates. In practice the Internal Revenue Service would construct the table using the actual interest rates that prevailed over the periods in question.

52. Brinner and Munnell, in "Taxation of Capital Gains," suggest that the deferral charge be levied implicitly by increasing the inclusion portion of the gain. The taxpayer would determine his inclusion proportion from a table based on his marginal tax rate and his holding period. The method selected here is less exact but considerably simpler.

Comments by Roger E. Brinner

I was somewhat constrained by the editor's three rules of order: the assumptions of a noninflationary economy, separate corporate and individual income taxes, and income rather than consumption as the appropriate tax base. Fortunately, James Wetzler discussed two of these three topics, so I consider them to be fair game. Thus in two of the six points I make, I touch on inflation and the separate corporate and individual taxes—topics that cannot be avoided in the case of capital gains taxation.

1. The toughest unresolved problems are related to the necessity of approximating accrual taxation in a tax system relying on the realization principle for capital gains. The deferral charge structure proposed by Wetzler is intended to be a compromise between the current taxation-upon-realization system and an exact accrual taxation system. The movement toward an accrual system should produce greater horizontal equity if done properly.

There are several elements to Wetzler's compromise. First, the gain is assumed to accrue evenly through the holding period. This compromise is virtuous because it produces a result similar to that of income-averaging. But his specific assumption that the asset value increases *arithmetically,* while he calls for a *compound* interest assessment, produces inappropriate results for assets held more than five years. Table 4-4 compares the results according to the original formula, with a new formula assuming the asset appreciates at a constant exponential rate. As should be expected, the greater the rate of asset appreciation, the more concentrated the absolute gains in the recent past and the lower the interest charge *per dollar of gain.* The results of the compound appreciation formula approach those of the original formula as the rate of appreciation approaches zero.[53]

The second proposed compromise is the use of the deferral charge corresponding to a 30 percent tax rate for all taxpayers. Table 4-4 (center panel) suggests that this is a reasonable approximation: the

53. The original formula leads to more than 100 percent of the gain being collected as a deferral charge for high interest rates and long-held assets. This is an intuitively implausible result although mathematically correct: the investor is assumed to be willing to invest in an asset with a steadily declining rate of return while his tax liabilities are compounding exponentially.

Table 4-4. Sensitivity of a Capital Gains Deferral Charge to Selected Patterns and Rates of Asset Appreciation, by Length of Holding Period[a]

Tax rate (percent)	Deferral charge per dollar of capital gain by length of holding period (years)								
	1	*2*	*3*	*4*	*5*	*10*	*15*	*25*	*50*
Original Wetzler formula: equal absolute appreciation in each year									
20	0.004	0.008	0.012	0.017	0.021	0.046	0.074	0.144	0.439
30	0.005	0.011	0.016	0.022	0.028	0.059	0.095	0.180	0.515
40	0.006	0.012	0.019	0.025	0.032	0.066	0.105	0.196	0.528
50	0.006	0.013	0.019	0.026	0.033	0.068	0.107	0.195	0.496
70	0.005	0.011	0.016	0.021	0.027	0.055	0.085	0.149	0.343
Appreciation at constant compound rate of 5 percent a year									
20	0.004	0.008	0.012	0.016	0.020	0.042	0.064	0.110	0.229
30	0.005	0.011	0.016	0.021	0.027	0.054	0.082	0.138	0.275
40	0.006	0.012	0.018	0.024	0.030	0.061	0.091	0.151	0.289
50	0.006	0.012	0.019	0.025	0.031	0.062	0.093	0.151	0.227
70	0.005	0.010	0.016	0.021	0.026	0.051	0.074	0.117	0.200
Appreciation at constant compound rate of 10 percent a year									
20	0.004	0.008	0.012	0.016	0.020	0.038	0.055	0.082	0.119
30	0.005	0.010	0.015	0.021	0.025	0.049	0.070	0.104	0.147
40	0.006	0.012	0.018	0.023	0.029	0.055	0.078	0.114	0.158
50	0.006	0.012	0.018	0.024	0.030	0.056	0.080	0.115	0.155
70	0.005	0.010	0.015	0.020	0.025	0.046	0.064	0.090	0.117

a. Assuming an interest charge of 5 percent a year.

deferral charge per dollar of gain peaks at a 50 percent tax rate, and the difference for the tax rates shown is a maximum of 2 percent at ten years, 4 percent at twenty-five years.

A third compromise that would be necessary is also highlighted by the table. Unless taxpayers are asked to calculate the effective compound rate of appreciation for each asset sold and then to refer to the appropriate tables of charges, a standard appreciation rate must be used. A comparison of the three blocks of charges suggests that this would create large errors only for assets held twenty-five years or longer. Even for fifty-year holding periods, however, a standardized rate of, say, 5 percent is likely to be better than no deferral charge at all, as in the current structure.

On the other hand, the goal of simplification suggests an alternative compromise. In place of any exact formula, an extra 0.5 percent of the gain could be assessed as a deferral charge for each year an asset has been held. The line corresponding to the 30 percent tax rate in the second section of table 4-4 indicates that this would be a fair procedure. It is worth noting that this extra 0.5 percent tax per year is a sharp contrast to a proposal by Congress that would reduce the tax burden by increasing amounts the longer an asset has been held. Neither inflation nor deferral justifies such a position.[54]

2. The appropriate interest rates that should be charged for the deferral of tax liabilities are not discussed. Because of the enforcement powers of the federal government, the taxpayer could not default on the loan. Therefore it would be reasonable to regard these interest-free loans as free of the risk of default. Hence some average federal government borrowing cost over the holding period of the gain would be appropriate when calculating the deferral charge.

Wetzler provides estimates of the interest charge per dollar gain for three different interest rates by holding periods (table 4-3). In fact, the taxpayer would not be faced with such a table. The Internal Revenue Service would merely provide one column relating holding periods to interest charges. (The calculations underlying the column would reflect the changes in interest rates through time.) That would be a fairly simple addition to the capital gains tax schedule.

Incidentally, Wetzler's revenue estimates are based on an 8 percent deferral charge, which is probably too high. Five or 6 percent would be more reasonable; thus his estimates should be scaled down by three-eighths or one-quarter. The revenue gain would be further reduced by adopting the compound appreciation formula presented in table 4-4 and the accompanying discussion.

3. The so-called rules-of-the-game argument—the fairness of changing the tax code abruptly—is not given proper emphasis. Wetzler does note that fairness may demand a reduction in the tax rates for high-income taxpayers, since as many tax experts have pointed out, only the early bird gets the tax shelter and not the people who invest later.[55]

This leads to the conclusion that in considering deferral charges on gains already accrued, no interest charge really would be fair. Thus interest should be charged only on gains that accrue from the time at

54. For a description of this proposal and alternative reforms, see Brinner and Munnell, "Taxation of Capital Gains," pp. 3–21.

55. For a recent example, see Martin Feldstein, "Compensation in Tax Reform," *National Tax Journal*, vol. 29 (June 1976), pp. 123–30.

which the charge is enacted, and even then it might be desirable to have a fairly long transition period to minimize the windfall losses.

4. The deferral procedure, under which a person is taxed as if a gain or loss has accrued evenly over the period an asset was held, might create additional instability in the market for capital assets. Investors would be motivated to realize losses immediately because the Treasury would behave as if any loss had accrued over the entire period the asset was held and would actually pay interest on the alleged overpayment of previous taxes. Of course, the reverse holds true for gains. This would be likely to amplify swings in the stock market and might have serious effects on the economy.

5. Wetzler defends 100 percent inclusion of capital gains in a world of dual taxation on the ground that it would bring the distortion facing upper-income groups closer to the distortion facing lower-income groups. I believe this is a poor rationale. Lower-income groups can and do opt to purchase land or homes to take advantage of preferential treatment. (Again, only the early bird gets the tax shelter. There may in fact be no preference that the market has not yet capitalized.)

Wetzler's response is that the capitalization actually does not proceed far enough for low-income individuals, because the capitalization reflects average tax rates and not their low rates. This may be true for stocks, but it certainly would not be true for land or homes. It seems clear to me that the value of a small lot or small home would represent the capitalization of the low tax rate of prospective buyers.

6. The proper solution to the capital gains problem in a noninflationary world is to have 100 percent inclusion *and* the deferral charge. The historical record, however, weakly supports an increase in the inclusion percentage without a deferral charge. If the average inflation-appreciation experience in the future duplicated the experience of the past twenty-five years, if the holding period averaged somewhat more than ten years, and if the average tax rate were approximately 30 percent, a constant 100 percent inclusion would be close to the correct proportion with a deferral charge. On these assumptions, the inflation loss would just be offset by the deferral benefit.[56]

56. See Brinner, "Inflation, Deferral and the Neutral Taxation of Capital Gains," pp. 565–73.

Comments by Alvin C. Warren, Jr.*

James Wetzler proposes the elimination of the preferential treatment of net capital gains (the 50 percent exclusion of section 1202, the alternative rate of section 1201, the limited step-up in basis under section 1014, and the deferral that is inherent in a realization-based income tax) as well as the detrimental treatment of net capital losses (the limitations on deductibility under section 1211, the step-down in basis under section 1015, and the deferral of losses). I certainly find these proposals attractive. He suggests that all these changes, save eliminating the benefits of deferral, will result in a net simplification of the tax law and can be implemented without serious administrative problems. As for deferral, he proposes two administratively feasible solutions: constructive realization of capital gains on assets transferred by gift or at death and a deferral charge (or credit), of which the second appears more attractive to him on balance.

Let me make explicit a point that I think is implicit in the paper: the simplicity gains without the deferral charge are not so clear, and there might indeed be a serious administrative problem created by the adoption of Wetzler's proposal without the elimination of deferral. As the paper indicates, eliminating preferential treatment of gains without a deferral adjustment is likely to increase the lock-in effect for taxpayers with unrealized gains. If the limitations on the deductibility of capital losses were repealed along with the preferential treatment of capital gains, taxpayers would have a tremendous incentive to accelerate their losses while deferring their gains.

Presumably that result would be no more acceptable than the other extreme, a complete denial of deductibility, so that an intermediate position of, say, the deduction of losses from the sale of property against gains from the sale of property plus a limited amount of other income would be permitted. Such a system would require defining those gains that could be fully offset against losses. Whether such gains were called capital gains or not, one would be back in the quagmire of defining a class of realized property gains that would be

---

* I wish to thank my colleague, Daniel I. Halperin, for the benefit of discussions on this subject and for his suggestions.

granted preferential tax treatment. Thus the elimination of preferential treatment for capital gains might not permit escape from the incredibly complex case law and statutory provisions that have developed to distinguish capital gains from ordinary income. In addition, the tax consequences of economic decisions would continue to be considered by a rational investor, since the after-tax return on investments would differ depending on whether the assets were part of a limited class of gains that could be fully offset by what are now called capital losses. To be sure, the benefits from manipulating the form of a transaction so that it qualifies for capital gains treatment would be less than they are with the 50 percent exclusion and the alternative tax, but they might not be insubstantial.

Adopting constructive realization would not eliminate the need for defining this special category of gains, although it would be likely to reduce pressure on the definition by cutting off the benefits of deferral at death. To the extent that the deferral charge made the taxpayer indifferent about the timing of his gains or losses, the problem would be eliminated. Indeed to the extent that the taxpayer became indifferent about the timing of his gains or losses, much of the complexity in the tax code that has to do with recognition (such as the provisions dealing with corporate reorganization, like-kind exchange, and so on) could also be eliminated. Exactly how much of that complexity would need to be retained would depend on the degree of the remaining taxpayer pressures for deferral, which I suppose would in turn depend on how closely the tax deferral charge approximated the nontax benefits of deferral.

One final footnote on simplification: even with a deferral charge, it is not clear to me that section 341, dealing with collapsible corporations, could be eliminated (as Wetzler suggests), since the abuse addressed by that provision may be as much a function of the rules of corporate taxation as of the difference between capital gains and ordinary income.

Wetzler suggests that the effects of inflation and bunching cannot be used to argue that full taxation of capital gains violates the principle of horizontal equity. But if the elimination of the 50 percent exclusion and the alternative rate is considered apart from a deferral charge, is it so clear that horizontal equity is advanced by enlarging the discrepancy in tax treatment between taxpayers who save out of unrealized gains and those who save out of realized gains? Equalizing taxes on taxpayers who realize gains, whether capital or ordinary, does of course seem an unambiguous improvement in horizontal equity. Rather than stimulating worry about which of those is the more relevant group for purposes of comparison, this observation seems to me another reason for adopting the deferral charge.

Yet even the deferral charge is not unquestionably an advance in horizontal equity. Wetzler rejects making an inflation adjustment solely for capital gains, in part because a complete adjustment for inflation would affect many other items of income. Surely the same is true for deferral, which creates benefits and detriments at many points in the tax system aside from capital gains and losses. If there is to be no comprehensive elimination of the advantages of deferral in such areas as deferred compensation, accelerated depreciation, and exceptions to the capitalization requirement, why should deferral be effectively eliminated here? Despite such questions, the discrepancy in treatment between realized and deferred gains from property is just too great, for me at least, to put off its elimination to the day when all the benefits of deferral might be dealt with.

Under the heading of horizontal equity, the paper also suggests that full taxation of gains and losses would eliminate the unfair current treatment of taxpayers with net capital losses—a suggestion I certainly agree with. But it should also be noted that that unfairness could be mitigated even without full taxation of gains by permitting full deductibility of losses where there had been no gains taken for some period in the past and by taxing subsequent gains as ordinary income.

Wetzler reviews three suggestions for alleviating bunching where there is full inclusion of capital gains: reduction of the steepness of the rate schedule, expansion of the current system of income averaging, and proration of the gain or loss over the holding period. Although bunching is a problem with any realization-based income tax, the problem would be aggravated by repeal of the preferential treatment of capital gains and by the introduction of a deferral charge.

Presumably the reason bunching is thought to be a problem is that a different tax would result under progressive rates if gains and losses were taxed as accrued rather than on realization. Accordingly the touchstone for eliminating the effects of bunching is approximation of the results of accrual taxation. Reducing the steepness of the tax rates in effect defines away the problem, since it only exists where there is progression. To the extent there is a problem, extending the current averaging provisions—which average the increase in total income rather than the gains from particular assets—would result in only the roughest approximation of accrual taxation, since the gain on each asset would not be averaged in accordance with its particular holding period.

In addition to the added complexity discussed by Wetzler, proration—which does average the gain or loss on each asset in accordance with its holding period—is subject to the objection that it would result in overaveraging and undertaxation when gains are accrued over a short period on assets held for a substantial holding period. In addition, a taxpayer who experienced great asset appreciation within a short period might be further locked into those assets in order to take advantage of the proration. Perhaps proration could be permitted for a restricted class of assets, such as closely held business interests, which are typically held for a long time and which are generally not used to produce recurring gains, while gains on other assets would be subject to expanded averaging provisions. Consideration might also be given to whether those provisions should be made applicable to declining as well as increasing income.

As Wetzler suggests, a comprehensive income tax base would in theory recognize gain or loss on an accrual basis. Accrual taxation is rejected, however, because of the difficulty of annual revaluation and liquidity problems. For some assets, such as publicly traded securities, the valuation objection is surely weaker than for others, and it would seem worthwhile to consider whether the liquidity objection is really significant enough to preclude accrual taxation where it is administratively feasible. My preference for accrual taxation where feasible is strengthened by the failure of the deferral charge always to give the same results as accrual, particularly in the case of a large gain or loss that accrues over a short period on an asset already held for a long period. Where accrual is not feasible, the deferral charge appears to be the second-best solution.

To conclude, I find the proposed elimination of special treatment for capital gains (and losses) and the introduction of a deferral charge (or credit) attractive. Only with the elimination of the benefits of deferring gains and accelerating losses is there hope of avoiding the complexity of both the capital gains definitional quagmire and the network of rules required to define recognition. The interaction of that proposal and the averaging provision seem to me to require further consideration, as does the potential for accrual taxation where administratively feasible.

CHAPTER FIVE

Homeowner Preferences

WILLIAM F. HELLMUTH

UNDER A comprehensive individual income tax based on the Haig-Simons definition of income, the income tax base would include imputed net rent for owner-occupied homes. Both Robert Murray Haig and Henry Simons were very explicit that imputed income would be included and that imputed rent on owner-occupied homes is an important imputed income item.[1]

Housing and other durable consumer goods provide services over a period of years. Consumers have a choice of purchasing financial assets that provide taxable monetary income or of purchasing homes that provide untaxed services over time. Simons pointed out that consumers' capital is not a uniform percentage of income for persons in the same income class, nor is it constant between different income classes; thus the omission of such income causes both horizontal and vertical inequities.[2]

---

1. See Robert Murray Haig, "The Concept of Income—Economic and Legal Aspects," in Haig, ed., *The Federal Income Tax* (Columbia University Press, 1921), pp. 7–8, 14–15, reprinted in Richard A. Musgrave and Carl S. Shoup, *Readings in the Economics of Taxation* (Irwin for the American Economic Association, 1959), pp. 59, 65; and Henry C. Simons, *Personal Income Taxation: The Definition of Income as a Problem of Fiscal Policy* (University of Chicago Press, 1938), p. 50 and chap. 4. Also see Chapter 1 in this volume.

2. Simons, *Personal Income Taxation*, pp. 114–15.

If homeowners' imputed net rent were taxable, it would obviously be necessary to calculate the amount of net rent. Generally this would be obtained by estimating a gross rent equal to the rent the housing unit would bring on the market and deducting the actual expenses, including mortgage interest, property taxes, maintenance expense, insurance, and depreciation. This net rent amount would be included in the homeowner's adjusted gross income.

Under current tax treatment all homeowners, whether they take the standard deduction for tax purposes or itemize deductions, benefit from the exclusion of imputed net rent in calculating their income. Further, homeowners who itemize deductions may deduct mortgage interest and real estate taxes to reduce their taxable income, even though the rental income against which these constitute expenses has not been included. Taxpayers who are tenants are permitted no comparable deductions.

Another tax preference for homeowners is the right, when an owner-occupied home is sold at a gain, to defer a tax on the gain if the seller purchases and occupies a new home that costs more than the one sold. This deferral of tax on rollover of a home generally does not apply to other assets sold at a gain. In addition, under certain conditions elderly taxpayers are permitted to exclude part or all of the tax on the gain from the sale of their homes.

The homeowner preferences have several important effects on the tax system and on the economy:

—They create horizontal inequities in the income tax system in that they provide tax savings for homeowners over tenants with comparable incomes, and differential savings between different homeowners with comparable incomes.

—They cause vertical inequities in the tax system. Since homeownership rises with income, the values of homes purchased increase as a proportion of income as incomes rise (that is, are income elastic), and the value of homeowner preferences is directly related to the marginal tax rate of the homeowner, high-income recipients benefit more from these preferences than do low-income recipients.

—They interfere with the allocation of resources between residential construction and other uses of resources. The tax expenditures favoring homeowners lower the cost of housing services and increase the after-tax rate of return on investment in homes, relative to other choices that consumers and individual investors have for the use of their funds. Tax incentives thus draw more resources into housing than would occur in the absence of such preferences.

—They also distort the housing market choices in favor of residential construction suitable for homeowners, creating a demand for more single-family homes and apartments for purchase than for rental units.

But these preferences, which provide higher effective rates of return for homeownership, need to be considered in the broader context of other preferences for other types of investment. Homeowner preferences do not exist alone in a tax system that is otherwise comprehensive and neutral between different forms of investment. Individuals and corporations that invest in rental housing are eligible for accelerated depreciation on the cost of the rental property. And businesses receive tax subsidies for investments in machinery and equipment, for export sales, for research and development expenditures, and for other selected activities.

Further, these homeowner tax preferences are relatively inefficient and expensive if they are considered as incentives to promote homeownership and the construction of more homes. The incentives are most valuable to those with higher marginal tax rates, the income class that would find it easiest to buy homes in the absence of tax incentives. And the incentives for homeownership are much weaker for families in the lower tax brackets whose income levels also make homeownership more difficult. Tax incentives are, of course, of no value to those whose income is so low that they pay no federal income tax. And to the extent that the tax preferences increase the demand for owner-occupied homes, the price of such dwelling units rises and puts them further beyond the reach of low- and modest-income persons. The greater value of these preferences for persons with high incomes and high marginal tax rates is likely to draw more resources into the construction of large and expensive homes; on the other hand, income-neutral incentives would be likely to result in more dwelling units to meet the housing needs of more people.

Income Excluded from Tax Base by Homeowner Preferences

Substantial amounts of income are now excluded from the individual income tax base by the three major homeowner preferences,

Table 5-1. Increase in Taxable Income and Income Tax Revenue Resulting from Changes in Certain Homeowner Tax Preferences, 1977 Levels

	Increase (billions of dollars)		Percent
Change	In taxable income	In tax revenue	increase in revenue
Include imputed net rent (all homeowners)	13.0	3.0	2.5
Eliminate deduction for real estate taxes (itemizers only)	26.0	5.8	5.7[a]
Eliminate deduction for mortgage interest (itemizers only)	28.4	5.7	5.6[a]
Eliminate deductions for both real estate taxes and mortgage interest (itemizers only)	54.3	10.7	10.6[a]
Include imputed net rent and eliminate deduction for both taxes and interest (all homeowners)	67.3	13.8	11.4[b]

Source: Brookings MERGE File.

a. The percentage increase shown is for all homeowners who itemize, although some do not deduct all of the items; for all homeowners, including nonitemizers who would have no increase, the increase would be 4.8 percent for elimination of the deduction for real estate taxes, 4.7 percent for elimination of the deduction for mortgage interest, and 8.8 percent for elimination of the deduction for taxes and interest combined. This last total is less than the sum of gain from the elimination of the two deductions separately, since some homeowners shift to the standard deduction.

b. This percentage increase combines a 4.2 percent increase for nonitemizers and a 12.8 percent increase for itemizers.

with consequent large effects on revenues. Estimates from the Brookings MERGE File shown in table 5-1 indicate that homeowners in 1977 will have imputed net rent of about $13 billion. Further, homeowners who itemize are expected to claim deductions of $26 billion for real estate taxes and $28.4 billion for interest on their mortgages. The possible revenue gains would range from $3 billion to $13.8 billion, depending on which preferences were eliminated.[3] These amounts for homeowner preferences do not include mortgage interest and real estate taxes paid by homeowners who do not itemize deductions. Moreover, part of the imputed rent is received by, and some of the interest and tax deductions are taken by, persons whose incomes are too small to be taxable. The loss of deductions for some taxpayers would be partially offset by shifting to the standard deduction, but this is allowed for in the revenue estimates in table 5-1.

A number of different studies have been made of the relation between housing values and gross and net imputed rent. These studies

3. Corresponding estimates in a 1976 study of tax expenditures by the Senate Budget Committee are given by income classes in table 5-9 in the appendix to this chapter.

Table 5-2. Income Tax Subsidy to Homeowners, Selected Studies

Calculation of imputed gross rental income and of subsidy	Study				
	Shelton[a]	Laidler[b]	Sunley[c]	Aaron[d]	James[e]
Percent of house value					
Imputed net rental income	4.0	6.0	8.0	4.0–6.0[f]	4.0–9.0
Property taxes	1.5	1.5	1.3	n.a.	2.0
Mortgage interest	3.0	...	...	n.a.	...
Maintenance	0.75–1.0	1.25	1.25	n.a.	...
Depreciation	1.0–1.5	2.25	...	n.a.	1.0–1.2
Imputed gross rental income	10.25–11.0	11.0	10.55	10.0–12.0	6.5–10.0
Percent of imputed gross rental income					
Subsidy	77.3–82.9	68.2	88.2	n.a.	n.a.
Percent of reduction in imputed gross rental income[g]					
Subsidy	19.3–20.7	17.0	22.0	n.a.	26.8

Sources: First four columns from Frank A. Clayton, "Income Taxes and Subsidies to Homeowners and Renters: A Comparison of the U.S. and Canadian Experience," *Canadian Tax Journal*, vol. 22 (May-June 1974), p. 299; and last column adapted from Franklin J. James (see note e).

a. John P. Shelton, "The Cost of Renting versus Owning a Home," *Land Economics*, vol. 44 (February 1968), pp. 63–68. Assumes ratio of imputed net rental income to equity of 8 percent and a mortgage interest rate of 6 percent; the homeowner is assumed to have 50 percent equity in the market value.

b. David Laidler, "Income Tax Incentives for Owner-Occupied Housing," in Arnold C. Harberger and Martin J. Bailey, eds., *The Taxation of Income from Capital* (Brookings Institution, 1969), p. 57. Assumes the ratio of imputed net rental income to house value and the mortgage interest rate are both 6 percent.

c. Emil M. Sunley, Jr., "Tax Advantages of Homeownership versus Renting: A Cause of Suburban Migration?" in National Tax Association, *Proceedings of the Sixty-Third Annual Conference on Taxation* (Columbus: NTA, 1971), pp. 377–92. Assumes the rate of imputed net rental income and the mortgage interest rate are the same.

d. Henry Aaron, "Income Taxes and Housing," *American Economic Review*, vol. 60 (December 1970), pp. 789–806.

e. Franklin J. James, "Income Taxes, Homeownership and Urban Land Use" (Urban Institute, 1976; processed), pp. 13–24.

f. Percent of equity.

g. Assuming average marginal tax rates of 25 percent for homeowners.

n.a. Not applicable.

are useful in showing what percentage of the gross rent is excluded from tax for the average homeowner. As shown in table 5-2, the portion of imputed gross rent that is excluded from income by homeowner tax preferences is variously estimated as between 68 and 88 percent. The smaller the amount of maintenance and depreciation relative to the gross rental, the larger the fraction of the gross rental that is excluded from income subject to tax. Applying a taxpayer's marginal tax rate to these percentages determines each unit's tax subsidy. Obviously the higher the marginal tax rate, the greater the tax subsidy portion of the gross rental. Homeowner tax preferences, as shown in table 5-2, have reduced the effective cost of housing, as measured by gross rents, by approximately 20 percent, assuming average marginal tax rates of 25 percent for homeowners.

Renters obtain some reduction in average rentals, resulting from the accelerated depreciation allowed to investors in rental housing. Franklin James estimated this reduction in rents at 11 percent, based on the assumption of a 25 percent tax bracket for the typical investor in rental housing.[4] Emil Sunley suggested the reduction in rents to tenants was somewhat higher, perhaps 17 percent, assuming the marginal investor in rental housing was in the 40 percent tax bracket.[5]

The demand for housing is influenced by the price of housing. The lower the price, the greater the quantity of housing demanded. Numerous studies have led to the conclusion that the price elasticity of demand for housing falls in the range of -1.0 to -1.5.[6] This means that a 1 percent decline in the price of housing will cause the quantity demanded to increase by 1 to 1.5 percent.

These estimates indicate the value of the tax preferences for housing in reducing the rentals, whether paid by tenants or imputed to owner-occupiers. The net subsidy for homeowners over tenants would generally fall in the 10 to 15 percent range for homeowners in the heavily populated $10,000 to $25,000 income brackets. With a price elasticity of -1.0 to -1.5, this indicates an increase of 10 to 20 percent in the demand for homeownership.[7] Obviously the value of the net subsidy from the tax preferences and the increase in demand for homeownership generally varies directly with a person's income level and marginal tax rate.

Thus removal of the tax subsidies would have the effect of raising the net cost of housing and of reducing the demand for owner-occupied homes. The demand for owner-occupied housing usually varies

4. Franklin J. James, "Income Taxes, Homeownership and Urban Land Use" (Urban Institute, 1976; processed), pp. 19–21, 24.

5. Emil M. Sunley, Jr., "Tax Advantages of Homeownership versus Renting: A Cause of Suburban Migration?" in National Tax Association, *Proceedings of the Sixty-Third Annual Conference on Taxation* (Columbus: NTA, 1971), pp. 377–92.

6. See Richard F. Muth, "The Demand for Non-Farm Housing," in Arnold C. Harberger, ed., *The Demand for Durable Goods* (University of Chicago Press, 1960), pp. 72–74; Margaret G. Reid, *Housing and Income* (University of Chicago Press, 1962), p. 381; Frank de Leeuw, "The Demand for Housing: A Review of Cross-Section Evidence," *Review of Economics and Statistics*, vol. 53 (February 1971), pp. 8–9; and Sherman J. Maisel, James B. Burnham, and John S. Austin, "The Demand for Housing: A Comment," ibid. (November 1971), pp. 410–13.

7. James, "Income Taxes, Home Ownership and Urban Land Use," pp. 19–25.

directly with income level, with an income elasticity of demand of about 1.5 (that is, for every 1 percent increase in personal income, the quantity of housing demanded rises about 1.5 percent). With the value of the subsidy provided by tax preferences rising with increases in taxable income from 14 percent up to 70 percent at the top marginal rate, the tax preferences add to the stronger demand for homeownership the higher a person's income.[8]

The Commission to Revise the Tax Structure estimated that the sweeping changes it recommended for a very comprehensive income tax base with much lower rates would have caused a small reduction in residential construction estimated at $2.5 billion for 1975, after the new tax structure was fully effective, with a consequently larger flow of capital to corporate investment.[9]

A Fully Comprehensive Income Tax Base

A comprehensive income tax base would include imputed net rent of homeowners in adjusted gross income. Generally the first step would require an estimate of the gross rent the dwelling unit would bring in an arm's-length-market rental. From the gross rent, the normal expenses of property taxes, interest on the mortgage (if any), maintenance, depreciation, and insurance would be deducted to obtain a net rental. In effect homeowners would treat their houses as investment property that they rent to themselves.

The inclusion of imputed net rent in arriving at adjusted gross income would apply to all homeowners. Further, those homeowners who now itemize their deductions would no longer be permitted the separate deductions now taken for mortgage interest and for property taxes, since these deductions would already have been used in calculating net rent.

The increase in individual income tax revenues would be large, estimated at $13.8 billion for projected 1977 incomes, assuming imputed net rent is included and no separate deductions are taken for mortgage interest and for property taxes (see table 5-1). All homeowners with taxable income would probably have some increase, with an average increase of 11.4 percent. (The distribution of this tax in-

8. Commission to Revise the Tax Structure, *Reforming the Federal Tax Structure* (Washington, D.C.: Fund for Public Policy Research, 1973), pp. 141–42.
9. Ibid., pp. 35, 140.

crease by income bracket and age group is discussed later and shown in tables 5-7 and 5-8.)

Including imputed net rent in the income of homeowners would present a number of major difficulties. One is the problem of obtaining accurate and consistent estimates of imputed net rent for millions of homeowning taxpayers. Imputed net rent is estimated now on an aggregate basis for various national income purposes. But the calculation of imputed net rent for approximately 45 million different individual and family units would be a complicated task for each taxpayer and for Internal Revenue Service review. There is no background or history in the United States for making estimates of imputed rent or home values on a nationwide basis, unlike the United Kingdom or Germany.

The United Kingdom included imputed rent in taxable income for over a century, from the beginning of its income tax until 1963. Imputed rent was discarded then instead of attempting to correct and update the assessments, which had become obsolete in the period of inflation and other major economic changes following World War II. Imputed rent was abandoned despite a recommendation in 1955 by the Royal Commission on the Taxation of Profits and Income that the taxation of imputed rent be continued.[10]

The Canadian Royal Commission on Taxation (popularly known as the Carter Commission after its chairman, Kenneth L. Carter) stated that the comprehensive tax base

would include imputed income, that is, the gains realized when a person uses or consumes his own personal services or his own property. In most circumstances, however, . . . the valuation and administrative problems involved in including such amounts in income are insuperable.[11]

The Carter Commission stated further specifically in relation to imputed rent:

The most prevalent example of an imputed property gain is imputed rent. . . . To ensure that all taxpayers bore their fair proportion of the total tax burden, it would be necessary to impute rental income to this [homeowner] taxpayer. . . .

10. Richard Goode, *The Individual Income Tax,* rev. ed. (Brookings Institution, 1976), p. 118. Goode cited the Royal Commission's *Final Report,* Cmd. 9474 (London: Her Majesty's Stationery Office, 1955), pp. 249–51. See also Simons, *Personal Income Taxation,* note on p. 112, for reference to both Britain and Germany.

11. *Report of the Royal Commission on Taxation;* vol. 3, *Taxation of Income* (Ottawa: Queen's Printer, 1966), p. 41.

. . . The exclusion from income of imputed rent is therefore a substantial tax preference for home ownership.

An incentive of this magnitude leads to inequities between owners and renters. If it were administratively feasible, we would recommend that imputed net rental income be included in the tax base or, to compensate for not doing so, that the deduction of some portion of the rent paid by individuals who do not own their own homes be permitted. . . .

Because of the administrative difficulty of properly and equitably determining the amount of the net gain, we suggest that imputed rent continue to be omitted from the tax base.[12]

Other approaches provide rough but reasonable approximations of imputed rent without the necessity of estimating or calculating gross rent, mortgage interest, property taxes, depreciation, maintenance, and insurance. A net worth approach would use the market value of the home less any outstanding mortgage. An annual net rent would be obtained by multiplying this net worth by a conservative rate of return. Alternatively, the *net* return on the market value of the home could be calculated by applying a reasonable interest rate to the market value of the home, less the actual interest on the mortgage, if any. The calculated net rent would vary inversely with the relative size of the mortgage and the mortgage interest rate.[13]

This approach still requires a periodic estimate or appraisal of the market value of each owner-occupied unit, the major administrative problem with any tax on imputed rent. And this problem is so likely to result in errors, inconsistencies, and litigation that this approach still creates really major problems from the viewpoint of administration and compliance. The problem of valuation is made more difficult by the rapid changes in real estate values in recent years, and the uneven rates of change between different areas and different types of housing.

An impressive case can be made for including imputed rent in a comprehensive income tax base. William Vickrey made the case very

12. Ibid., pp. 47–49.

13. The Commission to Revise the Tax Structure recommended the determination of imputed rent as follows: (1) the owner-occupant would determine the capital value of the home and would declare this value on his tax return, permitting review by the Internal Revenue Service; (2) Internal Revenue would establish guideline rates for communities by region, these rates to be either gross or net or both; (3) the taxpayer would apply the appropriate return to his declared capital value to get the annual rent; if the taxpayer chose the gross return, deductions for interest and taxes would be permitted. (*Reforming the Federal Tax Structure*, p. 39.)

persuasively in 1947 that although the valuation problems would be rough, no possible inequity due to inconsistent valuations "can be as great as the disparity between tenants and home-owners with equities [in value of their homes] that would remain, even with the deductions for taxes and mortgage interest eliminated."[14] He considered the likely increase in controversy small relative to the greater equity that would result from inclusion of imputed rent.

Comprehensive Income Plus Net Gains Approach

If Henry Simons's broad definition of personal income, including consumption plus accumulation during a period, is accepted as the basis for a comprehensive income tax, the concept and the measurement of the value of homeowner preferences become more complicated. This approach would call for the net change in the value of assets less liabilities to be included in the taxpayer's income subject to tax each year. For owner-occupied homes, a valuation would be required at the beginning of each tax year for the current market value less any outstanding mortgage debt. The net gain (or loss) would be included in taxable income each year. Accrued and unrealized gains based on changes in estimated or appraised values would be taxed just as would realized gains based on market sales. Difficulties would arise from both the problem of annual valuations and the liquidity problem of paying taxes on unrealized gains.

Given the difficulties of obtaining comparable and accurate property tax valuations on residences within local assessing districts and under statewide equalization programs, the administration of an income tax including both imputed rent and annual changes in the net value of owner-occupied homes on a national basis seems impractical. Although the Carter Commission did not consider the problems insoluble, it did recommend that Canada initially should include only realized gains in the tax base.[15]

Termination of Deduction for Mortgage Interest

Interest payments made by individuals may now be taken as itemized deductions to reduce income subject to tax. These deductions have been permitted since the income tax began in 1913. For indi-

14. *Agenda for Progressive Taxation* (Ronald Press, 1947), p. 24.
15. *Report of the Royal Commission,* vol. 3, p. 50.

vidual returns for 1973, the most recent year for which such detail is available, the deductions for interest paid on home mortgages accounted for $19.2 billion, or 60 percent of all deductions for interest paid, as shown in the following table (only 3,509 tax returns showed itemized deductions for investment interest):[16]

	Total interest deductions	*Deductions for interest paid*		
		On home mortgages	*On investment*	*All other*
Number of returns (millions)	24.8	19.4	...	22.0
Amount of deductions for interest (billions of dollars)	31.9	19.2	0.2	12.6

For a net income tax, only interest payments that are associated with the production of income subject to tax fit the concept of a deductible expense. Thus interest payments to finance income-producing investments, including securities and rental property, would qualify as deductions. Interest payments to finance a mortgage on owner-occupied housing, purchases of automobiles and appliances, and other consumption expenditures would not be deductible under this approach.[17] The table above shows that most of the interest deductions taken now are for interest payments on home mortgages, which are directly related to consumption.

It is relevant to note that the current tax law disallows deductions for interest payments on loans taken to purchase tax-exempt securities. This is comparable to the disallowance of deductions for mortgage interest payments to purchase a home whose imputed rental income is exempt from tax.

This approach to a comprehensive tax base would permit as deductions only interest payments that are costs of producing taxable income. A problem arises here of identifying the use to which a loan is put. An investor may mortgage his home to get funds to invest in

16. Internal Revenue Service, *Statistics of Income—1973, Individual Income Tax Returns* (Government Printing Office, 1976), table 2.7.

17. In 1972, individuals deducted $2.4 billion of interest on installment purchases, bringing to almost 70 percent the interest deductions related directly to housing and consumer goods. This detail does not appear in the 1973 data. Internal Revenue Service, *Statistics of Income—1972, Individual Income Tax Returns* (GPO, 1974), table 2.16.

securities. Or persons with other assets may borrow on the collateral of securities or business assets to buy a home without financing through a mortgage.

Richard Goode suggests that deductions for interest be allowed only for taxpayers reporting property income, with the maximum deduction for interest payments for any taxpayer not to exceed the amount of property income. This is less precise than allowing deductions only for interest payments that are for loans for business purposes or for the purchase of securities that are taxable. But the more precise approach assumes it is possible to trace which borrowed funds are used to earn income and which to increase consumption. Goode's recommended approach is administratively more practical, since it avoids the tracing of dollars and allows interest payments to be deducted up to the amount of property income. Under this approach, based on tax return data for 1970, at least two-thirds of that year's interest deductions would not have been allowed.[18]

The disallowance of interest deductions for home mortgages, in the absence of the inclusion of imputed rent in taxable income, would make the tax system more equitable among taxpayers and more neutral among different types of consumption. Especially if interest deductions for credit purchases of other consumer durables and for consumer installment contracts, credit cards, and charge accounts were disallowed, interest payments would be treated as other personal consumption payments. The choice between purchases with different methods of payment—immediate payment, noninterest-bearing credit, and interest-bearing debt—would be a market decision, unaffected by the deductibility of interest for tax purposes.

Some would argue that the ability to pay varies between two persons, A and B, with the same income, A owning a home without a mortgage and B owning a home of equal value with a large mortgage. A and B have probably made different choices between consumption and saving in the past, or are at different stages in their life cycles— A has a home that is fully paid for and B has a large mortgage. If the concept of an income tax emphasizes comprehensive *money* income and excludes imputed income and changes in net worth in the measure of taxable income, no inequity exists between A with the debt-

18. Goode, *The Individual Income Tax,* pp. 151–53. In Chapter 2 of this volume, John Due seems to support a limit on interest deductions but would permit an amount of $3,600 in addition to property income, and this would permit deductions for interest on a home mortgage of perhaps $45,000.

free home and B with the mortgaged home if no deduction is permitted for the interest on B's mortgage.

If the annual change in net worth covering major types of assets and liabilities were included in income subject to tax, it would be appropriate to include annual changes in the net worth of owner-occupied homes. But it would appear unfair to do this for owner-occupied homes only and not cover changes in the net value of securities, businesses, and farms.

About two-thirds of homeowners have mortgage debt. About three-quarters of those with mortgages itemize their deductions, and these itemizers account for over four-fifths of all interest on homeowners' mortgages, as shown in table 5-3. The homeowners with mortgages and accompanying interest payments are more concentrated by income class and by age than are all taxpayers or all homeowners. This fits the expectation that young families in their late twenties or early thirties are the most frequent homebuyers and typically carry mortgage payments for twenty to thirty years.

The exclusion of mortgage interest as a deduction would have its greatest impact on those in the $10,000 to $50,000 income brackets. Individuals and families in this income range include 55 percent of the population and account for 85.7 percent of the mortgage interest deductions. The deductions also are relatively heaviest for tax-filers between the ages of twenty-five and fifty-five, an age group that includes about 65 percent of all homeowners and accounts for 80 percent of the mortgage interest deductions. (See tables 5-4 and 5-5.)

The effect of the exclusion of interest deductions thus would focus on a smaller population than all homeowners; it would raise taxes for those homeowners with mortgages who itemize deductions, approximately 22.5 million out of 45.2 million homeowners, and out of approximately 72 million taxpayers. (This contrasts with imputed rent and real estate taxes that affect all homeowners.) But this part of the population is typically of an age in which incomes are rising and three decades of steady or rising incomes are ahead when a mortgage obligation is assumed.

Unlike the inclusion of imputed rent, which theoretically is desirable but administratively very difficult, exclusion of the deduction for mortgage interest is both theoretically desirable and administratively practical. By and large, it would make the income tax base closer to a measure of net income and the tax system more equitable between homeowners and tenants. It is claimed that it would introduce an

Table 5-3. Data on Homeowners with Mortgages, on Mortgage Interest, and on the Effect of Eliminating the Interest Deduction, by Comprehensive Income Class, 1977 Levels

Comprehensive income class (thousands of dollars)	All homeowners		Homeowners with mortgages			Homeowners with mortgages who itemize mortgage interest			Effect of eliminating mortgage interest deduction	
	Number (thousands)	Percent	Number (thousands)	Percent	Mortgage interest paid (millions of dollars)	Number (thousands)	Percent	Interest deduction (millions of dollars)	Increase in income tax (millions of dollars)	Percent increase in tax
Negative income	80	0.2	21	0.1	25	6	*	14	0	0
0–2.5	780	1.7	125	0.4	85	15	0.1	28	0	0
2.5–5	2,130	4.7	457	1.5	377	204	0.9	209	1	a
5–7.5	2,899	6.4	895	3.0	750	416	1.8	437	13	b
7.5–10	3,425	7.6	1,443	4.8	1,164	615	2.7	654	51	44.2
10–15	7,857	17.4	4,457	14.9	4,016	3,120	13.9	3,077	314	15.2
15–20	8,362	18.5	6,219	20.7	6,382	4,674	20.8	5,091	654	11.3
20–25	7,083	15.7	5,941	19.8	6,882	4,307	19.1	5,346	891	10.3
25–30	4,787	10.6	4,068	13.6	4,985	3,284	14.6	4,298	900	9.3
30–50	6,057	13.4	5,079	16.9	7,181	4,588	20.4	6,747	1,891	8.3
50–100	1,344	3.0	1,037	3.5	1,859	1,015	4.5	1,846	757	5.7
100–200	280	0.6	205	0.7	457	203	0.9	453	204	2.6
200–500	68	0.2	42	0.1	132	42	0.2	131	49	1.2
500–1,000	10	*	6	*	26	6	*	26	8	0.5
1,000 and over	5	*	4	*	14	4	*	14	5	0.2
All classes	45,169	100.0	29,999	100.0	34,334	22,500	100.0	28,371	5,739	7.3

Source: Brookings MERGE File. Comprehensive income, used here, in subsequent tables, and in the text, is defined in the appendix to this volume. Figures are rounded.
a. Negative tax of −$27.2 million when mortgage interest is deductible becomes − $25.9 million if interest deduction is eliminated.
b. Negative tax of −$10.6 million when mortgage interest is deductible becomes a $2.3 million positive tax liability if interest deduction is eliminated.
* Less than 0.05 percent.

Table 5-4. Selected Data on Homeowners, by Comprehensive Income Class, 1977 Levels

Percent

Comprehensive income class (thousands of dollars)	All taxpayers	All homeowners	Total value of owner-occupied housing	Amount of mortgage debt	Amount of mortgage interest	Amount of property taxes	Imputed net rent	Total imputed rent, interest, and taxes
Negative income	0.2	0.2	0.2	0.1	0.1	0.4	0.3	0.3
0–2.5	2.6	1.7	0.9	0.2	0.2	1.3	1.2	0.9
2.5–5	6.5	4.7	3.3	1.2	1.1	4.5	4.0	3.1
5–7.5	8.6	6.4	5.0	2.2	2.2	5.8	6.1	4.4
7.5–10	9.4	7.6	6.3	3.6	3.4	6.5	7.3	5.4
10–15	19.6	17.4	16.2	13.7	11.7	14.9	17.2	14.0
15–20	18.3	18.5	18.5	20.9	18.6	15.9	17.7	17.2
20–25	13.4	15.7	16.5	21.1	20.0	14.7	14.6	16.8
25–30	8.5	10.6	11.3	14.3	14.5	10.6	10.1	12.1
30–50	10.2	13.4	14.7	17.0	20.9	16.6	13.8	17.9
50–100	2.1	3.0	4.0	3.7	5.4	5.9	4.1	5.4
100–200	0.4	0.6	1.9	1.4	1.3	1.9	2.1	1.7
200–500	0.1	0.2	0.9	0.5	0.4	0.7	1.1	0.6
500–1,000	*	0.0	0.2	0.1	0.1	0.2	0.3	0.2
1,000 and over	*	0.0	0.1	0.1	0.0	0.1	0.1	0.1
All classes	100.0	100.0	100.0	100.0	100.0	100.0	100.0	100.0
Addenda								
Number of units (millions)	71.6	45.2	45.2	30.0	30.0	45.2	45.2	45.2
Percentage of all taxpayers	100.0	63.1	63.1	41.9	41.9	63.1	63.1	63.1
Dollar amount (billions)	...	...	1,162.0	333.7	34.3	40.1	13.0	87.4

Source: Brookings MERGE File. Figures are rounded.
* 0.05 or less.

Table 5-5. Selected Data on Homeowners, by Age Group, 1977 Levels
Percent of total

Age group	All taxpayers	All homeowners	Total value of owner-occupied houses	Amount of mortgage debt	Amount of mortgage interest	Amount of property taxes	Imputed net rent	Total imputed rent, interest, and taxes
Under 20	1.9	1.5	0.9	0.5	0.4	1.0	0.9	0.8
20–25	9.0	7.1	4.7	5.7	4.4	4.6	4.2	4.4
25–30	11.3	10.4	9.0	13.5	11.5	8.4	7.1	9.4
30–35	9.9	10.2	10.2	16.1	13.9	9.4	7.8	10.9
35–40	9.7	10.6	10.9	17.6	15.0	10.7	8.3	12.0
40–45	10.5	11.5	12.0	19.2	16.0	11.9	9.1	13.1
45–50	10.9	11.6	12.2	9.1	13.0	12.2	13.6	12.7
50–55	10.1	10.8	11.7	7.5	10.8	11.7	13.5	11.6
55–60	9.4	9.7	10.5	5.2	7.6	10.5	12.7	9.7
60–65	7.6	7.6	8.3	3.3	4.7	8.5	10.4	7.3
65 and over	9.7	9.1	9.5	2.2	2.8	11.2	12.4	8.0
Total	100.0	100.0	100.0	100.0	100.0	100.0	100.0	100.0
Addenda								
Number of units (millions)	71.6	45.2	45.2	30.0	30.0	45.2	45.2	45.2
Percentage of all taxpayers	100.0	63.1	63.1	41.9	41.9	63.1	63.1	63.1
Dollar amount (billions)	…	…	1,162.0	333.7	34.3	40.1	13.0	87.4

Source: Brookings MERGE File. Figures are rounded.

inequity between those taxpayers who own their homes debt-free and those who have a mortgage. The validity of this view, in my judgment, hinges on whether changes in net worth as well as net income are relevant and practical for a comprehensive income tax.

Exclusion of the deduction would make the tax system more neutral between investments that yield imputed income and those that yield taxable income. It would be more neutral between housing and other consumer goods and services, assuming interest deductions for other consumer purposes were also disallowed. Thus my recommendation is that deductions for mortgage interest and other interest deductions be terminated except to the extent that there is property income. This change would also contribute to the simplification of the tax system.

If the termination of interest deductions were undertaken separately or as one of only a few changes and not accompanied by any general tax rate reduction, some gradual transition arrangement might be desirable in fairness to persons who have taken on mortgages with sizable interest payments anticipating stability in the tax treatment of mortgage interest. A gradual transition might run ten to twenty years, given the relatively large sums involved for many homeowners with mortgages and the long maturities of many mortgages. If broad changes were made, including substantial rate reductions, there would be little or no need for transition arrangements.

Another transitional approach would permit the present system of high rates with its deductions, exclusions, and other preferences to continue for a limited period to coexist with the new comprehensive tax base with its lower tax rates. As current homeowners with mortgages repaid their mortgages the size of the annual interest deduction would decline gradually to a point where a voluntary changeover to the comprehensive system would save taxes. Interest on new mortgages would either not be deductible or would be deductible only for a percentage that declined each year over a limited transition period.

Nondeductibility of Property Taxes

Property taxes on owner-occupied homes, like mortgage interest payments, are now deductible, although as stated earlier the imputed rental income to which they relate is not taxed. Federal individual income tax revenue would increase by an estimated $5.8 billion under current tax rates if the deductibility of homeowners' property taxes were terminated (see table 5-1).

The major reason for allowing a deduction for homeowners' property taxes is to encourage the use of property taxes by states and local governments, particularly the latter. Currently, property taxes as well as other major state and local taxes, such as individual income taxes and sales taxes, are deductible. State excise taxes, other than those on gasoline, are not deductible. (Of course, if imputed rent were included in income, property taxes would be deductible expenses in calculating net rent.)

Homeowners deduct large amounts of property taxes as itemized deductions. It is estimated that 45 million homeowners will pay approximately $40 billion in property taxes in 1977. About $26 billion of these taxes are taken as itemized deductions by the 28 million homeowners who itemize deductions. The right to itemize mortgage interest and property tax payments puts many homeowners in the itemizing group and thus makes their other deductions valuable in reducing their income subject to tax. Of the 28 million taxpayers who itemized their deductions in 1973, 19.4 million took deductions for mortgage interest paid and 23.1 million took deductions for real estate taxes.[19]

Exclusion of the deductibility of property taxes on owner-occupied residences would be justified as excluding a selective tax on one form of consumption (housing services) for one group of persons (homeowners). Further, as stated above, these property taxes are expenses of obtaining one kind of income—imputed rent—where the income itself is not included in taxable income. Other property taxes for rental properties, businesses, and farms that are expenses of obtaining taxable income would continue to be deductible.

Deductions for real estate taxes in 1973 amounted to $13.8 billion on federal individual income tax returns.[20] These taxes were approximately one-third of the total of $39.4 billion of all taxes paid taken as itemized deductions. Since real estate taxes for businesses and farms would be deducted on Schedules C and F, respectively, it seems a reasonable assumption that practically all of the $13.8 billion represented real property taxes on homeowners.

Nondeductibility of homeowners' property taxes would probably

19. Internal Revenue Service, *Statistics of Income—1973, Individual Income Tax Returns,* pp. 50, 51, 56.
20. Ibid., p. 51.

have an adverse effect on local government revenue sources. Property taxes are still the main local source of revenue for all local governments. For fiscal year 1974–75, for example, property taxes yielded local governments $50 billion, 81.6 percent of their tax revenue from local sources. A large part of this revenue came from locally assessed real property, which accounted for 80.3 percent of taxable assessed values in 1975.[21]

The termination of deductibility for homeowners' property taxes would be a blow to local governments in the very sensitive area of property taxes on homes, a major source of revenue for municipalities, counties, and especially school districts. To the extent that the level of property tax rates and local budgets are major political issues, and even in some cases determined by referendums, local governments would face a more difficult time obtaining voter approval. The federal government, by excluding deductibility, would no longer be sharing the burden of the local property tax on homeowners, at least for those owners who itemize their deductions.

If the end of deductibility of property taxes were accompanied by an approximately offsetting reduction in rates for the federal income tax, taxpayers in general would be no worse off. But tenants and homeowners who do not itemize would gain relative to homeowners who itemize. Of course, this is desirable from the equity and efficiency standpoint. Perhaps consideration would be given to an increase in federal aid to local governments concurrently with the termination of deductibility of property taxes.

All in all, a good case on economic grounds can be made for the termination of deductibility, but there is certain to be major political opposition.

Termination of Deductibility for Both Mortgage Interest and Property Taxes

If for administrative or other reasons it is not possible to tax imputed rent, the next best step in seeking a comprehensive income tax base would be to end deductibility for both homeowners' mortgage interest and property taxes. As stated earlier, these deductions are

21. U.S. Bureau of the Census, *Governmental Finances in 1974–75*, series GF75, no. 5 (GPO, 1976), p. 18; and Bureau of the Census, *Property Values Subject to Local General Property Taxation in the United States: 1975*, series GSS, no. 80 (GPO, 1976).

now permitted without the related income being included in the tax base.

Based on Brookings MERGE File projections for 1977, the termination of homeowners' deductions for mortgage interest and property taxes would reduce itemized deductions by about $54.3 billion and would increase individual income tax revenues by $10.7 billion, as shown in table 5-1. (This change would account for about three-fourths of the revenue gain of $13.8 billion from a full shift to taxation of imputed net rent, where interest and taxes are subtracted from gross rent in calculation of net rent.) Terminating these deductions would thus remove the largest part of the difference between the current treatment of homeowners and the result that would obtain if imputed net rent were subject to tax. Thus this change would remove a major part of the tax preference enjoyed by homeowners over renters. But it fails to distinguish between homeowners with mortgages who itemize their interest deductions and other homeowners. About half of all homeowners itemize deductions for mortgage interest, as shown in table 5-3.

Ending these deductions would make the tax system simpler, more equitable, and more neutral in its effects on resource allocation. The reasons for ending each deduction separately, as indicated earlier, would also apply to removing them both.

Tax Deduction or Tax Credit for Tenants

If it is not possible to remove tax preferences for homeowners, consideration might be given to some step in favor of tenants, as the other way to remove the glaring inequities between these groups. A move to provide a deduction or credit for tenants, however, is a move away from, not toward, a comprehensive income base.

At present, economists are divided over the incidence of property taxes on rental housing. Some conclude that these taxes are largely shifted forward to tenants, at least when there is only a normal vacancy rate; others conclude that the incidence falls largely on the owners of capital.[22] A deduction or credit for tenants probably should

22. See especially Henry Aaron, "A New View of Property Tax Incidence," and Richard A. Musgrave, "Is a Property Tax on Housing Regressive?" *American Economic Review,* vol. 64 (May 1974, *Papers and Proceedings, 1973*), pp. 212–21 and 222–29, respectively; Dick Netzer, "The Incidence of the Property Tax Revisited," *National Tax Journal,* vol. 26 (December 1973), pp. 515–35; and Henry J. Aaron, *Who Pays the Property Tax? A New View* (Brookings Institution, 1975), chap. 3.

approximate the property taxes on the dwelling unit that are partly shifted forward in the rental payment. To make such a deduction or credit simple to administer and appropriate in amount, it should probably be stated as a percentage of the rent, with perhaps a maximum amount set.

Property taxes are estimated nationally to average 1.5 to 2.0 percent of the market value of residential real estate. Rentals are estimated at about 10 to 12 percent of market value. Average property taxes thus would fall in the range of 15 to 20 percent of rent. Assuming that only part of property taxes are shifted to tenants, a deduction of perhaps 8 to 10 percent of rent might be reasonable. If a credit were chosen instead of a deduction, assuming an average marginal tax rate for tenants of 20 percent, a tax credit would be set equal to 2 percent of the rental. A credit, in addition to being of equal value to each taxpayer regardless of tax rate, would benefit all tenants, whether they use the standard deduction or itemize.[23]

The estimated revenue cost of a 10 percent deduction for tenants would be $220 million for 1977 income levels, based on the Brookings MERGE File. Fewer than half of all tenants who pay income taxes would benefit, since even with this new deduction available, most tenants would still use the standard deduction.[24] The estimated revenue cost of a tax credit for tenants equal to 2 percent of rent would be $440 million. All tenants who pay taxes would benefit from a direct credit.

An upper limit on any deduction for the equivalent of property taxes might be set at, say, $400 or a credit of $80. These limits would correspond to an annual rent of $4,000, including $800 of property taxes. If such limits were included with a deduction or a credit, the revenue loss would be less than indicated.

23. It is interesting to note that Congressman Joseph L. Fisher, who is an economist and the former president of Resources for the Future, introduced a bill in 1976 (and again in 1977) to provide renters with a federal income tax credit of 5 percent of annual rent, up to a maximum of $75 for a married couple filing jointly or $50 for a single taxpayer. In explaining this bill, he questioned the justification of treating renters differently. He also pointed out that most renters use the standard deduction and thus a credit would benefit more renters than a deduction provision.

24. A renter who pays one-third of his income in rent, probably more than average, would receive a deduction equal to 3 percent of income; because the standard deduction is equal to at least 16 percent of income up to about $13,000 of adjusted gross income, a tenant who currently takes the standard deduction would be unlikely to elect to itemize because of the deduction equal to 10 percent of rent.

Distributional Effects of Homeowner Preferences

Homeowner preferences provide significant tax savings for homeowners over tenants. Effective tax rates for comprehensive 1977 incomes are higher for tenants than for homeowners for all income classes from $2,500 to $100,000, as shown in table 5-6.[25] These estimates for 1977 also indicate, as one would expect, that homeowners who itemize deductions have lower effective rates than those for all homeowners, at least for all income classes up to $50,000, which still includes 96 percent of homeowners.

A shift to include imputed net rent and to terminate deductions for mortgage interest and property taxes would increase the average effective rate of income tax on homeowners from 12.5 percent to 13.9 percent of comprehensive income. Homeowners who itemize deductions would have their effective tax rates increased from 13.7 to 15.4 percent (table 5-7). The average tax increase for all homeowners from the removal of these preferences would be about 11 percent. The increase for homeowners who do not itemize deductions, however, would average only 4 percent, since only the imputed net rent is added to their taxable income. But the average increase for owner-occupants who now itemize would average 12.8 percent, since taxable income is increased by the addition of imputed net rent plus mortgage interest plus real property taxes. The absolute increase in the effective rate would be smaller in the lower income brackets, but the relative increase would be larger in these brackets. The same increases, by age brackets, are shown in table 5-8.

If current preferences were changed to disallow mortgage interest and property taxes—the changes I recommend as a feasible part of a general move to a more comprehensive income tax base—those homeowners who now itemize would bear all of these increases. The changed tax rates, as shown in table 5-7, would raise average effective tax rates on itemizing homeowners from the current 13.7 percent to 15.1 percent. The current gap in effective rates between all homeowners and itemizers for income levels up to $25,000 would prac-

25. These calculations are based on data from the Brookings MERGE File and are consistent with the important earlier findings of Henry Aaron (based on 1966 data) in "Income Taxes and Housing," *American Economic Review,* vol. 60 (December 1970), pp. 791–93.

Table 5-6. Number of Tenant and Homeowner Taxpayers and Effective Individual Income Tax Rates with and without Homeowner Preference Tax Deductions, by Comprehensive Income Class, 1977[a]

Comprehensive income class (thousands of dollars)	Number of taxpayers (millions)		Homeowners		Effective tax rate (percent)[b] With homeowner preferences		Homeowners		Without homeowner preferences[c] Homeowners	
	Total	Tenants	Total	Itemizers	Total	Tenants	Total	Itemizers	Total	Itemizers
0–2.5	1.9	1.1	0.8	*	−1.6	−1.8	−1.3	−3.0	−1.3	−3.0
2.5–5	4.6	2.5	2.1	0.3	−0.9	−0.7	−1.0	−2.0	−0.9	−1.0
5–7.5	6.2	3.3	2.9	0.6	1.3	1.5	1.0	0.1	1.2	1.0
7.5–10	6.7	3.3	3.4	1.0	3.8	4.2	3.5	2.4	3.8	3.6
10–15	14.1	6.2	7.9	4.4	6.3	6.9	5.8	5.8	6.3	6.8
15–20	13.1	4.8	8.4	6.0	8.3	9.1	7.8	7.3	8.5	8.3
20–25	9.6	2.5	7.1	4.9	9.9	11.0	9.5	9.0	10.4	10.3
25–30	6.1	1.3	4.8	3.8	11.5	13.2	11.0	10.9	12.2	12.3
30–50	7.3	1.3	6.1	5.3	14.2	16.2	13.8	13.7	15.4	15.5
50–100	1.5	0.2	1.3	1.3	21.0	23.3	20.7	20.8	22.7	22.9
100–200	0.3	*	0.3	0.3	29.9	27.4	30.2	30.1	31.9	31.8
200–500	0.1	*	0.1	0.1	36.2	42.6	35.0	35.0	36.1	36.1
500–1,000	*	*	*	*	38.2	35.7	38.4	38.2	39.2	39.0
1,000 and over	*	*	*	*	42.6	41.8	42.7	42.7	43.1	43.0
All classes	71.6	26.5	45.2	28.0	11.9	10.3	12.5	13.7	13.6	15.1

Source: Brookings MERGE File. Figures are rounded.
a. Homeowner preferences are deductions from adjusted gross income of home mortgage interest and home property taxes.
b. In the income classes $0 to $5,000, net refunds and earned income credits lead to negative effective tax rates.
c. See table 5-7 for effect of other possible changes in homeowner preferences.
*0.05 or less.

Table 5-7. Effect on Homeowners' Effective Tax Rates of Eliminating Various Home-

Income classᵃ (thousands of dollars)	Number (millions)	Effective tax rates (percent)ᵇ					
		With home-owner prefer-ences	Imputed net rent taxable	Mort-gage interest not de-ductible	Property taxes not de-ductible	Neither interest nor taxes de-ductible	Imputed net rent taxable, interest and taxes not de-ductible
A. All homeowners							
0–2.5	0.8	−1.3	−1.3	−1.3	−1.3	−1.3	−1.3
2.5–5	2.1	−1.0	−0.8	−1.0	−0.9	−0.9	−0.6
5–7.5	2.9	1.0	1.4	1.1	1.1	1.2	1.7
7.5–10	3.4	3.5	3.9	3.6	3.6	3.8	4.3
10–15	7.9	5.8	6.1	6.1	6.0	6.3	6.7
15–20	8.4	7.8	8.1	8.2	8.1	8.5	8.8
20–25	7.1	9.5	9.8	10.1	10.0	10.4	10.7
25–30	4.8	11.0	11.3	11.7	11.6	12.2	12.4
30–50	6.1	13.8	14.1	14.7	14.6	15.4	15.6
50–100	1.3	20.7	21.0	21.5	21.8	22.7	23.0
100–200	0.3	30.2	30.7	30.8	31.3	31.9	32.3
200–500	0.1	35.0	35.4	35.2	35.8	36.1	36.6
500–1,000	*	38.4	38.8	38.6	39.0	39.2	39.5
1,000 and over	*	42.7	42.8	42.8	43.0	43.1	43.1
All classes	45.2	12.5	12.8	13.1	13.1	13.6	13.9
Addendum Revenueᶜ (billions of dollars)	...	121.3	124.3	127.0	127.1	132.0	135.0

Source: Brookings MERGE File. Figures are rounded.
a. The estimated 80,000 homeowners reporting negative incomes have been omitted from this table.
b. In the income classes $0 to $5,000, net refunds and earned income credits lead to negative effective tax rates.

tically disappear. (The effective rates now show little or no difference for income classes above $25,000.) Further, the relatively wide gaps in current effective rates between homeowners and tenants would be reduced by more than half at income levels up to $100,000 if home-owners were not allowed to deduct mortgage interest and property taxes (tables 5-6 and 5-7).

The termination of deductibility of interest and taxes for home-owners would represent an increase in average tax liability of almost 10 percent, with the percentage increase approximately even among all groups up to age fifty-five, with a declining percentage increase above that age (table 5-8).

owner Preferences, by Income Class, 1977

Income class[a] (thousands of dollars)	Number (millions)	*Effective tax rates (percent)*[b]					
		With home-owner prefer-ences	Imputed net rent taxable	Mort-gage interest not de-ductible	Property taxes not de-ductible	Neither interest nor taxes de-ductible	Imputed net rent taxable, interest and taxes not de-ductible
		B. Homeowners who itemize deductions					
0–2.5	*	−3.0	−3.0	−3.0	−3.0	−3.0	−3.0
2.5–5	0.3	−2.0	−1.8	−1.9	−1.1	−1.0	−0.8
5–7.5	0.6	0.1	0.5	0.4	0.7	1.0	1.5
7.5–10	1.0	2.4	2.8	3.0	3.1	3.6	4.1
10–15	4.4	5.8	6.2	6.4	6.3	6.8	7.1
15–20	6.0	7.3	7.6	7.9	7.8	8.3	8.6
20–25	4.9	9.0	9.3	9.9	9.7	10.3	10.6
25–30	3.8	10.9	11.1	11.8	11.6	12.3	12.6
30–50	5.3	13.7	14.0	14.7	14.6	15.5	15.7
50–100	1.3	20.8	21.1	21.7	22.0	22.9	23.2
100–200	0.3	30.1	30.6	30.7	31.2	31.8	32.2
200–500	0.1	35.0	35.4	35.2	35.8	36.1	36.6
500–1,000	*	38.2	38.6	38.3	38.8	39.0	39.3
1,000 and over	*	42.7	42.8	42.7	43.0	43.0	43.1
All classes	28.0	13.7	14.0	14.4	14.5	15.1	15.4
Addendum Revenue[c] (billions of dollars)	...	101.3	103.5	107.0	107.1	112.0	114.2

c. Total revenue that would be collected under the condition specified in the heading.
* Fewer than 50,000.

Another dimension of the equity effect, the variation in the understatement of tax liability and disposable income between individuals in the same income class, has been very carefully analyzed by Melvin and Anne White.[26] Their study showed that taking account of all features of the tax structure that caused understatement of taxable income relative to a comprehensive income base led to coefficients of variation in tax liability of 30 percent for people in equal circumstances. Horizontal inequalities would have been reduced by one-

26. "Horizontal Inequality in the Federal Income Tax Treatment of Homeowners and Tenants," *National Tax Journal*, vol. 18 (September 1965), pp. 225–39. Their study focused on taxpayers in the $3,000 to $25,000 range of comprehensive income based on incomes and tax structure for 1960.

Table 5-8. Effect on Homeowners' Effective Tax Rates of Eliminating Various Homeowner Preferences, by Age Group, 1977

Age group	Number (millions)	With home-owner prefer-ences	Imputed net rent taxable	Mort-gage interest not de-ductible	Property taxes not de-ductible	Neither interest nor taxes de-ductible	Imputed net rent taxable, interest and taxes not de-ductible
				Effective tax rates (percent)[a]			
		A. All homeowners					
Under 20	0.7	5.2	5.4	5.4	5.6	5.7	6.0
20–25	3.2	8.4	8.7	8.8	8.7	9.1	9.3
25–30	4.7	10.1	10.3	10.7	10.5	11.0	11.3
30–35	4.6	10.3	10.6	11.1	10.9	11.5	11.8
35–40	4.8	11.0	11.3	11.8	11.6	12.3	12.6
40–45	5.2	12.5	12.7	13.3	13.1	13.8	14.0
45–50	5.2	13.9	14.2	14.6	14.5	15.1	15.5
50–55	4.9	13.7	14.0	14.3	14.3	14.9	15.2
55–60	4.4	15.2	15.5	15.6	15.8	16.2	16.6
60–65	3.5	14.6	15.1	15.0	15.2	15.5	16.0
65 and over	4.1	12.3	12.6	12.4	12.9	13.1	13.4
All groups	45.2	12.5	12.8	13.1	13.1	13.6	13.9
Addendum Revenue[b] (billions of dollars)	...	121.3	124.3	127.0	127.1	132.0	135.0
		B. Homeowners who itemize deductions					
Under 20	0.2	9.3	9.5	9.7	10.3	10.6	10.9
20–25	1.3	9.6	9.8	10.3	10.2	10.8	11.0
25–30	2.8	10.6	10.8	11.5	11.2	12.0	12.2
30–35	3.2	10.9	11.1	11.9	11.6	12.4	12.7
35–40	3.4	11.7	12.0	12.7	12.5	13.3	13.6
40–45	3.7	13.4	13.6	14.3	14.1	14.9	15.2
45–50	3.7	14.9	15.2	15.7	15.7	16.4	16.7
50–55	3.3	14.6	15.0	15.4	15.5	16.1	16.5
55–60	2.8	16.6	17.0	17.2	17.4	17.9	18.3
60–65	1.9	16.4	16.8	16.9	17.3	17.7	18.1
65 and over	1.9	15.4	15.8	15.6	16.4	16.6	17.0
All groups	28.0	13.7	14.0	14.4	14.5	15.1	15.4
Addendum Revenue (billions of dollars)	...	101.3	103.5	107.0	107.1	112.0	114.2

Source: Brookings MERGE File. Figures are rounded.
a. The effective tax rate is calculated on the basis of a comprehensive income base.
b. Total revenue that would be collected under the condition specified in the heading.

third if the homeowner tax preferences (exclusion of imputed rent and deductions for mortgage interest and property taxes) had been removed. These preferences accounted for an understatement of 5 to 6 percent of comprehensive income and a reduction of 9 to 11 percent in mean tax liability for all the income classes between $3,000 and $25,000 in 1960. The termination of all the homeowner preferences would have reduced the variations between taxpayers in the same income classes most for lower-income taxpayers, with the dispersion reduced by 42 percent in the $3,000 to $4,000 income class, by 24 percent in the $9,000 to $10,000 class, and by 11 percent for the $20,000 to $25,000 comprehensive income class.[27]

If the homeowner preferences were removed separately, termination of the mortgage interest deduction would have reduced horizontal inequality as measured by the coefficient of variation by an average of 15 percent, focused heavily on lower and middle incomes. Removal of the property tax deduction would have reduced the variation by 13 percent, with a less regressive distribution of the increases than removal of the interest deduction. The inclusion of imputed net rent with no other changes would have reduced the variation also by 13 percent, with a lesser regressivity.[28]

Thus horizontal equity would be substantially improved if homeowner preferences were eliminated. The inequities occur not only between homeowners and tenants in the same income classes but also between homeowners with comparable incomes to the extent that housing represents different percentages of their incomes and is thus reflected differently in their tax preferences. Vertical equity would also be improved, since homeowners would fall with greater certainty into the taxable income class that measures their comprehensive income.

Economic Effects of Homeowner Tax Preferences

There are two economic effects of the favorable tax treatment of homeowners.[29] First, it lowers the net price of homeownership rela-

27. Ibid., pp. 232–33.
28. Ibid.
29. See the analyses in Aaron, "Income Taxes and Housing," pp. 796–99; James, "Income Taxes, Homeownership and Urban Land Use," pp. 39–43, 68–69; and Commission to Revise the Tax Structure, *Reforming the Federal Tax Structure*, pp. 120–23, 141–42.

tive to rental housing and nondurable consumer goods. (Durable consumer goods, such as cars, boats, appliances, and furniture, receive the same advantages as homeownership—exclusion of imputed rent and deductibility of interest on installment purchases and of property taxes, if any.) Second, it allows a lower before-tax rate of return on investment in owner-occupied housing than on other income-producing investments, which will yield equal after-tax rates of return because the income from housing is not fully taxed.

To the extent that consumers are sensitive to the reduction in the price of owner-occupied housing, more consumers will become homeowners, some will buy larger or better-quality housing, and more homebuyers will be apt to use large mortgages to finance their purchases. (Even when homebuyers have other financial assets, they often take out mortgages for a higher percent of value due to the high visibility of the mortgage interest deduction, the greater ease of selling with a large mortgage, and the reluctance to liquidate other assets.) Further, because single-family homes account for 94 percent of all owner-occupied housing,[30] homeowner preferences generally direct resources into this type of housing.

With an increased demand for housing for purchase, the price of such housing usually rises and resources shift to the construction of more and larger houses for sale. With more consumers becoming homeowners, the demand for rental housing declines, rental rates decline, and relatively fewer rental units are built. With tax incentives in the form of accelerated depreciation available to owners and investors in rental housing—subsidies that bring forth more rental housing than would occur in their absence—the prices of housing both for ownership and for rental are reduced relative to the prices of other consumer goods and services. The increase in the demand for housing, both for rental and for purchase, leads to a higher rate of return on housing, a shift of capital to housing, and a higher rate of return to capital generally, because housing is very capital intensive.

Several studies support the view that the quantity of housing demanded rises with a decline in price, generally indicating a price elasticity of demand of −1 to −1.5. This means that a reduction in homeowners' costs due to tax subsidies of perhaps 10 to 15 percent would

30. U.S. Bureau of the Census, *Statistical Abstract of the United States, 1976* (GPO, 1976), p. 747.

"increase demand for owner-occupied housing by at least 10 percent and perhaps more than 20 percent."[31]

Homeowners receive a subsidy determined by the value of the housing services they consume and by their marginal tax rate. Generally, new homeowners have large mortgages and relatively little equity, making for large interest deductions and small imputed net rents.[32] With the rates of interest relatively high on new mortgages in recent years, interest deductions have grown rapidly and imputed net rent has grown slowly.

In a study in 1976 Franklin James calculated the effect of income tax subsidies for homeowners, comparing them with tax subsidies for rental housing. While tax subsidies are more valuable for rental housing than for owner-occupancy for households with incomes below $4,000, for all higher income levels tax preferences are more valuable for homeowners. Moreover, the value of these preferences for homeowners rises as incomes rise, from a net tax subsidy of 3 to 4 percent of imputed gross rent for those with incomes of $4,000 to $6,000 up to a 27 percent subsidy for those with incomes over $25,000. The rising marginal tax rates together with an income elasticity of 1.5 causes the rise in the effective subsidy as incomes increase. James concluded that between 1946 and 1970, income tax subsidies for homeowners resulted in 2.8 million more owner-occupants than there would have been without the subsidies.[33]

A further factor, neglected in the discussion so far, has been the steady rise in real estate values since World War II. Homeowners are very aware that they benefit from such increases. In addition, homeowners who sell at a gain but reinvest in a more expensive house are allowed to defer the tax on this gain. Individuals who invest in securities or real estate other than homes for their own occupancy do not get to defer taxes on their gains. The estimated tax saving for individuals who sell their home at a gain and buy another is $890 million for fiscal year 1977. The saving from the tax deferral is the equivalent of an interest-free loan. (The distribution of this tax saving by income classes is shown in table 5-9 in the appendix to this chapter.)

31. Aaron, "Income Taxes and Housing," p. 799.

32. Richard Goode, "Imputed Rent of Owner-Occupied Dwellings under the Income Tax," *Journal of Finance,* vol. 15 (December 1960), pp. 513–15.

33. James, "Income Taxes, Home Ownership and Urban Land Use," pp. 22–25, 39–43, 68–69. His data were based on 1969 income levels.

Effect of Terminating Homeowner Preferences

Terminating the deductions for mortgage interest and property taxes would raise the average price of housing services to homeowners. The amount of this increase in the price of housing would probably range between 10 percent and 16 percent for the bulk of taxpayers in the $10,000 to $25,000 income brackets.[34]

In terms of resource allocation, the advantages now enjoyed by housing over other types of consumption and investment would be removed. At present, net income from other investments generally is subject to income tax, but income on equity in owner-occupied housing is not taxed. The differential tax causes the market before-tax rate of return on other investments to be higher than the rate of return in purchasing a home, because investors seek equivalent after-tax rates of return.

For example, assuming a 40 percent corporate tax rate, corporate investments must earn 10 percent before tax to match the 6 percent tax-free return on housing. In terms of economic efficiency and the allocation of resources, too little capital is invested in areas other than housing and too much in housing. The misallocation of resources results from the allocation of resources to earn only 6 percent in housing when, with a neutral tax between the different uses, these resources would earn a higher return in the corporate sector.

The removal of the tax preferences for housing would make the before-tax and after-tax rates of return from housing and other investments comparable. The net rate of return on housing would drop relative to other investments, and a shift of resources would take place. The market system would be more important, relative to the tax system, in determining investment and resource allocation decisions.

A welfare loss due to the present overallocation of resources to housing as a result of tax subsidies would be removed. David Laidler estimated that the omission of imputed income of homeowners from the tax base caused an overinvestment in housing stock of approximately $60 billion in 1960. By income class, the overinvestment increased from approximately 20 percent for homeowners in the $3,000 to $7,000 income brackets to approximately 35 percent for owners with incomes above $15,000. Laidler calculated the welfare loss in

34. Ibid., p. 24.

terms of Marshallian consumer surplus to be in excess of $500 million for the year 1960.[35]

Effectiveness and Efficiency of Tax Subsidies for Homeowners

There is no clear statement of the purpose of homeowner preferences in the tax system. The deductions for mortgage interest and for homeowners' property taxes are parts of broader policies generally permitting deductions for interest payments and for state and local taxes that have been in effect since the beginning of the federal income tax. Similarly, imputed rent has been excluded from income.

The national goal generally has been the provision of safe and decent housing for all. The federal government provides assistance through direct expenditure programs for low-income housing projects, homeownership assistance through mortgage interest subsidies, rental housing assistance and rent supplements, and subsidized housing for the elderly and the handicapped. The government also provides direct loans or loan guarantees for homes to veterans, certain residents in rural areas, and other homebuyers inadequately served by the private mortgage market.

Budget outlays for the major housing programs in the Department of Housing and Urban Development are estimated at $3 billion for fiscal year 1977.[36] Net direct loan outlays for housing programs for fiscal 1977 are estimated to bring net repayments of $1.5 billion.[37]

35. David Laidler, "Income Tax Incentives for Owner-Occupied Housing," in Arnold C. Harberger and Martin J. Bailey, eds., *The Taxation of Income from Capital* (Brookings Institution, 1969), pp. 51, 55–64. These income brackets would need to be adjusted for 1977, but the magnitude of the welfare losses would be greater due to higher prices and more homeowners, partly offset by tax rate reductions since 1960.

36. *The Budget of the United States Government, Fiscal Year 1978,* pp. 173–74.

37. *Special Analyses, Budget of the United States Government, Fiscal Year 1978,* pp. 96–97. Excluded are estimated loan guarantee commitments for housing during fiscal 1977 of approximately $24 billion that usually do not involve any budget outlays (p. 102). A staff study of the Joint Economic Committee presented a full catalog of the gross budgetary cost of housing subsidies for fiscal year 1975 as follows (in billions of dollars):

Direct cash subsidies	1.7
Tax subsidies	12.9
Credit subsidies	1.1
Total	15.7

Tax subsidies thus accounted for 82 percent of the total. See *Federal Subsidy Pro-*

These direct budget outlays for fiscal 1977 for housing are dwarfed by the tax subsidies to homeowners of $5.4 billion for deductibility of mortgage interest, of $4.5 billion for deductibility of property taxes, and the $890 million from the deferral of tax on capital gains on sales of their principal residence. There are also tax expenditures for rental housing in the form of depreciation in excess of straight-line depreciation to owners of rental housing, estimated at $505 million for fiscal 1977. Of this total, $405 million goes to individual owner-investors and $100 million to corporate owners.[38]

Thus the federal budget effects on the housing markets are much greater through the tax preferences to homeowners than they are through direct expenditure programs. Further, these larger tax expenditure features benefit mostly the middle- and upper-income groups, plus elderly homeowners. The direct expenditure programs assist mainly lower- and modest-income persons. Henry Aaron has shown that government housing programs clearly are of most benefit to middle- and upper-income groups.[39]

The tax subsidies to homeowners provide little or no assistance for low-income housing. Tax preferences are provided in such a manner that the benefits vary directly with (1) the level of income and the marginal tax rate, (2) the market value of housing a family owns, and (3) the relative size of the mortgage to the value of the housing (assuming imputed net rent is not going to be taxed).

In 1969 George Romney, then secretary of the Department of Housing and Urban Development, was aware of the uneven effect of tax preferences and other housing programs. According to a press report of his opinions on this subject:

"[The] most fundamental aspect of housing and urban problems" is that the housing and tax policies of the past had helped most Americans

grams, A Staff Study prepared for the Subcommittee on Priorities and Economy in Government of the Joint Economic Committee, 93 Cong. 2 sess. (GPO, 1974), pp. 5–13, 87–94.

38. *Special Analyses, Budget of the United States Government, 1978,* pp. 129–30.

39. Aaron, "Federal Housing Subsidies," in *The Economics of Federal Subsidy Programs,* A Compendium of Papers Submitted to the Joint Economic Committee, 92 Cong. 2 sess. (GPO, 1972), pt. 5, pp. 584–87. Aaron pointed out that the income tax savings to homeowners were then "more than 10 times as large as benefits under the next largest program, low-rent public housing. . . . Indeed, yearly tax savings to households with incomes of $50,000 per year or more are nearly as great as annual benefits under low-rent public housing and larger than annual benefits under any other housing program" (p. 585).

to move into decent homes but that the same Americans were denying the support needed in establishing policies and laws that would do the same for low-income citizens who "live under deplorable conditions in our core cities."

"The people who benefit usually are not aware that they are being helped" . . . referring to both the tax write-offs for interest paid on home mortgages and housing loans guaranteed by the Government.[40]

The homeowner preferences provide upside-down subsidies—the greater the need, the smaller the subsidy.[41] For example, with the deductibility of mortgage interest, the subsidy to the home buyer varies directly with the taxpayer's marginal tax rate: for a family with taxable income over $200,000 and a 70 percent marginal rate, the Treasury in effect pays $70 of every $100 of mortgage interest; for a middle-income household with $15,000 of taxable income and a 25 percent marginal rate, the Treasury absorbs $25 of each $100 of interest; for a family with less than $1,000 of taxable income, the Treasury covers $14 of each $100 of interest; and for those individuals and families whose income is below the taxable level, the Treasury gives no subsidy on mortgage interest.

These tax subsidies are obviously powerful but inefficient and inequitable. Other federal housing programs have upper limits either on the income of the recipient, the size of the subsidized mortgages, or the value of the housing unit. There are no limits on the deductions that a homeowner may take for mortgage interest and property taxes. (The Tax Reform Act of 1976 did put restrictions on deductions for a second, or vacation, home.) These features are not designed to get more housing units for each buck of tax subsidy. There is no overall limit on the amount of these tax expenditures. As with other tax expenditures, there has been no periodic review to determine whether homeowner preferences are contributing to a priority national objective and whether they are doing this efficiently. The executive agencies, such as the Department of Housing and Urban Development and the Office of Management and Budget, do not seem to be analyzing and evaluating these tax subsidies. At least now under the Congressional Budget and Impoundment Control Act of 1974, the President's

40. *New York Times*, October 24, 1969, quoted in Stanley S. Surrey, *Pathways to Tax Reform: The Concept of Tax Expenditures* (Harvard University Press, 1973), p. 233.

41. Surrey, ibid., pp. 204, 232–36; Aaron, "Federal Housing Subsidies," p. 585; and Laidler, "Income Tax Incentives," pp. 53–54.

annual budget is required to contain a report on tax expenditures.[42] If tax preferences for homeowners are continued and if the promotion of more widespread homeownership is accepted as a national goal, major revisions should be considered to attempt to make the preferences more effective and more efficient.

The mortgage interest deduction could be replaced by a credit, which would make the tax subsidy of equal value to all taxpayers regardless of the marginal tax rate. For example, a tax credit equal to 30 percent of the mortgage interest would remove the present inequity between homeowners with mortgages in different tax brackets. Such a credit would of course be more valuable than the current interest deduction to home buyers whose income and personal exemptions place them below this marginal tax rate, single persons in general with taxable incomes up to $12,000, and married couples with taxable incomes up to $20,000 who file jointly. Further, if such credits were made refundable, they would assist people who are not currently subject to income tax, including the elderly.

The use of a credit rather than a deduction might also be considered for property taxes. This again would have the federal government sharing evenly with all homeowners in proportion to their real estate taxes.

Another approach would be to place a limit on the amount of mortgage interest and property taxes that could be deducted. Such a limit would aim to assist everyone to obtain satisfactory housing but would place a cap on the amount of subsidy that any taxpayer could receive. For example, interest might be allowed as a deduction on a mortgage up to a maximum mortgage of say $45,000 (approximately three times the median family income). And property taxes might be deductible on market values of up to say $60,000 (four times the median income). Such limits might need to be adjusted periodically to reflect changing levels of income. A case could be made for regional differentials, but this would complicate the tax administration.

An upper limit on deductions would be similar to some features already in the tax law. For example, the personal exemption is set currently at $750 as a crude measure of subsistence costs per family member.

If tax preferences for homeownership are continued, these changes

42. For example, see *Special Analyses, Budget of the United States Government, Fiscal Year 1978,* Special Analysis F, pp. 119–42.

would revise the preferences to make them more equitable among different income classes, to strengthen the tax incentives for families with modest income, and to make the preferences more efficient in assisting more people to obtain satisfactory housing for a given amount of revenue forgone. Before such changes are made, however, the whole gamut of other factors that affect homeownership, such as mortgage terms and interest rates, should be considered, since non-tax subsidies might well be more effective than tax expenditures. But the larger question of whether homeownership should be subsidized at all requires attention first.

Appendix

Table 5-9. Distribution of Revenue Gains from Termination of Homeowner and Related Tax Preferences, by Adjusted Gross Income Class, Fiscal Year 1977

Adjusted gross income class (thousands of dollars)	Deductions for interest		State and local taxes			Deferral of capital gains tax
	Mort-gage	Con-sumer debt	Property tax	State gasoline tax	Other	
	Percentage distribution					
0–7	1.3	1.4	2.2	3.2	1.0	6.7
7–15	23.6	23.7	19.8	32.3	12.9	23.9
15–50	65.9	66.0	62.7	60.3	57.3	56.9
50 and over	9.1	9.0	15.3	4.2	28.8	12.5
All classes	100.0	100.0	100.0	100.0	100.0	100.0
	Millions of dollars					
Revenue gain	4,710	1,075	3,825	600	6,680	890

Source: Committee on the Budget, United States Senate, *Tax Expenditures: Compendium of Background Material and Individual Provisions,* 94 Cong. 2 sess (GPO, 1976), pp. 49, 73–76, 79–80, 157. Figures are rounded.

Comments by Jerome Kurtz

I will address some of the practical problems of implementing the taxation of imputed rent on owner-occupied homes. It seems to me that in building the stairway to the paradise of a comprehensive tax base, imputed rent should be one of the last steps.

William Hellmuth suggests two methods of computing net imputed rental income. One is to estimate gross rental value and subtract expenses; the other is to assume an arbitrary interest return on the net investment in the property. I will discuss some of the problems in doing one or the other, but before that let me mention some general problems of implementing either system. These may appear to be fringe matters, but in this area the fringes are important.

The first problem is that of defining a home, and that will involve difficult problems of drawing a line. For example, how should farmers (who seem to have a great deal of legislative influence) be treated? They live on farms or ranches that produce very small incomes, considering the value of the property. Presumably they tolerate low rates of return on their assets because they like to live on a farm or a ranch. It seems to me that additional income should be imputed to them for living on the farm rather than elsewhere.

Other difficult line-drawing problems occur to me. Mobile homes should clearly be included; if so, campers, houseboats, and recreational land cannot be excluded. If a summer home is included, why not a hunting preserve?

While owner-occupied homes are singled out for taxation because they are the largest single class of consumer assets, not enough is known about the ownership of other consumption capital goods to conclude that inclusion only of homes will improve vertical equity. Horizontal equity might be improved, but the question of vertical equity should not be ignored. For example, people invest large sums in antiques, art, and collections of various kinds. To exclude the imputed income from such consumption assets—while including the imputed income of consumption assets owned throughout the scale of incomes—may not improve equity.

It goes without saying that simplification will not be served by taxing imputed rent, no matter what method is used. Inevitably the tax return will be made more complicated and the valuation problems will complicate compliance and tax administration. The question is whether the result is worth the effort.

Another factor that cannot be completely ignored—one mentioned by Richard Goode—is the importance of the taxpayer's perception of equity. Taxpayers generally think in terms of money income, or things that are essentially equivalent to money income; they would have great difficulty in understanding why imputed rent should be taxed.

If imputed rent were taxed on the basis of current values, the tax burden would increase as the value of the taxpayer's home increased. Many people would not view themselves as significantly better off— and therefore having greater taxpaying capacities—because their homes have increased in value. They probably do not view their homes as investment assets; they are not in the business of selling their homes. Homes are the places in which they live, the same places they have always lived. Their money incomes may remain essentially the same, yet their taxes would increase for reasons that would be relatively incomprehensible to most of them. The question is one of ability to pay. I am not sure that a person who lives in a house that appreciates at a faster rate than money income has an increase in his ability to pay taxes.

As to the mechanics of introducing imputed rent into the tax base, the more accurate method is to estimate gross rents and subtract the deductions. But I am not sure how to estimate gross rental values. I have the impression that homes do not command rents that represent a fair return on their value. One reason is that renters are unwilling to make the kind of financial commitment that a homeowner is willing to undertake. The homeowner may be making more of a commitment for his housing because he is hedging against future rent increases.

If that is so, consideration must be given to whether rental value means the amount that would be paid under a long-term lease or a short-term lease; if the former, then when should the lease be considered to have begun? It would not seem entirely inappropriate to regard the homeowner as having entered into a long-term lease at the time of acquisition of the property. According to this analysis, current values may be the wrong measure of imputed income.

Alternatively, suppose a taxpayer leases a house for ten years at a flat rental. Does he have imputed income if, toward the end of the lease term, the current rental value is higher than that which he committed himself to pay in the beginning? How should people living in rent-controlled housing be treated? They may be the beneficiaries of as much imputed income by reason of governmental controls as those who own their own homes.

Once having determined gross rental value, an estimate of expenses must be made. How should depreciation be figured? If the precedent of rental housing is followed, losses rather than gains will be generated on imputed income. Much of the rental housing built today shows no taxable income for eight or ten years. The accounting losses are rather substantial. Since houses turn over about every eight years on the average, this may be a roundabout way of giving tax shelters to middle-income people.

The problems of estimating the cost of repairs and maintenance boggle the mind. It is an extraordinarily difficult problem in business just to distinguish between repairs and capital additions. In addition, in an owner-occupied home, it would be necessary to distinguish between normal repairs and repairs that are incurred solely because the property is a home. One may paint every two years rather than every four. One may keep the property in a condition that would be uneconomical if one were renting the property. Such excess maintenance is really current consumption rather than repairs that are related to the imputed rent. Separating these items seems impossible.

These problems would lead, I think, to taxation based on a net rate of return on either the entire property, or only on the value of the equity. The simpler method is to impute a net rate of return only on the equity. The simpler approach would be inaccurate, however, because it fails to take account of the interest paid on mortgages. Obviously a homeowner paying a lower rate of interest on his mortgage has greater net imputed income than another who is paying a higher interest rate. If only net equities are considered, such differences are ignored.

It must be recognized that the price of achieving this degree of simplicity creates inequities because repairs, maintenance, and other expenditures affecting net income from the property are ignored. The taxpayer may not have realized any real net-imputed income in a particular year, yet he would be taxed in an arbitrary way to achieve greater simplicity.

The question of horizontal equity is frequently illustrated by comparing the owner-occupant of a home with one who rents and has a savings account. The interest on the savings account is taxed and no deduction is allowed for the rent. If the renter cashes in his savings account and buys a house, he avoids adding to his taxable income and improves his tax position while not affecting his ability to pay. While this comparison is valid, the owner-occupant could also be compared with a renter having investments in assets that are appreciating and on which there is no realization.

The appreciation in the value of a home is realized by the occupant by the consumption of the home at the appreciated value. But the owner-occupant may have two motives in owning—investment and consumption. For many people their home is their biggest investment. Taxation based on full fair market value would be equivalent to taxing unrealized appreciation due to the investment rather than the consumption element of the home.

In addition, housing may go up in value because of changes in interest rates. Since interest rates are a cost of construction, rents on newly constructed rental housing will rise as interest rates rise. To some extent, therefore, the tax on imputed income may reflect changes in market interest rates.

I would conclude that net-imputed rent might be included under an *ideal* income tax. Many other reforms are more urgent, however, and I would give the taxation of imputed rent a low priority on the tax reform agenda.

Comments by Melvin I. White

William Helmuth has provided a generally sound and comprehensive treatment of homeowner tax preferences. To adhere, therefore, to the stricture that a discussant be neither picayune nor counselor of perfection is not easy, but I shall try.

First, an observation about Hellmuth's use of price elasticity in estimating the effect of tax preferences on housing demand. The incentives for homeownership are described at one place as being weaker in the lower brackets than in the higher brackets because lower marginal tax rates imply smaller implicit price reductions resulting from the preferences. Presumably the price elasticity of housing demand is assumed to be the same across income brackets, but he does not say so.

I am uncertain as to Hellmuth's procedures for estimating the effect on the demand for homeownership of a net subsidy of 10–15 percent for homeowners over tenants in the $10,000 to $15,000 income range. He applies the price elasticity coefficient of -1.0 to -1.5 to the net subsidy percentage to reach an estimated 10–20 percent increase in demand for homeownership. But if the price elasticity is a housing demand elasticity, this procedure does not appear to allow for the switching from tenantry to homeownership induced by the subsidy differential, resulting in an underestimation of its impact.

For the alternative of imputing a rate of return to the owner-occupier's investment, rather than imputing an annual gross rent (from which net rent is derived), there are two contending methods that do not appear to be clearly distinguished. One is to impute a net return to the homeowner's equity; the other is to impute a return to the total value of the home and then subtract mortgage interest payments. The first does not allow for variation in taxable income owing to variation in interest rates. The second method does. The fact that I prefer the latter, whereas perhaps Hellmuth prefers the former, may reflect differing views (which I discuss below) about the validity of deducting interest on consumer debt. It also seems to me that if a rate of return imputation is used, it automatically includes an allowance for an average amount of capital gains, and that therefore appreciation in the value of the house should not engender additional tax liability.

In his discussion of the deductibility of interest, Hellmuth appears to share a persistent misunderstanding about the proper tax treatment of interest expense on consumer debt. Contrary to what he maintains, under a comprehensive economic definition of income, interest expense is properly deducted even when no income is generated by the use of the borrowed funds. For example, consider a vacation trip: if the vacationer finances the trip by drawing down his assets, he thereby forgoes interest earnings, which reduces his taxable income, and the deduction of the interest expense is implicit; if he finances the trip by borrowing, the interest expense is explicit. In general, consumption today implies lower Haig-Simons income in the future, regardless of how the consumption is financed. To consistently alter this requires both imputing an interest income to the person who draws down his own assets for consumption purposes and the disallowance of the deductibility of interest payments by the borrower-consumer. But then the result is a concept of income that fundamentally differs from the Haig-Simons definition in that it considers consumption as well as saving as a source of interest income.

With respect to mortgage interest, the reason for entertaining non-deductibility is *not* that housing is a consumer good. Rather it is that investment in a home generates investment income that is not taken into account under the tax law. The disallowing of the interest deduction—wrong in principle—may then have the empirical "second-best" rationale of offsetting in part the unfairness of failing to treat the investment income properly.

Hellmuth includes in his discussion the results of the study I did with Anne White of the contribution to horizontal inequality of the homeowner preferences. It has been some time since the study was done, and during this time income levels have changed drastically and there have been several tax reform acts. It is hard to say how reflective these results are of present conditions. Moreover, it should be kept in mind that the study did not take into account the benefits to tenants of income tax subsidies through accelerated depreciation that would have reduced the inequality coefficients that were obtained.

In evaluating the impact of terminating the interest deduction, Hellmuth suggests that fairness requires that some transitional arrangements be provided. The reasoning is that homeowners have adjusted to the expectation of mortgage interest deductibility—and presumably have been willing to spend more than otherwise on housing.

This concern for the possibility of creating an inequity when a tax preference is eliminated calls to mind the position on tax reform developed by Martin Feldstein.[43] His approach to the relation between tax preference elimination and horizontal equity implies a complete reversal of the approach that I and others have been taking and teaching: instead of horizontal inequity being reduced when tax preferences are removed, it may be increased. Instead of thinking about transitional arrangements, Hellmuth perhaps should be thinking about compensation arrangements. The horizontal equity cost should then be balanced against efficiency gains—such as the cited reduction in welfare loss of $500 million in 1960. When looked at from this perspective, the case for tax reform in the homeowner area does seem to lose attractiveness.

43. Martin Feldstein, "Compensation in Tax Reform," *National Tax Journal,* vol. 29 (June 1976), pp. 123–30.

CHAPTER SIX

Treatment of the Family

MICHAEL J. MC INTYRE *and* OLIVER OLDMAN*

AFTER SIXTY-ODD YEARS of income taxation, three issues have emerged as the dominant ones in the treatment of the family: (1) what the tax burden on single persons should be in relation to the burden on married couples, (2) how the costs of supporting children and other dependents should be taken into account in assessing tax burdens, and (3) what the tax burden on married couples with only one wage earner should be in relation to the burden on equal-income married couples with two wage earners. The first of these issues is a refinement of one of the classic questions in the design of an income tax: *who is the taxpayer?* Current law looks principally at property rules in answering that question. Our analysis suggests that in a normative tax system based on the comprehensive tax base ideal,[1] the appropriate taxpayer is the person benefiting from the income.

* The authors are grateful to Richard D. Pomp of the University of Connecticut School of Law for his thoughtful comments on a draft of this paper. The paper summarizes our views on the taxation of the family. Space limitations prevent us from fully developing our concept of the benefit rule. Since this concept is new to the tax reform literature, we have prepared a much longer paper, on which this one is based, that deals with many of the details (see "Taxation of the Family in a Comprehensive Simplified Income Tax," *Harvard Law Review,* forthcoming). We have also greatly abbreviated our discussion of imputed income, our analysis of the tax treatment of the poor, and our historical survey of the development of current law.

1. By comprehensive tax base ideal we mean a tax system that treats personal consumption plus the net change in savings as the theoretically correct definition of income. For an explanation of this definition, see Chapter 1.

The second major issue—the tax treatment of the costs of raising children—involves an analysis of the meaning of consumption in the comprehensive definition of income. Under the Internal Revenue Code, family allowances in a variety of forms are given (1) to exempt low-income families from tax on an amount approximating the subsistence level, as determined by official government poverty statistics; and (2) to provide "relief" to middle- and high-income families with children or other dependents. One would at least initially assume that the expenses of subsistence and the support costs of children constituted consumption. In fact, since both "subsistence" and "support costs" are such elastic concepts, depending more on societal views than on actual calculations of expenses, their exclusion from the definition of consumption could unhinge the concept from its grounding in market values.

We have met this difficulty of reconciling family allowances—which we think are an essential part of the code—with a normative tax system based on the comprehensive tax base ideal by developing justifications that do not depend on an esoteric definition of consumption. In discussing low-income relief we frankly acknowledge that relief for the poor in the income tax is an accommodation for the imperfections of the welfare system. Our recommendations, as a result, call for a simplified system of tax relief for the poor that would be phased out for persons above the poverty level.

The discussion of allowances for the costs of raising children for persons above the poverty level is an extension of the analysis of who the proper taxable person is under an income tax. Those who focus on whether child support is consumption of the parents have implicitly concluded, without serious discussion, that the children are not the proper taxpayers on income received by the parents and spent in child support. In our view the benefit rule for attributing income to particular taxpayers would make income consumed by the children taxable to the children. From that insight, we conclude that some form of income splitting is the result most in accord with the ideal of the comprehensive tax. For reasons of practical administration, however, the income-splitting result should be implemented through a system of deductions or through a special rate schedule for families. We have tentatively opted in favor of the deduction approach. If all our recommendations for reform of the tax treatment of the family were adopted—including our suggestions for the treatment of trusts and the consolidation of the income of children with that of their parents—a taxable unit approach, with multiple rate schedules, would have substantial administrative advantages. To be consistent with our analysis, however, the relationship among the rate schedules should be based on the distribution of burdens achieved through income-splitting.

The third issue of this paper—the treatment of two-job couples—requires an analysis of the imputed income concept. A direct corollary of the conclusion that married couples should be treated as splitting their consolidated income is that equal-income couples should pay equal tax. The view is persistently put forth, however, that two-job couples with the same pecuniary income as one-job couples typically enjoy less imputed income from self-performed services and as a result should pay less tax. Analysis shows, however, that special allowances for two-job couples create far more inequities than they remove. We therefore conclude that imputed income from self-performed services should not be taken into account in assessing tax burdens under an income tax unless a compelling case for an adjustment can be made on grounds of economic efficiency. Surely the type of allowance that would be indicated on efficiency grounds—large allowances for affluent two-job married couples and none at all for single persons and low-income two-job couples—is so obviously unfair as to have almost no political appeal.[2]

2. For a discussion of the relationship between efficiency (the maximization of goods and services) and fairness (the just distribution of tax burdens), see Arthur M. Okun, *Equality and Efficiency: The Big Tradeoff* (Brookings Institution, 1975). No attempt has been made to deal with the merits of efficiency arguments in this paper, although we believe that most persons arguing for some form of taxation of self-performed services are doing so, at least implicitly, on efficiency grounds. If we did discuss the merits, we would begin by examining the implicit assumption of all efficiency arguments—that the maximization of economic goods is a desirable social goal. What are the arguments for always encouraging market activity at the expense of leisure and self-performed services? Probably because some kinds of activities are rewarded by money and other activities are not, the choice between these activities and paying jobs is already distorted in favor of the latter. Some possible gains are evident in a tax system that leans against this distortion. For example, citizen participation in the political processes of the country is desirable but is inhibited by the economic incentives that pull people away from volunteer work. On the other hand, there are understandable arguments for encouraging market behavior in other situations. None of the efficiency literature we have seen, however, addresses itself to this fundamental point. For a discussion of efficiency arguments, see Harvey S. Rosen, "Applications of Optimal Tax Theory to Problems in Taxing Families and Individuals," OTA Paper 21 (U.S. Department of the Treasury, Office of Tax Analysis, 1977). This paper gives references to much of the literature.

Relative Tax Burdens of Single Persons and Married Couples

The most important, difficult, and emotional issue in the taxation of the family is the proper relationship between the tax burdens on single persons and those on married couples.[3] How one confronts this issue determines in large measure one's response to most of the other issues in the taxation of the family. Most writers on this controversy fall into one of two camps. The first camp maintains that marital status should be irrelevant to taxation and that everyone should be taxed on his or her own income under a single rate schedule without regard for marital status. The second camp argues for the consolidation of the incomes of husbands and wives, making the marital unit a taxable entity under the tax laws, with a rate schedule different from that used by single persons. The basis for this recommendation is that husbands and wives typically pool their incomes, so that the income of either one of two spouses is a poor index of the economic situation of the married couple.

The conflict between these two camps is reflected in the history of the changes in the tax treatment of the family under the Internal Revenue Code. Without much reflection, Congress and the courts started out taking the first viewpoint but later switched to the second. Similar seesawing is evident in the periodic changes in the tax systems of the member countries of the Organisation for Economic Co-operation and Development.

Our approach to the taxation of the family in large measure reconciles the two camps, for it preserves the principle that individuals should be taxed on their own income, but it also takes into account the real changes in economic circumstances that typically accompany marriage. In contrast to the approach of all other writers with whom we are familiar, we focus initially on the rules for attributing income to particular taxpayers. Only after tentatively deciding what the attribution rules should be do we move on to face the question of what the appropriate taxable unit is. When that issue is reached, we find, paradoxically, that it no longer has much theoretical importance—

3. Throughout this paper, "single persons" refers to unmarried individuals other than surviving spouses and heads of households—that is, persons filing under the rate schedule provided in the Internal Revenue Code, section 1(c).

that the choice is essentially between equally satisfactory administrative techniques.

Current Law

Personal income taxes are imposed under current law according to four different rate schedules. These rate schedules, in the order of their increasing relative burdens, are (1) the joint-return schedule, (2) the head-of-household schedule, (3) single-person schedule, and (4) the separate-return schedule. Although all the rate schedules begin at 14 percent and have a top marginal rate of 70 percent, the width of the tax brackets differs under each schedule, resulting (after the first bracket) in different tax burdens under each schedule for equivalent taxable incomes. The joint-return schedule has the widest brackets and thus yields the lowest relative tax.

The legal structure of the current system employs two taxable units, individuals and married couples. Heads of households, although given a separate rate schedule, are nevertheless taxed as individuals, since the income of other household members is not consolidated with the income of the head for assessment purposes.

Because married couples using the joint-return schedule are required to consolidate their individual incomes, the use of that schedule may not be desirable, although it gives the lowest available rates for equivalent taxable incomes. For married couples with only one income-earner, the consolidation requirement is a nullity. For two-income couples, however, consolidation means that the couples can use the low marginal rates at the beginning of the rate schedule only once. As the incomes of the individual spouses become more equal, the advantage of the wider rate brackets is offset by consolidation until at some point the couple would find a tax advantage in filing as two single persons.

In popular language, married couples who pay more in tax than they would if they had not married are said to pay a "tax on marriage." A variety of features of the tax law can result in a tax on marriage for husbands and wives who each have their own sources of income. For other married couples, these same features can give a tax benefit from marriage.

Since a single person could get this tax benefit by marrying someone with relatively low or zero income, single persons are said to suffer a "tax on remaining single." Here, we are only concerned with

Figure 6-1. Additional Tax on Married Couple Compared with Tax if They Were Single and Had the Same Combined Income, by Selected Income Levels, 1976ª

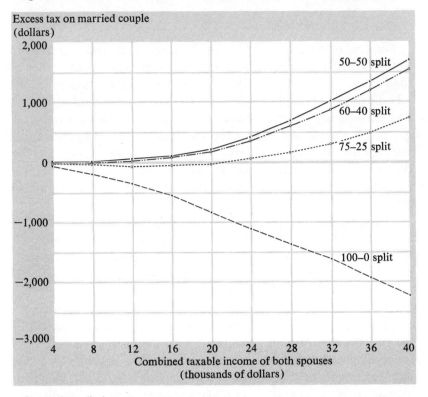

Source: Appendix A.
a. The figure shows the "tax on marriage" calculated from the 1976 statutory rate schedules. It does not show the possible tax-on-marriage effects from (1) the definition of taxable income, or (2) tax credits.

the tax "penalties" caused by the current system of multiple rate schedules. Other nonneutralities of the tax system as to marriage are discussed later.

Figure 6-1 illustrates the nonneutrality of the rate system as to marriage. For equal-income couples at high income levels, the marriage tax amounts to an additional tax on combined taxable income on the order of 3 to 4 percent. The class of taxpayers now disadvantaged by the consolidation requirement, however, is not a substantial part of the taxpaying public. As the figure indicates, the income split between spouses must be at least as even as 60 percent to 40 percent for marriage to become a major tax issue for the overwhelming majority of taxpayers. The combined taxable income of the spouses, moreover, must exceed $12,000 before the extra tax becomes significant. The number of married couples who satisfy both of these conditions is small, probably 3 or 4 percent of the total.

Although the percentage of two-income couples with relatively evenly divided income is not large, it can be expected to increase sharply in future years as "equal pay for equal work" becomes a social reality and as more and more married women enter the labor force. Unless the rate schedules are changed, moreover, the effect of inflation will be to push moderate income couples into higher tax brackets, where the marriage tax applies. For relatively high-income couples, the additional tax from marriage can be substantial, amounting to $400 for couples with combined incomes of $24,000, with a maximum of $4,800 for couples with incomes over $100,000.

The tax on remaining single becomes significant at much lower income levels than the tax on marriage does, and thus far more single persons are affected by it than two-income married couples are affected by the tax on marriage. For taxable incomes of $16,000, the extra tax is already $570, and at $24,000 the additional tax is $1,130. The maximum additional tax of $12,110 is reached at a taxable income level of $200,000.

The tax on remaining single has been a feature of the law in community property states since the beginning of the income tax and in common law states since 1948. The special rate for single persons added to the Internal Revenue Code in 1969 reduced the amount of the additional burden on single persons but did not eliminate it.

The tax on marriage has been a feature of the rate structure only since 1969. Before that time persons who married had generally lower tax rates, and never higher ones, than if they had not been married. Repeal of the 1969 schedule for single persons would therefore end this aspect of the tax on marriage. At the same time, it would increase the tax on remaining single in the upper-middle-income range (for example, from 34 percent to 45 percent for a taxable income of $50,000.

The potential tax advantage to a single person in marrying an impecunious spouse remains as long as married couples are allowed, in effect, to split their incomes. Current law permits income splitting under two distinct mechanisms. The first is by allowing married couples to use the joint-return rate schedule rather than to file as single persons. The tax effect of using the joint-return schedule is nearly equivalent to the result that would be achieved by splitting the consolidated income between the spouses on a 75–25 basis and by requiring each spouse to pay tax on his or her aliquot share under the rate schedule for single persons. The second mechanism is the recognition for tax purposes of the property rule of community property states that splits consolidated marital income on a 50–50 basis.

An end to some form of splitting, however, means an end to the result under current law of equal-income couples paying equal tax. Our reasons for believing that equal-income couples should pay equal taxes under an ideal tax system are discussed below. But in addition to the arguments based on theory, there are practical reasons for opposing a change in the consolidation requirement for married couples, at least with respect to property income. Without minimizing the nontax consequences of shifts in legal title from one spouse to another, it is a safe prediction that many married couples with property income would create new partnerships and otherwise reshuffle their property interests for the purposes of tax minimization. The burden of the tax would therefore be a function of property shifts that would have little effect on the overall economic position of the spouses. In other words, the taxes on marital status would be replaced by a tax on the higher income-earner holding income-producing property.

Treatment under a Comprehensive Income Tax

Under a comprehensive tax, what rules should apply in determining who the taxpayer is? In particular, when the candidates for taxation on an income item are members of the same family, who should be selected as the taxable person? The answers given to these questions determine in large measure what the relative burdens on single persons and married couples will be.

The answers given under current law to these questions are ostensibly simple but lack support in any normative model of the income tax. For earned income, the taxpayer is the person who performed the services that generated the income. For property income, the taxpayer is the person who holds legal title to the underlying property. The community property exception treats the earned and property income of either spouse as income of the marriage partnership, attributable in equal shares to each member of the partnership. Other exceptions have been created to deal with property arrangements, usually involving trusts, that shifted legal title to income-producing property to an entity under the control of the original owner of the property. The rules for determining the taxpayer have become more and more intricate, but the underlying theme in resolving disputes has been to see who has the most important property interest in the income.

A rule attributing income to the beneficiary or user of the income would be more compatible with comprehensive taxation than the property-interest rule of current law. Under a comprehensive tax, income is the sum of personal consumption plus the net change in savings. The only purpose of determining the amounts of an individual's consumption or savings is to tax someone on those amounts. What better candidate for taxation on those amounts than the one who did the consuming or saving? Taxing consumption to the consumer and savings to the saver is, in a nutshell, the benefit (or user) rule we are advocating.

Although we reject the property-interest rule as the theoretically correct answer to Who is the taxpayer? we consider it an essential tool in the practical administration of a tax on consumption plus the net change in savings. However refined one may get in developing an ideal definition of income, it is not *uses* of income but *sources* of income that provide the practical basis for identifying the tax base and computing and collecting the tax. Our benefit rule would be a nightmare for a tax administrator forced to apply it directly, since the only data available to the administrator relate to sources of income. But we have developed detailed rules, presented in broad outline below, for indirectly applying the benefit rule, using the data already available on sources of income. For single persons outside a family group, we assume that the benefit rule (applied to uses of income) and the property-interest rule (applied to sources of income) give nearly identical results. We also assume that the property-interest rule gives an accurate index of the total resources available to various family groups. Portions of the family income are then attributed to individual family members by formulas developed in accordance with the benefit rule.

Our use of the property-interest rule as an indirect method of administering the benefit rule is entirely compatible with the strategy of administering a comprehensive tax. In administering a tax on consumption plus the net change in savings, it was already necessary to assume that income transactions were a good proxy for uses of income. That assumption was based on the belief that there was a rough equivalence between a taxpayer's sources of income and his consumption plus his net change in savings. But that assumption is unwarranted if there is not also a close correspondence between the owner of income and the user of income.

An important implication of the benefit rule is that equal-income couples should pay equal tax. Our proposed formula for allocating income between spouses is a 50–50 split. Any formula approach, however, will cause equal-income couples to pay the same tax, unless the formula is based in some way on the income sources of individual spouses. A formula based on relative incomes is unacceptable, since it would be a back-door exchange of the benefit rule for the property-interest rule. Our endorsement of equal tax for equal-income couples is based on the same a-dollar-is-a-dollar insight that underlies the comprehensive tax. Basing tax liabilities on property rules instead of on economic enjoyment is akin to the source distinctions that the comprehensive tax was first developed to combat.

For married couples without children, the adoption of the benefit rule would amount to a return to the 1948–69 situation, with income split between the spouses and no tax on marriage resulting from the rate structure. But single persons whose marginal tax rate is above the minimum level would find under the benefit rule that they could reduce their tax burdens by marrying a person with little or no income. From the standpoint of tax theory this result is not undesirable. The tax benefits available to a single person from marriage to an impecunious spouse are seldom achieved with a mere paper change in legal status. The tax benefit is accompanied in almost all instances by a decrease in the amount of income available to the individual for satisfying his or her personal needs. This typical decrease in per capita consumption and savings makes it inappropriate to characterize the tax on remaining single as a *penalty* for not marrying.

Assume, for example, that a single person with an income of $20,000 is considering marriage to a person with no income and no prospects of one. Under the benefit rule a person with a salary of $20,000 married to a person with no salary is considered for tax purposes to have split the salary with his or her spouse and as a result to have taxable income of only $10,000. Under a benefit rule, therefore, the total tax after marriage will be decreased, since under a progressive rate structure, two persons with $10,000 of income pay less than one person with $20,000. The lower tax is justified, however, since the person with wages of $20,000 has less personal consumption and savings after marriage than before. To claim that there is a tax penalty on remaining single is to claim either (1) that persons do not typically pool incomes after marriage, or (2) that differences in property rights rather than differences in the enjoyment of incomes should determine tax liability. The first claim is contrary to all data collected on the subject. The second is contrary to the underlying insights of the comprehensive tax.

Our explanation of the benefit rule may be satisfying to some tax theorists; it is unlikely to be completely satisfying to all single persons if they find that the practical effect of our proposals is to increase their tax burdens. These proposals, however, are made in the context of a major broadening of the tax base, coupled with a significant decrease in the tax rates. Taking into account our proposed changes in the rate schedule, over 98 percent of all single persons would be at least as well off, in relation to married couples with the same income, as they now are under the 1969 schedule. The 66 percent of single persons with incomes (comprehensively defined) of less than $7,500 would get no rate advantage at all from marriage.

For upper-income single persons, however, these rate proposals will not be good news. A single person with an income (comprehensively defined) of $50,000 would pay almost a third more in tax than a married couple with the same income, and at $100,000 the maximum differential of almost 50 percent would be reached. The increase in tax on account of single status is tabulated in table 6-1.

A high relative tax on upper-income single persons should provoke objection under the standards of equity presented in this paper only if upper-income couples do not in fact split income on a 50–50 basis. The data on upper-income splitting is sketchy, and it may be that a less generous splitting formula is appropriate for upper-income taxpayers. A less generous formula would reduce the differential burden on single persons. The only practical method for implementing a variable splitting formula is through separate rate schedules for single persons and married couples, a route we have sought to avoid in the interests of administrative simplicity and public acceptability. Multiple rate schedules constructed on the basis of empirical data on in-

Table 6-1. Federal Income Tax of Single Persons Compared with That of Married Couples under Proposed Splitting Rate Schedule, by Taxable Income
Amounts in dollars

	Tax liability		Difference	
				As percent of married
Taxable income	Single person	Married couple	Amount	couple's tax
500	52	52	0	0.0
1,000	105	105	0	0.0
2,000	210	210	0	0.0
5,000	557	533	24	4.5
10,000	1,208	1,113	95	8.5
15,000	1,962	1,741	221	12.7
20,000	2,811	2,416	395	16.3
24,000	3,563	2,994	569	19.0
30,000	4,809	3,924	885	22.6
50,000	9,990	7,525	2,465	32.8
100,000	29,855	19,980	9,875	49.4
200,000	79,855	59,710	20,145	33.7
400,000	179,855	159,710	20,145	12.6
1,000,000	479,855	459,710	20,145	4.4

Source: Calculated from proposed splitting rate schedule and based on Richard Goode, *The Individual Income Tax*, rev. ed. (Brookings Institution, 1976), p. 229.

come-splitting patterns are nevertheless entirely consistent with the approach to the taxation of the family set forth in this paper. In the absence of data to the contrary, however, we assume that a 50–50 split is appropriate.

The reduction in the relative burdens on middle-income single persons and the increase in the relative burdens on upper-income single persons results from our proposal for a change in the rate structure of current law. The current rate schedules are highly progressive at low- and middle-income levels, but the rate of increase in progression tapers off rapidly at income levels above $50,000. There is no apparent logic to this pattern. The basic structure of the current rate schedules has remained unchanged since World War II—its effects on the middle class are an accidental by-product of inflation. Our proposal is for a new rate schedule for single persons with uniform width brackets. Under this proposal, the rate of increase in progression is constant until the top bracket of $100,000 is reached. A similarly shaped splitting schedule for married couples can be derived from the basic schedule. Figure 6-2 compares the proposed rate schedule

**Figure 6-2. Federal Income Tax Schedules of Single Persons and Married Couples
Filing Jointly under 1976 Law and under Proposed Alternative**

Marginal tax rate (percent)

Schedule for single persons,
1976 law

Joint return schedule,
1976 law

Schedule for single persons,
proposed

Joint return schedule,
proposed

Taxable income (thousands of dollars)

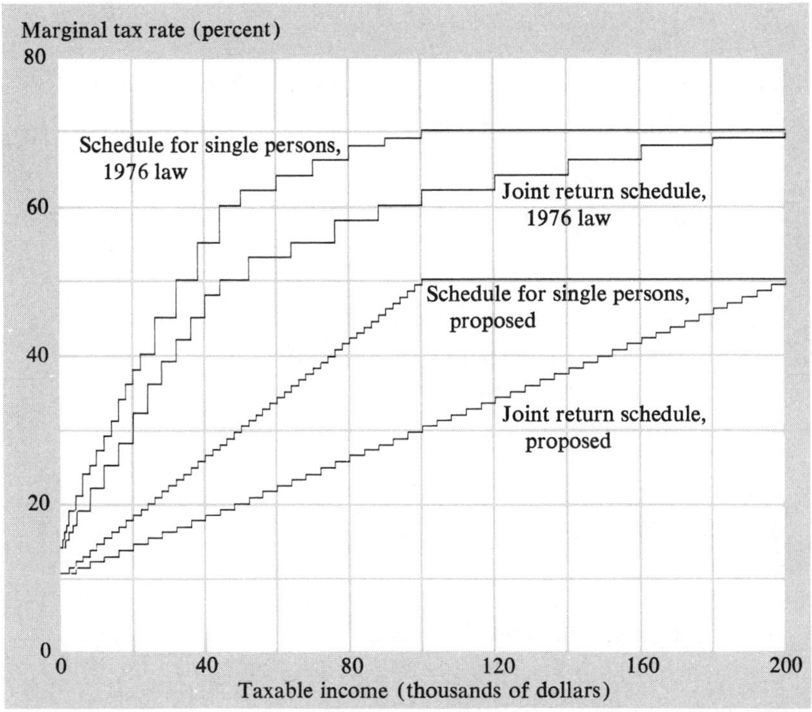

Source: Schedules for proposed alternative derived from Brookings MERGE File on the assumption that the maximum tax rate would be 50 percent and that the revenue yield of the old and new systems would be the same.

for single persons and the joint return derived therefrom with the
same schedules of the current law.

Differentiating Tax Burdens
Due to Family Responsibility

The main arguments presented here are a development of the case
made in the preceding section for using the benefit rule in determining
the appropriate taxable person. Since children are the beneficiaries
of some fraction of the income received by their parents, the benefit
rule suggests that the children rather than the parents are the appropriate taxpayers on a portion of the family income. Although for
assessment purposes the parents must remain the taxpayer, the bur-

den to be imposed on the total family income should be determined under a splitting rule. The practical effects of splitting can be achieved directly through splitting formulas or indirectly through either a system of family allowances or a special rate structure for families. The choice of techniques depends in large measure on how refined one wishes to be in devising the splitting formulas. The use of a special rate structure is by far the most flexible device because it allows for complicated adjustments without involving the taxpaying public in difficult arithmetical computations. The use of deductions or other allowances, however, involves minimum changes from current law and for that reason may be the most acceptable politically. Because the tax treatment of poor families involves a mix of tax and welfare issues not necessarily germane to the general treatment of the family, an analysis of the tax treatment of families below the poverty levels is deferred until later.

Family Allowances under Current Law

Family allowances, for the purposes of this paper, are tax deductions, credits, or other relief measures given on account of family responsibilities but without regard to actual cash expenditures by particular taxpayers. The major allowances—the personal exemptions, the personal tax credits, and the special rate schedules for heads of households and surviving spouses—are described briefly below.

Exemptions for dependents first became part of the income tax law in 1917, when a deduction of $200 for each dependent child was granted. Relative to the exemptions for single persons and married couples, the dependency exemptions were small from 1917 to 1944, when the per capita system of exemptions found in current law was adopted. The amount of the exemption is now $750.

In addition to dependency exemptions, taxpayers are currently entitled to a tax credit of either $35 per dependent or 2 percent of taxable income (with a ceiling of $180), whichever is greater. The dependency credit is of primary benefit to low- and moderate-income taxpayers with many dependents. The alternative of the percentage credit largely offsets the effects of the dependency credit in differentiating among the tax liabilities of families of different size. The limitation on percentage credit has created a new tax on marriage, since a married couple has a ceiling of $180 and two single persons have an aggregated ceiling of $360.

Overlooked in most discussions of family allowances are the tax breaks granted to one-parent families through the rate structure. A single person with children or other qualifying dependents generally pays tax under the schedule for heads of households, which produces a lower burden for equivalent taxable income than the schedule for single persons (above the first income level). A recent widow or widower with minor children ("surviving spouse" in the language of the Internal Revenue Code) can use the even lower joint-return schedule for the two years following that of the death of the spouse.

The tax saving from the rate reductions for heads of one-parent families is a function of income, increasing absolutely as income rises, until the top marginal rate of 70 percent is reached. As a percentage of taxable income, the saving is most important for individuals with incomes above $20,000 and below $30,000.

Although provided through a rate reduction, the benefits to one-parent families could be recast into a system of family deductions with no real change in tax burdens. Although the system of deductions duplicating current benefits must be a complex pattern of variable percentage deductions, the results could be approximated by allowing heads of households a deduction of 5 percent of taxable income (otherwise computed) and surviving spouses a deduction of 11 percent of taxable income (otherwise computed).

The decision made in 1948 to allow married couples to split their incomes was viewed in part as a relief mechanism for traditional two-parent families, even though it applied to all married couples, irrespective of the presence of children. The rate relief subsequently enacted for one-parent families was viewed as providing a qualifying taxpayer with a portion of the benefits that a one-income couple in a common law jurisdiction enjoyed from income splitting. In light of this history, therefore, it is instructive to consider the rate reductions for one-parent families as a form of income splitting, with one segment of the income taxed as if received by the parent and the other segment taxed as if received by a phantom spouse. The schedule for heads of household enacted in 1951 provided for an income split of 75 percent to the parent and 25 percent to the phantom spouse. With the 1969 changes, the new schedule is now roughly equivalent to a split of 90 percent to 10 percent.

Family Allowances under an Ideal Income Tax

Advocates of the comprehensive tax base ideal find it difficult to justify either an allowance for child support or a disallowance. To say that amounts spent by parents on their children constitute consumption on the part of the parents presupposes that the parents are engaging in an exchange of some sort with their children—food and clothing in return for smiles and cuddles. On that theory, a rigorous supporter of comprehensive taxation should then find the exchange resulting in income to the child as well. On the other hand, excluding child support from consumption is an equally unhappy result, for food, clothing, shelter, and other goods and services purchased on behalf of the child are the very heart of the popular ideas of consumption.

The children-as-consumption dilemma arises from the implicit assumption that the parents constitute the proper taxpayer on income earned by the parents and expended on their children. That implicit assumption is of course entirely consistent with the property-interest rule of current law. As noted earlier, however, the property-interest rule is inconsistent with the basic insights underlying comprehensive taxation. Under the benefit rule advocated in this paper, income spent or saved by parents for the benefit of their children is properly taxable to the children. Making the children taxable on some fraction of the family income is an extension of the income-splitting rule developed above for married couples.

Application of the benefit rule to children requires the development of splitting formulas for attributing income received by the family to individual family members. The patterns of income splitting vary with family size and income level. Any splitting formulas that try to approximate the patterns must be somewhat complex—too complex to be implemented directly, since the calculations required of the taxpaying public would be lengthy. Fortunately, the results of such formulas can be reasonably approximated through a series of dependency deductions. The convertibility of a splitting formula into a set of deductions was illustrated in the discussion of the special rate schedule for heads of households. The effect of a deduction for children is to treat some portion of the family income as attributable to the child, with the child taxed at a zero rate. A deduction of $1,000 for the first child and $500 for each additional child gives results for middle-income taxpayers that reflect realistic estimates of splitting patterns.

If a refined income-splitting approach is desired, the most accurate method is to adopt one or more new rate schedules for families. For example, a rate schedule could be constructed for married couples with one child that could give results equivalent to whatever splitting formula is desirable. The splitting formula can be complex without adding at all to taxpayer compliance problems, for the necessary calculations will be done by the tax administration and embedded in the rate schedule. The special rate schedule for heads of households again illustrates this technique.

Our income-splitting suggestion implicitly assumes that the income of dependent children will be consolidated with that of the parents. Consolidation is particularly important in the case of property income, since shifts in property income are easily accomplished under current law. Consolidation should be the price tag for splitting. We would find it acceptable, however, to allow children to file separate returns if the parents were denied all dependency allowances on account of such children.

Tax Relief for the Poor

Current law, through a variety of mechanisms, now exempts most poor families from the personal income tax. This result is good social policy; it is also in harmony with the comprehensive tax base ideal, since it equalizes the tax burdens of the "welfare poor," who cannot reasonably be taxed, and the "working poor," whose economic condition is presumptively the same. The current methods of achieving relief for the poor, however, are needlessly complex and rigid. We propose a direct exemption through a single mechanism, which would simplify administration and clarify the tax policies being pursued. In this discussion the related problems of the social security tax, which bears heavily on the poor, are ignored. The federal definition of poverty is taken as a given, despite the obvious ambiguities that are submerged in the government poverty level figures. The definition of poverty is primarily the responsibility of those concerned with direct expenditure programs for the poor and is only secondarily a tax problem.

We first of all recommend the elimination of the exemptions with respect to a taxpayer and spouse. For persons above the poverty level, the tax benefits now granted through the personal exemptions could be provided instead through an adjustment in the rate schedule(s). For persons below the poverty level, the exemptions would be incorporated into the low-income allowance. Besides simplifying the computation of tax burdens, the elimination of the personal exemptions would make it easier to adjust the low-income allowance for inflation. Untying the dependency allowances from the taxpayer exemptions is a minimum first step in reforming the present inadequate system of family allowances.

We similarly recommend the elimination of the $35 tax credit (or 2 percent of taxable income up to a credit of $180). This credit would be incorporated into the low-income allowance. Its removal for persons above the poverty level would eliminate the undesirable tax on marriage that it creates.

Whether deductions for dependents should be incorporated into the low-income allowance depends on the approach adopted for the treatment of dependent children. If dependency deductions were entirely eliminated, the low-income allowance should be the full amount of poverty-level figures. If our income-splitting recommendations were to be implemented through a system of dependency deductions, however, then the low-income allowance group should be the poverty level amount for a particular family group minus the dependency deductions already granted.

We recommend that our expanded low-income allowance be gradually phased out.[4] The allowance could be reduced $1 for each $4 of income over the poverty level. A low-income allowance of $2,500 would be phased out entirely for incomes above $12,500 under our one-to-four formula. This rate would ensure taxpayers near the poverty level against being faced with a high marginal tax rate on income above the poverty level and would remove the low-income allowance for middle-income taxpayers. The phaseout would be independent of

4. Under 1976 law, the low-income allowance is an alternative to the percentage standard deduction. As adjusted gross income increases, the benefits of the low-income allowance are partially offset by the loss of the percentage standard deduction. At some point—$10,625 for a single person and $13,125 for a married couple filing a joint return—the low-income allowance vanishes and the percentage standard deduction takes over. Proposals of the Carter administration under consideration by Congress would convert the low-income allowance and percentage standard deduction into an exemption that would vary with marital status but would be independent of income level. As tax relief for the poor, the Carter proposal is defective, in that it gives benefits that bear no consistent relationship to poverty levels. As an alternative to itemized deductions, it is defective in that it bears no consistent relationship to average deduction levels for any sizable percentage of the taxpaying population.

any standard deduction that might survive reform resulting in a comprehensive tax base. A standard deduction is intended to replace itemized deductions and is unrelated to the issue of poverty if the itemized deductions qualify under the comprehensive tax base ideal.

The present low-income allowance system is least generous, in terms of apparent need, to single persons. The allowance for single persons is nevertheless substantially more than half the allowance for a married couple. The low-income allowance, as a result, acts to impose a tax on marriage.

The tax on marriage from the low-income allowance results from the apparent finding that a typical married couple needs less money on a per capita basis to maintain a minimum standard of living than a typical single person living apart. Unless a definition of poverty is desired that requires the tax collector to ascertain the living arrangements of persons claiming the low-income allowance, one is forced to use estimates of need based on aggregate data. The only method for eliminating the tax on marriage is to convert the low-income allowance into per capita relief. A per capita approach, however, will give too large a benefit to the average married couple or too small a benefit to the average single person.

Relative Burdens of One- and Two-Income Married Couples

Our argument that equal-income couples should pay equal tax assumed that a satisfactory definition of taxable income had been agreed upon. The tentative definition of income advanced by supporters of a comprehensive tax base, although broad in comparison with the definition under current law, does not attempt to take into account the imputed income arising from services performed by family members for the benefit of themselves or other family members. For two-income couples in which both spouses have full-time jobs, the time available for performing services on their own behalf is less (by about eight hours a day) than the time available to typical one-job couples. On the assumption that less time means less self-performed services, a tax system that fails to take into account the differences in patterns of imputed income from self-performed services is said to discriminate against two-job couples. Quite clearly, if imputed income should be taxable in principle under a comprehensive tax and is omitted only for administrative reasons, taxpayers with less than the average amounts of imputed income from self-performed services are being treated unfairly.

The case against any allowance for two-job couples, however, is stronger than the case in favor of such an allowance. First of all, the argument that in principle self-performed services constitute income is unpersuasive. The impossibility of arriving at a workable definition of self-performed services has long been recognized in the literature —Henry Simons called the problem "clearly hopeless."[5] Self-performed services undoubtedly constitute income within at least some of the myriad meanings of that word. But we see no tax policy objective that requires the inclusion of self-performed services in the definition chosen as the base for a personal income tax. More specifically, no principle requires that Simons's definition of income, which would tax "the market value of rights exercised in consumption,"[6] be elaborated to include benefits obtained without the exercise of any market rights.

Second, the distribution of self-performed services among the tax-paying public is much more complex than is generally supposed, even if the concept of self-performed services is limited to the household and "handy-person" services that are often purchased in the market. The performance of services is related much more to life style, aptitude, and inclination than it is to leisure time available. Persons without children, for example, have little or no self-performed child-care services. Small children and retired persons often have insignificant amounts of handy-person or household services. Similarly, persons who rent have less of many categories of self-performed services than the typical homeowner.

Even if our general objections to the taxation of self-performed services are rejected, we think that the typical proposals for tax relief for two-job couples are seriously defective. Here, only two of the many proposals being made are discussed: (1) the deduction granted under pre-1977 law to two-job couples and heads of one-parent families for child-care expenses, and (2) an earned-income allowance for two-job couples.

5. Henry C. Simons, *Personal Income Taxation: The Definition of Income as a Problem of Fiscal Policy* (University of Chicago Press, 1938), p. 53.
6. Ibid., p. 50.

The basic idea of the child-care deduction is to equalize the tax treatment of purchased child-care services and self-performed services by in effect making both kinds of services exempt from tax. A deduction for purchases of any type of service will be fair between persons who typically perform the service themselves and those who purchase. A deduction will be unfair, however, between those who purchase and those who neither purchase nor perform the service themselves.[7]

A deduction for child-care expenditures is therefore unfair to those without children, assuming that the purpose of the deduction is to adjust for the failure of the tax system to tax imputed income from child-care services. If self-performed child-care services were really income, the proper adjustment would be a huge deduction for taxpayers without children, with a more modest deduction for those with children who purchase child-care services. This result follows directly from the common observation that persons without children have little or no imputed income from child-care services but that *all* persons with children, even those who hire babysitters on a regular basis, perform large amounts of child-care services themselves.[8]

7. An example illustrates the point. Assume a universe with only three taxpayers, A, B, and C, each with pecuniary income of 100. The required revenue yield of the tax system is 30; each of the taxpayers therefore has a tentative tax bill of 10. Assume A mows his lawn, B hires someone to mow, and C has no lawn and never purchases lawn-mowing services or performs them himself. If mowing for oneself should be taxable in an ideal income tax system, then A should pay more tax than B or C; and B and C should pay the same tax. For example, A should pay 14 and B and C should pay 8. If only B is allowed a deduction for mowing, however, then the tax on A and C will be increased to make up for the revenue loss. A and C, for example, would each pay 11 and B would pay 8. This is not unfair to A, who has more income than B, but it is unfair to C, who has the same income as B. The only fair solution is to give the deduction to both B and C. Assume further that B purchases some mowing services and also performs some for himself. The only way to approximate the "ideal" solution of taxing mowing services would be to give a big deduction to C (perhaps 30), a smaller deduction to B (say 10), and no deduction to A. A possible result would be that A paid 13, B paid 11, and C paid 6.

8. The limitations on the child-care deduction in the pre-1977 law were partly due to some of its supporters viewing it as a proper business expense deduction. Most tax specialists would agree, however, that child-care costs are essentially personal expenses, not business expenses. For a statement of this viewpoint and an analysis of the credit of current law, see Michael J. McIntyre, "Evaluating the New Tax Credit for Child Care and Maid Service," *Tax Notes*, vol. 5 (May 23, 1977), pp. 7–9.

The earned-income allowance for two-job couples suffers from its own collection of infirmities. The most frequently proposed allowance would grant a tax deduction of 25 percent of the earnings of the lower-income spouse, or a tax credit of 10 percent of those earnings, subject to a ceiling of $1,000 in tax benefits.[9] The allowance is supposed to make up for the difference in self-performed services between one- and two-job couples resulting from the greater amounts of leisure available to one-job couples. As suggested above, the amount of self-performed services does not relate well to the one-job, two-job classification unless "self-performed services" is defined so broadly as to be nearly meaningless. Even if one assumes the correlation of leisure and self-performed services, two other serious defects remain in the proposed earned-income allowance.

First of all, there is no acceptable justification for limiting the allowance to two-job couples. If the allowance is an adjustment for leisure, it should also be available to single persons, since they have the same leisure available to them on a per capita basis as two-job couples. Moreover, a case can even be made for giving some part of the allowance to one-job couples to make up for the greater amount of leisure enjoyed by couples and single persons supported entirely by property income. In addition, persons who habitually work long overtime hours should get a bigger allowance than persons working a forty-hour week. Extending the earned-income allowance to all equally deserving cases, however, would mean that the size of the allowance would have to be much smaller than is generally proposed. Since from 80 to 90 percent of total adjusted gross income reported for tax purposes is earned income, an allowance available to a substantial part of the population would have to be very small or it would cause a massive shift of tax burdens to property income.

The other difficulty with the earned-income allowance arises from the practical problems of distinguishing part-time from full-time workers. It is common for one spouse in a two-job couple to work on a part-time basis. Since the rationale of the earned-income allowance is based on loss of leisure, the allowance should be a function of hours worked and, equivalently, of leisure forgone.

9. For a clear presentation of alternative earned-income allowances and estimates of their distributional impact, see Joseph A. Pechman, *Federal Tax Policy,* 3d ed. (Brookings Institution, 1977).

The common proposal for an earned-income allowance nevertheless makes the allowance a percentage of the earnings of the lower-income spouse and does not take into account at all the actual hours worked. This approach is based on two simplifying assumptions. First, the percentage allowance is limited to a fixed amount. It is assumed that the level of the limit can be pegged high enough so that most persons eligible for the maximum allowance will be full-time workers and most persons denied the maximum will be part-time workers. The second assumption is that for persons who are not eligible for the maximum benefits, the amount of income earned is a good proxy for the number of hours worked.

Neither of these assumptions has much intuitive appeal. The second assumption appears particularly unreasonable. Our guess is that there are, first of all, a significant number of part-time workers who are highly compensated on an hourly basis. It probably is also common for lower-income spouses to take jobs that are essentially full time but that pay close to the minimum wage. Since the tax consequences of being denied or granted a deduction of 25 percent of earnings are substantial, the simplifying assumptions implicit in the proposal for a percentage allowance undoubtedly mask from view an unacceptable degree of unfairness, even assuming the merits of some form of earned-income allowance.

Conclusion

Tax reform discussions over the past thirty years have been dominated by the ideal of the comprehensive tax base. According to this ideal, the starting point in defining income under a personal income tax is the market value of consumption enjoyed during the tax year plus the net change in savings. In recent years as the impact of that ideal on federal tax policy has grown, the concept has been subjected to detailed scholarly examination. The debate over the usefulness of the comprehensive tax ideal has been spirited and informative. Critics have pointed out the inconsistencies of those who have relied on it too heavily, but supporters have succeeded in enlarging the areas of general agreement.

The comprehensive tax nevertheless has played a very minor role in the debate over the taxation of the family. Critics and supporters alike assert that it is neutral on what we consider the primary issue in the taxation of the family—the determination of the taxable person. The explanation given is that the ideal addresses itself to problems in the definition of income, while most issues in the taxation of the family relate to other elements of the tax system.

This is an inadequate explanation. We agree that a particular mode of taxation for the family cannot be deduced by pure logic from the comprehensive tax ideal and that a variety of approaches to the taxation of the family could be consistent with it. The comprehensive tax base ideal, however, presents a set of tax rules, internally consistent on matters of importance and organized around a few insights about what a fair income tax should be doing. Normative rules for the taxation of the family should be organized around these same insights. In exploring possible normative rules, we found the range of alternative treatments of the family that are consistent with comprehensive taxation to be surprisingly narrow.

We have found, in fact, that our emphasis on the benefit rule has shed light on a number of intractable problems in rationalizing generally accepted treatment of the family with the comprehensive tax. Our analysis, for example, gives the first consistent explanation for child-dependency deductions, although the deductions have been defended by a majority of comprehensive tax advocates. An extension of our benefit rule would rationalize the practice in current law of applying the income tax to gifts only once. If income is taxable to the person enjoying the income, then in theory the donor should not be taxed; the tax paid should be considered an advance payment on behalf of the donee. The benefit rule, however would suggest that a gift of appreciated property should trigger a realization of gain. Another desirable result of the benefit rule is that it would highlight the folly of allowing trusts, which neither consume nor save within the meaning of the Haig-Simons definition, to be treated as taxpayers. The income of trusts should in every possible case be attributed to either the beneficiary or the owner of the trust. When the beneficiaries and owners are so separated from the trust as to be reasonably unavailable as taxpayers, then the trust should be taxed according to the general taxing scheme for corporations, with a high flat rate and an additional tax (without credit for taxes paid by the trust) on "dividends" to the ultimate beneficiaries.

In judging proposals for reform, an important consideration must be their contribution toward the simplification of the tax laws. One expected by-product of the development of normative rules for a tax system is the reduction in arbitrary distinctions in the law. Normative rules cannot eliminate all or even most ad hoc decisionmaking, but they at least give a framework for the system that can be readily understood. We believe, therefore, that our proposals for change in the taxation of the family will be simpler to understand than the multitude of inconsistent features of current law.

The major contribution to simplicity of our proposals is not so much in what they change as in what they leave alone. The consolidation of marital income, which we want to continue, requires far less time and energy than was required in policing a system of separate taxation. Our rejection of any tax allowance for imputed income strikes a major blow for simplification. Some of our recommendations for change also should make a positive contribution to the goal of simplicity. If, as we suggest, the income of children could be consolidated with that of the parents—and if this were handled properly —it would end a variety of tax avoidance techniques, thereby reducing conflicts between the Internal Revenue Service and the taxpayers and freeing the courts for other business. Our proposal concerning trusts would add to complexity in the short run, but by eliminating the tax advantages that motivate the formation of the majority of trusts, the long-run results are likely to be on the side of greater simplicity. Our low-income allowance, which would replace a patchwork of special relief measures, would undoubtedly be easier to administer than present law and would probably make it possible for many low-income taxpayers to prepare their own returns.

Most changes in the law unfortunately result in additional complexity for at least a year, until the taxpaying public learns the new rules. Many of our changes, however, fit into old patterns of taxation, even if the theory supporting them and the overall impact on burdens are radically changed. We therefore anticipate no significant administrative problems in implementing our proposals. If some of our more refined income-splitting notions are implemented, we would expect to see some trade-off between fairness and simplicity, but for the bulk of our reform suggestions, we see net gains both in fairness and simplicity.

Appendix A

Table 6-2. Increase or Decrease in Individual Income Tax Burden from Marriage[a]
Taxable income in thousands of dollars; amounts in dollars

	Income split between husband and wife (percent)							
	100–0		75–25		60–40		50–50	
Taxable income[b]	Amount	Percent change[c]	Amount	Percent change[c]	Amount	Percent change[c]	Amount	Percent change[c]
4	−70	−1.8	−25	−0.6	−8	−0.2	0	0.0
8	−210	−2.6	−40	−0.5	−16	−0.2	0	0.0
12	−370	−3.1	−80	−0.7	4	0.0	40	0.3
16	−570	−3.6	−60	−0.4	64	0.4	80	0.5
20	−850	−4.2	−40	−0.2	160	0.8	200	1.0
24	−1,130	−4.7	40	0.2	336	1.4	400	1.7
28	−1,390	−5.0	140	0.5	584	2.1	680	2.4
32	−1,630	−5.1	280	0.9	856	2.7	1,000	3.1
36	−1,950	−5.4	460	1.3	1,168	3.2	1,320	3.7
40	−2,250	−5.6	660	1.6	1,520	3.8	1,680	4.2

Source: Calculated from 1976 statutory individual income tax schedules.
a. Excess of the joint return tax over the tax on two single individuals with the same combined income. A negative figure indicates a decrease in burdens on account of marriage.
b. Aggregate taxable income of couple. Table ignores possible differences in definition of taxable income on account of marriage.
c. Increase (decrease) in tax over aggregate taxable income.

Appendix B: Distribution of Tax Burdens by Income Classes under Proposed Splitting Arrangements

Table 6-3 shows the distribution of burdens by income class for various family groups under a comprehensive income tax, with tax treatment of the family according to present law and according to our proposals. This distribution is compared with that of 1976 law.

Many of the differences in the tax results under our proposed plan and under 1976 law are due to the changes in the tax base recommended by the authors of other papers in this volume. Isolating the differences due to our proposals for changes in the taxation of the family from those resulting from the expansion of the tax base is not easily done, since some change in the rate schedules of current law is unavoidable if the tax base is to be expanded and if the revenue yield of the tax system is to remain constant. In an effort to isolate the effects of our proposals, Joseph J. Minarik computed the tax liabili-

Table 6-3. Distribution of Tax Burdens by Income Class under 1976 Law and under a Comprehensive Income Tax with Proposed and Present-Law Treatment of the Family, by Marital Status and Size of Family, 1977
Percent

Comprehensive income class[a] (thousands of dollars)	1976 law[b]	Comprehensive income tax	
		With proposed treatment of family[c]	With present-law treatment of family[d]
All filers			
0–2.5	0.0	0.0	0.0
2.5–5	0.3	0.1	0.2
5–7.5	1.1	1.1	1.1
7.5–10	2.2	2.4	2.4
10–15	8.0	8.7	9.0
15–20	11.7	13.0	13.0
20–25	13.0	14.2	14.0
25–30	11.6	12.1	11.7
30–50	22.6	21.6	20.6
50–100	12.6	10.4	11.2
100–200	7.5	6.1	7.1
200–500	5.3	5.3	5.2
500–1,000	1.3	1.7	1.5
1,000 and over	2.9	3.3	2.9
Single persons			
0–2.5	0.0	0.0	0.0
2.5–5	1.5	0.4	1.3
5–7.5	5.9	4.9	5.2
7.5–10	9.5	8.5	8.6
10–15	21.7	20.5	20.5
15–20	15.8	16.5	15.4
20–25	10.6	11.0	10.3
25–30	7.0	7.2	6.9
30–50	11.8	11.0	11.3
50–100	7.3	7.3	7.8
100–200	4.0	5.4	5.7
200–500	2.9	4.0	3.9
500–1,000	0.9	1.4	1.4
1,000 and over	1.2	1.8	1.7
Heads of households			
0–2.5	0.0	0.0	0.0
2.5–5	0.2	0.0	0.2
5–7.5	2.4	2.2	2.9
7.5–10	6.5	6.9	8.0

Table 6-3 (continued)

Comprehensive income class[a] (thousands of dollars)	1976 law[b]	Comprehensive income tax	
		With proposed treatment of family[c]	With present-law treatment of family[d]
10–15	20.2	22.1	23.3
15–20	16.3	17.8	17.2
20–25	12.4	12.8	11.7
25–30	9.1	9.3	8.5
30–50	11.0	10.1	9.5
50–100	5.7	5.6	5.9
100–200	7.2	5.7	6.0
200–500	7.1	4.9	4.6
500–1,000	0.7	0.9	0.8
1,000 and over	1.1	1.6	1.4
All married couples			
0–2.5	0.0	0.0	0.0
2.5–5	0.0	0.0	0.0
5–7.5	0.1	0.2	0.2
7.5–10	0.6	0.9	0.9
10–15	4.7	5.5	6.2
15–20	10.7	12.0	12.4
20–25	13.5	14.9	14.8
25–30	12.6	13.4	12.8
30–50	25.3	24.5	23.0
50–100	14.0	11.3	12.1
100–200	8.1	6.3	7.4
200–500	5.7	5.6	5.4
500–1,000	1.4	1.8	1.6
1,000 and over	3.2	3.6	3.1
Married couples with no children			
0–2.5	0.0	0.0	0.0
2.5–5	0.0	0.0	0.0
5–7.5	0.2	0.5	0.5
7.5–10	1.0	1.8	1.7
10–15	5.7	7.3	7.5
15–20	10.6	12.3	12.1
20–25	12.8	14.1	13.5
25–30	12.5	12.8	12.2
30–50	25.4	23.1	22.2
50–100	14.1	11.2	12.6
100–200	7.6	5.9	7.2
200–500	5.3	5.3	5.4
500–1,000	1.9	2.3	2.1
1,000 and over	2.7	3.4	3.0

Table 6-3 (continued)

Comprehensive income class[a] (thousands of dollars)	1976 law[b]	Comprehensive income tax	
		With proposed treatment of family[c]	With present-law treatment of family[d]
Married couples, one or two children			
0–2.5	0.0	0.0	0.0
2.5–5	0.0	0.0	0.0
5–7.5	0.1	0.0	0.1
7.5–10	0.5	0.6	0.7
10–15	5.2	5.6	6.3
15–20	12.1	13.3	13.7
20–25	14.8	16.3	16.1
25–30	13.0	14.1	13.4
30–50	25.9	25.4	23.9
50–100	13.3	10.6	11.5
100–200	6.5	5.0	6.0
200–500	5.9	5.6	5.4
500–1,000	1.1	1.4	1.2
1,000 and over	1.6	2.0	1.8
Married couples, three or more children			
0–2.5	0.0	0.0	0.0
2.5–5	0.0	0.0	0.0
5–7.5	0.0	0.0	0.0
7.5–10	0.1	0.0	0.2
10–15	2.4	2.4	3.9
15–20	8.2	9.3	10.8
20–25	12.3	13.9	14.7
25–30	12.1	13.1	12.9
30–50	24.0	25.4	22.7
50–100	15.0	12.8	12.6
100–200	11.8	9.2	10.2
200–500	6.0	5.8	5.4
500–1,000	1.3	1.6	1.3
1,000 and over	6.8	6.6	5.3

Source: Brookings 1970 MERGE File, projected to 1977.
a. See appendix to this volume for definition of comprehensive income.
b. Without earned-income credit.
c. McIntyre-Oldman proposals for treatment of the family combined with comprehensive income tax base.
d. Present-law treatment of the family combined with comprehensive income tax base.

ties resulting from the comprehensive tax base[10] on the assumption that the tax treatment of the family would follow the pattern of the current law as much as possible. (See last column of table 6-3.)

10. See the appendix to this volume for the definition of comprehensive income.

The effects of the composite reform packages made up of the independent recommendations of the authors of other papers in this volume on relative tax burdens vary for different family groups. Most single persons have their relative burdens reduced, although most heads of households have an increase in relative burdens at income levels above $7,500. The overall impact on income classes is to reduce relative burdens at low-income levels and upper-middle-income levels and to increase them at middle- and high-income levels. Most of this change is due to the changes in the tax base, but some is due to the rate structures shown in figure 6-2. The reduction in burdens at the bottom, however, results from our improved low-income allowance.

Comments by William D. Andrews

Michael McIntyre and Oliver Oldman begin their paper by saying that the taxation of the family involves a complex, difficult, and emotional issue: what the tax burden on single persons should be in relation to that on married couples. The paper is true to its subject; it is complex and difficult. But it contains much of value and interest.

First, the authors are exactly right in reading Simons, at least the Simons part of the Haig-Simons definition, to indicate that the subject matter of the tax is consumption and accumulation, the uses of income rather than its sources. That bears on the treatment of the family because at least one typical pattern involves a single major earner whose money income goes to support a household containing another adult and one or more children. Since the underlying subject of the tax is the uses of income, the burden should be shaped to fit the income-using unit, the household, rather than the individual earner. McIntyre and Oldman are quite right in concluding that it would be senseless to try to divide consumption among the individuals who share in a particular household. Consumption is predominantly a household function rather than an individual function in our society.

The same thing is true of accumulation to a considerable extent. It is different, of course, but realistically, much accumulation is for a family rather than for just the individual whose efforts may have produced the income that supports the family. Incidentally, the family that shares in accumulation may be different from the household that shares in consumption, since the former often embraces adult children who have established their own households.

The family problem is mainly that of constructing appropriate rates for different sorts of households. McIntyre and Oldman would approach that problem by focusing on the question that lawyers typically pose: who is the taxpayer? Their answer is that the individuals (at least the adult individuals) within the household are the true taxpayers, and they conclude that this leads to complete splitting—the pre-1969 solution—as the correct way of setting household rates. They would extend this analysis to children by allowing exemptions as deductions, as a kind of partial splitting mechanism.

But I think that leaves unresolved the problem they describe as the tax on remaining single. Moreover, that problem should be put together with another: the problem of the difference between a marital household in which only one person goes to work and one in which both adults are employed.

The aspect of Simons's analysis that needs to be pursued further in relation to this problem is the difference between a one-earner household and a two-earner household, not in terms of sources of income but in terms of consumption. If one thinks of two such households with the same money income, and then takes the Simons formulation seriously, the question to consider is whether those two households really have equal total consumption, and the answer becomes a clear negative. The fact is that a household in which one adult is the earner and the other adult stays at home has a larger real income and real standard of living than a household does that receives the same money income for which two people have to work.

Now of course it would not be prudent to try to reflect that difference by assigning a value to services performed by the spouse at home. Nor should anyone even inquire whether the nonworking spouse does something at home or just enjoys his or her leisure. Not having to work enhances real welfare in either case.

The difference in welfare between a one-earner couple and a two-earner couple can be taken into account indirectly, and that is the line that ought to be pursued. Serious attention should be given to the provision of an earned income credit for the income of the second worker in a two-earner couple. One possibility is that the rate schedule for single persons adopted in 1969 may really make sense because it benefits persons living together who each work for a salary without the services of an unemployed adult at home. But then an equivalent benefit should be extended to married couples in which both spouses work. It would be useful to plot the tax burdens produced by the present rate schedule for the separate incomes of two working persons at different income levels and different divisions of the income, and then see whether an earned income credit for the spouse with the smaller earned income could be devised to approximate that result over some substantial range.

I suggest a generous allowance—even more generous than those that are usually proposed. It might begin with $1,000 completely tax free. That would tend to compensate for the larger low-income allowance offered unmarried persons under present law, and it might provide some shelter for the expenses incurred by a second adult going to work. Then something less than 100 percent of earnings over $1,000 could be exempted up to a maximum total exemption of $9,600. At the 50 percent maximum rate of tax on earned income, this would produce a maximum tax saving of $4,800, just what the single rate schedule would produce under the present law.

This might not necessarily be the right final answer, but it would be an answer that would remove the tax on marriage for two people who both work. (It is constructed to do just that.) It would also maintain some reduction in rates when the income of a single person is devoted to the support of more than one person. But there ought to be a study that would try to answer the further question of whether the result bears some kind of sensible relationship to the value of homemaking services or the withheld time or leisure that distinguishes the two-earner from the single-earner family.

All of what has been said so far relates to earned income, not property income. In the case of simple investment income, there is no loss in welfare in the sense of leisure sacrifice associated with it, and therefore it may make little difference to the welfare of a household whether its income belongs to one person or another. Any special credit or deduction for the unearned income of a lower-income spouse is therefore unjustified, even though that leaves the problem of a tax on marriage in some cases.

One solution might be to somehow reinstate the pre-1969 rates for single persons with unearned income—to confine the 1969 relief for single persons to earned income. But it is not clear whether such a change would be worth the effort.

Property income raises another problem at a higher point up the income scale. Unjustified discrimination persists in tax burdens between families with a significant amount of property income, some of which goes to children (or trusts for children) under current property rules, and other families that either do not have property income to be allocated to children in that manner or have not made such arrangements. As in the case between spouses, however, there are reasons for taxing children's earnings at less than their parents' marginal rates, since the children's work entails a sacrifice of time, which might otherwise have been devoted to valuable educational endeavors. So again the question arises whether additional distinctions should be drawn between earned and unearned income, distinctions that may be quite consistent with the Simons version of the Haig-Simons ideal, since they indirectly reflect differences among households in real resources available for consumption and (human capital) accumulation.

Comments by Harvey E. Brazer

Michael McIntyre and Oliver Oldman make an interesting and valuable contribution to a rather sparse literature on the subjects of the appropriate unit for taxation under an income tax and the case for allowances for dependents. This is not to say, however, that I can agree with either their analysis or their conclusions.

One source of difficulty is the attempt to tie the choice of taxable unit and the dependents' allowance to the comprehensive tax base concept. If I understand correctly the approach taken, it begins with a denial that $Y = C + \Delta NW$, where Y is income, C is consumption, and NW is net worth. Since this identity is not logically necessary, according to the authors, it does not follow that all expenditures for a family member made out of some income source constitute consumption. They then argue that income accrues to the person who enjoys the benefits of consumption from income from whatever source. It is this assertion that leads to the guts of the policy positions that follow.

Thus the preferred unit for taxation is the family, with income-splitting permitted to the married couple. Objections in terms of the definition of marital status are met generously by permitting income-splitting privileges to any two (or more?) people who pool their incomes and constitute a shared household. This position, it seems to me, is one that contains the ingredients for its own demise. Short of periodic Internal Revenue Service inspections and complex filing rules for less than full-year sharing arrangements, it is difficult to see how it would be possible to deny the right to income-splitting to any two people who choose to claim it.

Nevertheless, as McIntyre and Oldman see it, there remains the problem of how to deal with single-person households. It is either necessary to go back to the 1948–69 system and again face the ire of single people and the political pressures that led to present law provisions or to resort to a multiplicity of tax schedules and continue to face the penalty on marriage now sustained in the income tax. The authors of this paper seem rather complacent about the latter prospect. While aware of the fact that the rate schedules account for only a part—and in the lower- and middle-income brackets only a small part—of the tax penalty on married couples, they never present the full picture. Obviously in many cases the most important tax deterrents to marriage are found in features such as the following: (1) the low-income allowance—$2,100 for a married couple and $3,400 for two single persons; (2) the tax credit for child care may be only $800 for a couple with four children but $1,600 for two single people, each with two children; (3) the tax credit of $35 per capita or 2 percent of income up to $180 may be $180 for a couple but $360 for two single people; (4) the opportunity may be available for one of a pair of people (of opposite sexes) to itemize deductions while the other takes the standard deduction; and (5) the medical expense floor may be more easily circumvented by two single people. This does not, of course, exhaust the list of sources of income tax deterrents to marriage, in addition to the rate schedules. Calculations I have presented elsewhere indicate that where income is divided equally, or can be by manipulating titles to property or through alimony agreements, a married couple with a combined adjusted gross income in the range of $10,000 to $40,000 can save between $250 and $2,500 a year, or more if circumstances are especially favorable, by means of a divorce decree or the decision not to marry under the law.[11] Nothing

11. *American Families: Trends and Pressures, 1973,* Hearings before the Subcommittee on Children and Youth of the Senate Committee on Labor and Public Welfare, 93 Cong. 1 sess. (GPO, 1974), p. 209.

of substance or practice need be different, of course, in the two circumstances.

Thus neither the pre-1969 system nor the one that supplanted it seems to me to be acceptable, let alone attractive. Economists as well as lawyers have seen the optional joint return or even the mandatory joint return as an important requisite for the attainment of horizontal equity. This follows, not from the McIntyre-Oldman "benefit rule" and the demands of the comprehensive tax base, but from the notion that the household rather than the individual is the unit whose economic well-being should govern the relative size of its contribution to the public fisc under an ability-to-pay approach to taxation. It is this conception of the basis for determining tax obligations that leads one to the comprehensive tax base, not the other way round, as the paper under discussion seems to suggest.

As a one-time adherent to the view that the household should be the unit for taxation, I am now persuaded that there is no clear-cut logic that leads to this choice. Instead, we face something of a dilemma, one that will permit some of us to opt for one alternative and others for another. The choice, as I see it, is between seeking neutrality among households—call them families, couples, whatever you will—defined as one or more persons who pool income for their mutual benefit and share an abode, and neutrality among people irrespective of their marital status, living, or sharing arrangements. I prefer the latter option because I believe that marriage or its dissolution through death or divorce, cohabitation of a sustained or sometime sort, or what have you, are simply not the concern of the Internal Revenue Code.

The system that I prefer is essentially the Canadian system and, assuming state community property rules can be ignored for federal income tax purposes, it is very close to the U.S. approach before 1948. I recognize that it is far from an ideal system, for it is open to manipulation through real or spurious transfers of title to property and probably has other defects as well. It is, rather, a difficult choice between far less than perfect alternatives. I do not believe that a first best option is available under a graduated income tax with a complex system of credits, exclusions, and deductions. I simply opt for neutrality between individuals with respect to their choice of marital or living arrangements as preferable to either the present or the pre-1969 approach.

I am even less satisfied with the McIntyre-Oldman benefit rule as a justification for dependents' allowances for children. The fact that children benefit from parents' expenditures to provide them with consumption goods and services moves me not at all. Here, surely, is a classic case of interdependence of utilities. My utility is a function only in part of my own consumption; into that function the consumption (more accurately the utility) of my children enters as an argument, perhaps even with substantially greater weight attached to it than attaches to my consumption. Certainly they benefit from consumption I make possible, but so do I. I therefore would not treat a disposition of income for consumption by children in any more (or less) favored way than any other consumption.

Similarly, in an age of actual or prospective overpopulation, I find entirely unpersuasive the suggestion that an allowance for children is justified by the parents' serving a societal function by conceiving and rearing children. Like any other deduction, a children's allowance is a tax subsidy, a device that reduces the net cost of having children. Unabashedly, I regard this as lacking in social merit. The decision to have children in various numbers is for most taxpayers a voluntary choice, properly regarded in the same light as any other consumption choice and no more a reduction in taxpaying capacity than alternative choices. If one is to make a case for its special, but not necessarily specially deserving, nature, it may be seen in the fact that the decision to consume by rearing children is far less readily reversible than are other consumption choices.

Finally, I would note simply that the exemption for dependents is indeed an income-conditioned children's allowance, costing $8 billion to $9 billion a year. It differs, however, from the one many of us would design in that its value is zero at income levels where it is most needed and rises to as high as $525 per child at income levels at which that sum is a bagatelle.

CHAPTER SEVEN

The Definition of Taxable Business Income

E. CARY BROWN *and* JEREMY I. BULOW

THE PURPOSES of this paper are to define business income in a way that is congenial in the main to economists, to consider the situations and assumptions that permit this definition to be carried over as an acceptable basis for taxation (that is, that tax liabilities arise and tax payments are asserted consistently on the basis of this definition of income), to see where and how the definition may break down, and to consider possible remedial action.

This menu is indeed a large one. We will have to concentrate on major aspects of the definition of taxable business income. We will not consider taxable personal income, personal deductions, or exemptions, nor will we discuss whether income, rather than some other tax base such as consumption or wealth, *should* form the basis for taxation. We will assume that the income tax base, defined in this particular way, would apply to businesses being taxed under either an in rem business income tax or an in personam tax imposed on firms as part of a comprehensive personal income tax. We thereby also exclude a discussion of the consolidation of common business interests and the business capital unit for which income is defined—whether it is the common stock, all equity capital, or all contributed capital. However these decisions are reached, the basic issues in defining taxable business income remain essentially the same. Lastly, to complete our long list of omissions, we will not consider the problems posed by inflation. These have been thoroughly discussed at a previous Brookings conference and elsewhere. In general the techniques or procedures that can be worked out to deal with changing prices depend basically on the initial inflationless definition of income. Put in another way, we are discussing the definition of taxable *real* business income and thus turn to our topic surrounded by the cocoon of a constant general price level.

Income Defined

Over the years economists have continued to lean toward the Haig-Simons definition of income—that income consists essentially of consumption plus or minus changes in net wealth over a particular period of time[1]—as the one that, if systematically applied, leads to the fewest anomalies or inconsistencies.[2] This definition seems to have been adapted from much older definitions of income developed by accountants and economists for application to a business. For example, Alfred Marshall (1890),[3] Lawrence R. Dicksee (1892),[4] Henry R. Hat-

1. The initial statement was Robert Murray Haig's in "The Concept of Income—Economic and Legal Aspects," in Haig, ed., *The Federal Income Tax* (Columbia University Press, 1921), chap. 1. It was later developed in Henry C. Simons, *Personal Income Taxation* (University of Chicago Press, 1938), chap. 2; J. R. Hicks, *Value and Capital: An Inquiry into Some Fundamental Principles of Economic Theory* (Oxford University Press, 1939), chap. 14; William Vickrey, *Agenda for Progressive Taxation* (Ronald Press, 1947), chap. 1; and Sidney S. Alexander, "Income Measurement in a Dynamic Economy," in Sidney S. Alexander and others, *Five Monographs on Business Income* (New York: Study Group on Business Income, American Institute of Accountants, 1950), pp. 1–95.

2. Nicholas Kaldor differed from this view in *An Expenditure Tax* (London: Allen and Unwin, 1955), chap. 1 and app. He argued that the conventional definition of income breaks down under changes in interest rates, since income cannot then be defined in principle. The argument is made with respect to a stream of consumption that remains constant despite the increase in capital value of the asset providing it. It would appear to apply less strongly to a business unit.

3. From the first edition in 1890 of the *Principles of Economics* (London: Macmillan) to the eighth and last in 1920, Marshall defined profits essentially as follows: "When a man is engaged in business, his PROFITS for the year are the excess of his receipts from his business during the year over his outlay for his business; the difference between the value of his stock and plant at the end and at the beginning of the year being taken as part of his receipts or as part of his outlay, according as there has been an increase or decrease of value" (p. 136, 2d ed., 1891).

4. *Auditing: A Practical Manual for Auditors* (London: Gee, 1892).

field (1909),[5] Arthur L. Dickinson (1913),[6] and John B. Canning (1929),[7] defined income essentially as the change in net worth or proprietorship, adjusted for proprietors' contributions or withdrawals. Hence applying the Haig-Simons definition of income to the business firm means that income will consist of accrued changes in net worth, plus distributions and less net contributions of capital.

This is not the sole definition in the literature, however, and there is some difficulty in implementing it, primarily in measuring the change in wealth. But the bulk of the profession returns to this definition as the most reasonable, or the least ambiguous, or the most satisfying for the purposes of income taxation. Conceptual and implementation problems stud the landscape to be sure, and these may require some compromising.

It should be noted that the Haig-Simons definition of income is one based on the *use* of income and is identically equal to one based on the *source* of income—wages, interest, rents, business income, transfer receipts, and gains and losses. That is to say: $C + S = Y = W + I + R + P + T_r + G$, where $C =$ consumption, $S =$ saving, $Y =$ income, and the other symbols stand for the items in the preceding sentence in the order given.

Perfection of Markets and Degrees of Certainty of Outcomes

The major difficulty in implementing a definition of income that relies on change in net wealth is in reaching a meaningful measurement of this change. In many cases market values can be used, but the

5. *Modern Accounting: Its Principles and Some of Its Problems* (Appleton, 1909); and *Accounting: Its Principles and Problems* (Appleton, 1927).

6. In both the first edition (1913) and the second (1918) of *Accounting: Practice and Procedure* (Ronald Press), Dickinson made the following interesting comment on realization: "In the widest possible view, profits may be stated as the realized increment in value of the whole amount invested in an undertaking; and, conversely, loss is the realized decrement in such value. Inasmuch, however, as the ultimate realization of the original investment is from the nature of things deferred for a long period of years, during which partial realizations are continually taking place, it becomes necessary to fall back on estimates of value at certain definite periods, and to consider as profit or loss the estimated increase or decrease between any two such periods" (p. 67, 2d ed.).

7. *The Economics of Accountancy* (Ronald Press, 1929). Canning was a disciple of Irving Fisher but defined business income in the same general way as the others we have cited.

extent of reliance on such values depends on the perfection of markets and the degree of certainty about future events.

Competitive Markets and Certainty

With competitive markets and conditions of certainty with respect to all present and future events, measuring income in the way implied in the definition would not be difficult. All necessary valuations could be taken for all assets from the prices observed in such competitive and rational markets.

Financial assets and liabilities usually have fairly satisfactory markets except, perhaps, for accounts receivable (although there are factors who buy them). Under our assumptions, these market prices would be used in periodic valuation. Finished inventories and goods in process would be valued at the discounted value of selling prices less selling expenses; materials would be recorded at the buyers' market price. Depreciable assets would be quoted continuously throughout their lives, and therefore the decline in their value could be determined from the market in every period. (We have no such information on this depreciation pattern at the present time.) The vexed question of the valuation of research and development, patents, and advertising would be settled by resort to their particular markets. Improper book valuations caused by inaccurate accounting procedures would be correctable by market information.

From this quick review of the Haig-Simons definition applied in a world of competitive markets that are operated under conditions of certainty, one can conclude that the definition could be readily and systematically applied to the determination of taxable income. Business income would be some rate of interest on capital. Mistakes in income or expense allocation would be corrected by the appropriate market. While the simplicity of achieving this result is delightful, this is unfortunately a restricted and not very interesting world.

Competitive Markets and Uncertainty

The situation does not change much when it is assumed that the competitive markets are operating under conditions of uncertainty. Although uncertainties characterize the durability of assets, the collectibility of accounts, and the future selling prices of inventories, the competitive markets will continue to yield information that can be used in the valuation process. What is new is the possibility of unforeseen changes in important economic variables—the interest rate, attitudes toward risk, major improvements in products, technical changes, and so on. Large swings in asset values could occur in any one year, both upward and downward, as these unforeseen changes become visible. These swings in particular asset values would make possible large amounts of unforeseen gain and loss. Because of uncertainty, there may also be swings in the total value of an enterprise that are greater or less than the changes in particular asset values. Such changes would be attributed to goodwill—Canning's master valuation account.[8]

While many factors give rise to unforeseen gains and losses, very few large ones occur because of unexpected increases or decreases in the physical productivity of assets. Machines, for example, may have longer or shorter lives than expected; firms may discover oil. Generally, however, these risks are diversifiable and need not have a substantial effect on income. Instead, most unforeseen gains and losses are due to changes in the market value of firms that continue to produce similar physical outputs, and the altered market value results from changes in relative prices. For example, a change in the price of a firm's product is an obvious case of a factor that leads to a change in its market value. The introduction of a more efficient machine by a competitor reduces the value of a firm as its economic rent declines. A change in interest rates modifies the capitalization factor and the capital values of a firm.

While the latter case is not substantially different from the previous ones—all involve changes in relative prices in a firm producing the same output—it has traditionally provided one of the most difficult problems in defining income. On the one hand, it is pointed out that although liquidation of the asset would create more resources for the firm, its retention would not; that the expected stream of income has not changed; and hence that no true gain can be included in income. On the other hand, comparing firms with varying lengths of income streams at the time the interest rate changes reveals a substantial difference between a firm in a short position on future income—with cash—and one with a long position holding consols or perpetuities. The tax law surely should recognize such a difference between firms in some way.

8. Canning, *Economics of Accountancy,* p. 42.

Still another view of the interest rate change is that on day 1 there was a certain stream of resources (say $10) that one could expect from a given capital investment (say $100). On day 2, a new transformation rate between present and future (say 5 percent interest) has been decreed by forces outside the firm, and new investments (of say $100) can only expect a lower income stream (say $5). By virtue of its long position it gains (say $100) by not having its future income stream diminished. In other words the new numeraire is a flow of $5 a year from the $100 value.

While we think that the theoretical case for including these unforeseen gains and losses from interest rate changes in income is persuasive, it may not convince everyone, at least not Kaldor.[9] To the unconvinced, we offer important practical grounds. First, there is no operational way to separate gains and losses from interest rate changes from those of other sources. Second, there are important differences between firms in the relative asset and liability effects resulting from interest rate changes, and these differences should be recognized. We therefore favor the full inclusion of all gains and losses in our taxable income definition under these assumed market conditions. We recognize the possiblity of large swings in income, however, and the need for some type of averaging, depending on the particular structure under which firms would be taxed.

Imperfect Markets

We now move to the world of imperfect markets characterized by a few sporadic market transactions. The implementation of our definition of income becomes much more difficult, and new issues come to the fore. The presence of markets for all assets and liabilities, secondhand or new, in the previous situations meant that firms could buy, sell, or borrow at the market price and that banks could lend on these values. The income (or loss) as determined by the definition we favor can also be seen to be readily convertible into cash or its equivalent (where there are perfect markets). Indeed accrued income is equal to the firm's capacity to make a distribution while maintaining its initial market value. The existence of such a capacity does not depend on the realization of this income by sale or disposal of the assets.

9. See note 2.

In sharp contrast, imperfect markets force upon us the fact that large discrepancies may arise between the notion of accrued income, somehow estimated or appraised, and the actual income that the imperfect market would reveal if business were transacted. There also may be a large difference between notional accrued income and the ability to pay or the change in disposable income.

A second major problem in a world of imperfect markets is how much reliance to place on markets for assistance in income determination. In one sense the present definition of income in the tax law largely follows the Haig-Simons definition with competitive markets, basing valuations on markets whenever they provide satisfactory information; that is, when relevant transactions take place. Consider, for example, depreciable assets. In a world of perfect markets the market value would be used when the asset was purchased and also in every period of its life until it is scrapped or otherwise disposed of. Under present practice the market is also used at the time of purchase. This price is then presumed to be the value of the asset when adjusted by tentative coefficients, called depreciation rates, that measure the percentage decline in value. Finally, when the asset is disposed of, a final market value for the asset is realized and a gain or loss recorded as a final adjustment of the tentative valuations throughout the asset's life. Clearly, the market is used whenever it can be. But because few transactions are taking place despite the multitude of assets, continuous market valuation is impossible. Income no longer can be surely accrued. We are pushed to the use of the market when the firm uses it, namely to a realization criterion.

To sum up:

1. With competitive markets under conditions of certainty, the definition of income as the accrued change in net worth plus net capital withdrawals can be easily implemented.

2. Competitive markets under conditions of uncertainty can also deal with this definition of income easily and equitably, although unforeseen gains and losses can arise and the averaging of income becomes necessary because of large potential shifts in income.

3. Imperfect markets create two problems:

a. Accrued income diverges from disposable income because markets are not always present or precise enough to permit conversions of asset values into cash.

b. Accrued income can no longer be estimated continuously or period by period because markets are no longer continuously giving information. The requirement that accurate market values be used is not met because there may be gaps in market transactions and in information. In these situations it may be impossible to determine the amount of accrued income (positive or negative) until a market transaction takes place. Therefore postponing the recognition of gain or loss may be necessary until the gain or loss has been realized.

Divergence of Present Tax Law from Economists' Definition of Income

We have stated a concept of income—accrued changes in net worth *plus* net distributions of capital—that we believe to be consistent and equitable and that we modified under imperfect markets from accrued changes to realized changes in net worth. How much will this change from accrual to realization qualify our original view? What will the character of the deviations be?

Actual effective rates deviate in many ways from the statutory rate schedule applied to the income concept we favor. These deviations— some of which are being reduced or phased out by the Tax Reform Act of 1976—can be grouped in several categories.

1. *Special tax rates* may be enacted for particular groups or for particular forms of income. Examples are the now vanishing low rate on Western Hemisphere trade corporations, the special rate on capital gains and losses, the treatment as capital gains of certain timber income, coal and iron royalties, and certain agricultural income.

2. *Direct tax base reductions,* as an alternative form of subsidy to lowered tax rates, also lower the effective rate. Three major examples at the present time are exempt state and local interest, the excess of percentage over cost depletion, and the excessive bad-debt reserves of certain financial institutions.

3. *Subsidies of factor inputs* operate to reduce costs and increase after-tax returns, as in the cases of the investment tax credit and the work incentive program.

4. *Deferment of tax* is the most generally used device for tax subsidy and takes various forms:

a. *Expensing capital outlays* such as exploration and development costs, intangible drilling costs, certain agricultural outlays, excess first-year depreciation, and construction-period interest and taxes.

b. *Five-year amortization* of longer-lived facilities used for pollution control, of railroad rolling stock, of low-income rental housing rehabilitation, and of child-care facilities.

c. *Accelerated depreciation* on structures and on depreciable assets covered by the asset depreciation range.

d. *Direct postponement of tax* through such provisions as domestic international sales corporations for some export income, the unrepatriated earnings of controlled foreign subsidiaries, and some earnings of shipping companies on deposited construction funds.

The purpose of these provisions is to increase the value of particular assets or of a firm's net worth by reducing or postponing taxes through the acceleration of deductions. The benefits to the firm can be stated in present-value terms and become the equivalent of a subsidy. These provisions are not intended to improve the definition of income. Their purpose could be clarified by conversion to subsidies and moved to the expenditure side of the budget.

The treatment of installment sales may be somewhat different. The payments of installments are considered a realization of income, despite the market transaction at the time of sale that provided a clearly defined price. We do not see that the method of financing transactions should determine the timing of the recognition of income. Our view would be to include in taxable income the full gain from the sale of personal property, without the present special treatment of a particular method of finance.

Two major types of expenditures—for research and development and for advertising—are now expensed. On the basis of our present view, they should be capitalized and allocated over the economic life of the asset. The nature of these activities, however, appears to us to preclude any very precise ex ante determination of their economic lives. Although it is clear that successful patents may have value for a considerable period of time, an advertising campaign is much more apt to be short-lived. Research and development costs connected with the improvement of products or the creation of new ones can be distinguished from the cost of developing oil wells. The disparity of product in the first case contrasts with the more homogeneous product of the second. The latter is much more susceptible to averaging over large numbers and more readily predictable in duration than a successful piece of research that develops a new product of uncertain market.

Given the difficulty of estimation under conditions of uncertainty, and given the absence of a market that can place a value on such assets as are created by advertising and research and development outlays, we see no other way but to continue the present treatment. Allowing the expensing of assets with a relatively short life is probably not a major compromise with the fairness of the definition of income. With a 50 percent tax rate and an after-tax discount rate of 5 percent, the subsidy of allowing expensing rather than economic depreciation rises from the equivalent of a 2 percent investment tax credit when the economic life is two years, 10 percent for ten years, and 17 percent when a life of twenty years is expected.[10] Since these assets are typically short-lived, the implicit subsidy of expensing does not seem too large.

On the whole, therefore, we find that while there is a substantial difference between present taxable income and what might be termed a more appropriate definition, it stems primarily from the use of the tax system to subsidize or provide incentives to worthy causes, activities, and industries. The specific changes from the present structure that arise solely from the definitional viewpoint do not seem to be major, and the major definitional problems do not loom large so long as we accept the notion of realization as fundamental to a definition of income in a world of incomplete and imperfect markets.

Seriousness of Divergence of Realized from Accrued Income

This tentative conclusion, however, may mean that by giving up the accrued income standard for practical reasons in favor of the realization concept, we have given up too much—so much as to make the gain not worthwhile. For example, will failure to apply the accrual concept result in serious and arbitrary variations in the income

10. The formula is

$$C = \frac{r\tau}{r + \delta}$$

for the exponential case, where r = after-tax rate of return, τ = tax rate, and δ = exponential rate of decay = $2/n$, where n is economic life. Use of exponential decay overstates the subsidy because the asset is not all written off over its economic life.

tax from firm to firm or from firm to nonfirm? Such a judgment is very difficult to make, and it is equally difficult to decide whether some kind of adjustment for tax postponement à la Vickrey could improve things.[11]

Since this section focuses on the difference between accrued and realized changes in net worth, problems will be found only when there is a difference between accrued or realized capital gains and losses on financial assets and on productive assets—inventories, depreciable assets, and land. Accrued capital gains that are not taxed until realized may be postponed indefinitely if the asset has a potentially infinite life, such as land and equity shares. If the life is short, as for inventories, the value of the postponement becomes trivial. The in-between cases are provided by depreciable assets and bonds, where the remaining life may vary between one year and perhaps a hundred years. In the case of a fall in interest rates, for example, bonds and depreciable assets would rise in value, and a rigorous accrual approach would write up the value of the asset and include that gain in income, just as if the asset were sold. For the rest of an asset's life, its depreciation base would be larger; more depreciation would take place over the depreciable asset's remaining life that would be precisely equal in the aggregate to the gain in the year of interest rate change. For bonds, there would be an added amortization of bond premium over the life of the bond, precisely equal to the gain in value when the interest rate changed. Under strict accrual accounting these added deductions should also be subtracted from income. While the additions and subtractions wash out in aggregate over an asset's life, they of course do not in present-value terms. The realization criterion would not have recognized the gain in the value of the asset when the interest rate changed or the added depreciation or amortization deductions so long as these assets were held by the firms over their economic lives. We therefore must try to get some grasp of the order of magnitude of the present value to the firm of ignoring these accrued gains and enlarged deductions under a realization concept, compared with including them fully in income under the accrual concept.

Consider, for example, the case of depreciable assets. Assume a tax rate of 50 percent and an after-tax interest rate change from 10 to 5 percent. The present value to the firm of not recognizing this gain

11. See Vickrey, *Agenda for Progressive Taxation*, pp. 172–76.

under the realization concept is 2 percent of the asset value when the remaining life is 10 years, 6 percent for a twenty-year asset, 12.5 percent for a forty-year asset, and 50 percent for a perpetuity.[12] For most depreciable assets with lives of thirty years or less, the gains in equity from making this adjustment do not seem to justify the costs involved in making them. For the really long-lived assets, the equity case is more pressing.

Assets such as land and equities may have large gains from interest rate changes that go untaxed indefinitely. These gains probably represent the largest deviation of accrued income from the realization concept. They are, moreover, the most difficult to deal with. The market for land is often imperfect and cannot be resorted to for serious pricing except from a realized transaction. Equities, on the other hand, can be valued in a virtually perfect market for many securities. In these cases the market could be used to overcome the unfairness of long postponement of gains. Periodic assessments could be made to include these gains or losses in income. The influence of taxes on the sale of such assets would thereby be sharply curtailed. A substantial averaging method would also be necessary.

Conclusion

Theoretically, one would like to have taxes based on income measured as the increase in the value of the firm plus net capital distributions. Ideally, then, for firms whose securities are traded in perfect capital markets these gains can be determined by market values. The corporate tax system, however, does not permit us to use equity values in determining taxable income, and we have accepted this constraint in our work.

The definition of income we favor means that all capital gains and losses should be included in current income, with allowances for averaging. For assets and liabilities with readily identifiable market values, such values could also be used for tax purposes. For other assets, however, such as used equipment and research and develop-

---

12. The formula for the present value computation is

$$\frac{(r_1 - r_2)r_2\tau}{(\delta + r_2)^2}$$

where r_1 = the initial after-tax interest rate, r_2 = new after-tax interest rate, δ = exponential rate of decay of net receipts from an asset, and τ = tax rate.

ment expense, markets are not generally available, and we must resort to a realization-based system of measuring income. We believe that in these cases the costs of switching to an accrual system would exceed the benefits from doing so. Among the reasons for this view is that a tax policy based on the realization concept does not provide nearly as large a tax break for depreciable assets as for assets with liquid markets, because producers cannot selectively realize gains or losses in depreciable assets.

Many of the special provisions in the current tax law do not represent conceptual problems in the definition of income but rather constitute subsidies, or tax expenditures, meant to encourage certain types of activities. While we may disagree with many of these subsidies, they are not issues to be dealt with in defining income.

In conclusion, then, while we would favor a more accrual-based tax system in some areas, and while the definition of income indeed presents some difficult conceptual issues, the current definition of business income requires modest modifications to be made to conform fairly well to an economist's definition.

*Comments by Daniel I. Halperin**

Income from a business could be determined by valuing the holdings of the owner (stock or partnership interests) at the beginning and end of the accounting period. The most likely application of this procedure—the case of the publicly held corporation—seems precluded by the editor's instructions not to consider the integration of the corporation and individual income taxes. Therefore I do not consider whether it would be impractical to extend this approach to the closely held business and, if not, whether it would be discriminatory to apply it at all. Further, I assume, as E. Cary Brown and Jeremy Bulow do, that determining income (or accretion) at the firm level by measuring the value of assets, including inventory and machinery, is just not in the cards. I do not share the belief that accrual taxation is so impossible as to be unworthy of consideration. For the purposes of this comment, however, I will assume that the decision has been made to compute business income on a realization basis, whatever the de-

* I wish to thank my colleague, Alvin C. Warren, Jr., for his help and suggestions.

cision might be about the basis for computing investment assets held by corporations and individuals.[13]

As Brown and Bulow note, most of the current departures from an economic definition of income are not due to conceptual problems of income measurement but to efforts to favor various forms of economic activity. This probably was not the original justification for all these provisions, nor is it a very good reason for maintaining some of them, but it seems a fair characterization of at least the stated reasons for opposing change. Therefore the major question probably is whether a move to a comprehensive tax base requires expenditures designed to accomplish the same purpose in all or some of these areas. The paper does not deal with this issue, which is fortunate for me, since I lack the expertise to comment on it intelligently. If income is to be determined on a realization basis, the principal conceptual questions would seem to be the proper period for deducting expenditures that are likely to provide continuing utility beyond the end of the taxable year and the acceptability of the cash method of accounting for income.

The accounting profession is of course vitally concerned with the question of matching expenditures to related income. But the principle that costs that provide "no discernible future benefits"[14] must be expensed reflects a traditional bias toward understating income and leads to immediate expensing of such items as advertising and, apparently, research and development costs, all of which have uncertain future utility. In general the accountants' approach leads to deductions of expenses (for example, interest and taxes to carry vacant land) that may not enhance future income prospects, even though the income to which the expenditures relate is yet to be realized. This bias

13. Brown and Bulow conclude that for most assets, the equity gains from taxing unrealized gains would not justify the administrative costs of valuation. Their computation appears to assume a method of depreciation at least as rapid as that of double declining balance. I would want more development of the economic justification for using this mode of depreciation rather than straight line. If straight line is "correct," it could make a substantial difference as to when annual measurement would be worthwhile. Moreover, accelerated depreciation would present a more serious continuing tax shelter problem.

14. See, for example, American Institute of Certified Public Accountants, Accounting Principles Board, Statement 4, *Basic Concepts and Accounting Principles Underlying Financial Statements of Business Enterprises* (AICPA, October 1970), par. 160. A fair examination of the use of the word "discernible" might suggest that "demonstrable" is closer to the intended meaning.

may prevent overall acceptance of accounting principles, but it would certainly indicate the likelihood that more rapid expensing of costs than is allowed for accounting purposes is unlikely to result in accurate income measurement.

Turning to the issue of capital recovery, if the accountants do not have the answer, the tax law could turn back the clock twenty years and allow "reasonable" depreciation on a case-by-case basis. It seems worthwhile, however, to try for more certainty and thus for simplicity.

Guideline lives for depreciation would appear to be an acceptable means of avoiding excessive administrative costs, as would an automatic repair allowance along the lines of present Internal Revenue Code section 263(f). These rules would serve their purpose if they were mandatory rather than elective and obviously should more closely approximate actual economic lives. The current guidelines (for purposes of the asset depreciation range system) appear much too liberal in their assumption that future lives will be much shorter than the period over which present equipment is used, nor is there any justification for the 20 percent reduction from the guideline life. Straight-line depreciation should probably be the norm unless there is a better economic defense for accelerated depreciation than I know of. Moreover, for real estate and perhaps for other assets, straight-line depreciation is far too liberal. On the liberalization side, amortization of goodwill and other intangibles should certainly be considered, as well as some allowance for reserves, such as self-insurance, if the valuation problem proved manageable.

Expenditures for advertising, research, promotion, and other start-up costs may present insoluble difficulties. Brown and Bulow suggest that if these costs were properly amortizable over two years at an exponential rate of depreciation, immediate deduction is the equivalent of a 4.5 percent investment credit. At a 50 percent tax rate this is equal to a *taxable* government subsidy for 9 percent of the cost. Perhaps this is too small to worry about, but it may be worthwhile to consider the possibility of deferring some of these expenditures, at least for those that are significantly in excess of the prior year's outlay if there is no reason to encourage the particular expenditure.

It is difficult to be more specific because these questions have not played a prominent role in debates over tax reform. The same can be said for cash method accounting. Acceptance of realization may require the use of the cash method if the primary concern is liquidity. This would explain the installment method and other means by which even accrual-basis taxpayers may report income from deferred payment sales (in the regular course of business or otherwise) as cash is received. If the problem is valuation, however, a market appraisal exists at the time accountants would recognize income under the accrual method (which would probably leave room for deferral for truly contingent payments).

Further, if accrual accounting is to be required for merchandising firms, it should probably be mandatory for large service businesses (accounting, law firms, and so on). The cash basis would then be reserved for the truly small business, which may have some claim for a simplified accounting procedure.

Comments by John B. Shoven

Although Jeremy Bulow and I have recently collaborated on papers about the taxation of business income,[15] I believe I can be fair in discussing this paper on the same subject that Bulow and E. Cary Brown have prepared.

This is a good paper, but I have some frustrations with the narrowness of its scope. Part of the problem is that Brookings has dealt with many of the important business income tax issues at previous conferences and plans to discuss others at future meetings.[16] Nevertheless, it is difficult to deal properly with the definition of business income without considering inflation, the possibility of integrating the individual and corporation income taxes, and the application of the individual income tax to capital and business income. Therefore I will violate the rules of the conference a bit and discuss some of these important issues briefly because they are not discussed in the paper. Before I do so, however, let me state why I think the paper is basically a sound document offering solid reasoning on many important points.

Brown and Bulow deal with the implementation of a Haig-Simons

15. "Inflation Accounting and Nonfinancial Corporate Profits: Physical Assets," *Brookings Papers on Economic Activity, 3:1975*, pp. 557–98; and "Inflation Accounting and Nonfinancial Corporate Profits: Financial Assets and Liabilities," ibid., *1:1976*, pp. 15–57.

16. See, for example, Henry J. Aaron, ed., *Inflation and the Income Tax* (Brookings Institution, 1976).

definition of income for business. They correctly interpret that definition as meaning that business income is equal to the distributions of the firm augmented by changes in net worth. They talk about implementing this concept of income in three different economic environments. The first, which will be familiar to economic theorists, is a world in which there are perfect and complete markets and no uncertainty. In such an economist's heaven, there is no difficulty in determining Haig-Simons income. Net worth would simply be the market value of assets minus the market value of liabilities, and calculating the change in net worth (to include in income) over a particular interval of time would be trivial. The second world adds uncertainty to the first, but since there are still complete markets, adding uncertainty does not really create any difficulties in calculating Haig-Simons business income. Finally, in coming down out of the theoretical clouds to the real world, some problems are encountered. Unfortunately, there are not perfect markets, not even adequate ones for most used physical assets. Since there are no market values for determining net worth and changes in net worth, one must impute values to assets and liabilities. The current system can be interpreted as trying to impute values to assets using adjusted original cost, the adjustment being given by the depreciation schedule that attempts to reflect the effect of wear and tear and obsolescence.

In dealing with the adequacy of adjusted original cost as an approximation of the value of an asset, inflation cannot be ignored. Unless the adjustment explicitly takes the change in price levels into account for assets with long useful lives, their value will be grossly distorted.

The authors enumerate the major deviations of the actual tax base from the Haig-Simons definition of income. They point out that special tax preferences provide subsidies to particular industries, certain payouts are expensed when they should be depreciated, and taxes on some incomes are deferred. The difference between accrual taxation and realization taxation in particular can be substantial for assets and liabilities with long lifetimes.

The following are among the issues that are not discussed in the paper:

1. The existence of a separate personal income tax is not taken into account. If the personal income tax followed the Haig-Simons definition, equity and bond appreciation would be included in the base.

Further, all business distributions would be included in the base. Therefore there would be no need for a separate business income tax. Some of the participants in this conference do not think that capital income should be taxed at all; it is even more doubtful that it should be taxed twice.

The current personal income tax system, however, does tax business income. Dividends and interest are fully taxed—except for the odd $100 dividend exclusion—and capital gains are partly taxed. Because capital gains are more lightly taxed at the personal level, perhaps dividends should be taxed more lightly than retained earnings if there is a separate business income tax.

The importance of the definition of business income does not depend on the existence of a business income tax. In fact, business income statistics have many uses other than as a tax base. I believe that the Haig-Simons definition of income provides the most informative and useful figures that a firm can record on its performance, and that it gives management an accurate guide regarding the wisdom of its investment decisions. But I question the need for a business income tax—even defined according to Haig and Simons—considering the existence of the personal income tax.

2. The current system is based on nominal figures that get less meaningful at higher inflation rates. I assume that Brown and Bulow agree that if inflation continues at high rates, it would be necessary to adjust business income to real values.

3. How should multinational corporations report their U.S. income, particularly in a world with floating exchange rates? Should they be forced to revalue their foreign assets and liabilities to current dollar values using the new exchange rates each year? If so, income will fluctuate widely. A related issue concerns the proper treatment of the earnings of the foreign subsidiaries of these companies.

4. To what extent should firms be allowed to choose the income they report? Currently, firms are offered a choice of inventory accounting methods and an even broader choice of depreciation accounting methods. They have substantial discretion regarding the timing of their income, because gains and losses on assets and liabilities are taxed on a realization basis. This clearly provides the opportunity to alter the timing of reported income, and there is substantial evidence that this opportunity is used to smooth the pattern of earnings. Should firms be allowed to have this long-run averaging and

smoothing ability? I personally vote no. Corporations not only have accounting alternatives and discretion in the timing of reported earnings but also are allowed to report higher income to their stockholders than to the Internal Revenue Service. The justification of such a practice is less than readily apparent.

5. To what extent should the total operations of the firm be consolidated in business income reporting? Currently, several large activities of firms are "off the balance sheet." This would include the performance of company-owned pension funds and much of a firm's leasing activities. Should a firm be forced to consolidate its pension fund assets into its accounts and reserves? In 1973 and 1974 pension funds owned by businesses lost a total of $55 billion in the stock market. These losses were not reported in annual reports and were not available as a tax deduction. The issue is to what extent those losses were real and whether they should be included in the calculations of taxable income. Another example of off-balance-sheet activities is the insurance reserve of Allstate Insurance, a Sears, Roebuck subsidiary. In 1974 the reserve sustained a $500 million loss in the stock market.

6. The banks are now discussing with the Financial Accounting Standards Board when they should revalue their less than secure loans. Nonfinancial corporations have similar problems, and railroads have numerous nonproductive assets. When should the fact that these assets are no longer valuable be reported?

To conclude, I am generally sympathetic with the Haig-Simons definition of income and the interpretation in this paper of that definition for business income. I am not sympathetic to business income taxation, however. If there must be a separate tax on business income, a number of major issues must be resolved. These include adjustments for inflation, the treatment of multinational corporations, the timing of income and expenses, the consolidation of off-balance-sheet activities, and the write-off of worthless loans and assets.

CHAPTER EIGHT

Summary of the Conference Discussion

EMIL M. SUNLEY, JR.

THE PRECEDING chapters provided the background for the two-day conference of tax lawyers and economists held at the Brookings Institution on December 10–11, 1976. This chapter summarizes the conferees' lively and wide-ranging discussion of the analytical and practical issues of designing a comprehensive income tax.

The Economic Definition of Income

The definition of income for tax purposes that has received the most support is the Haig-Simons concept. According to Haig, "Income is the *money value of the net accretion to one's economic power between two points of time.*"[1] It is the power to satisfy economic wants—consumption plus accumulation—and not the satisfactions themselves. After reviewing alternative definitions, Richard Goode concludes in the first paper that the Haig-Simons definition is the best one to use

1. Robert Murray Haig, "The Concept of Income—Economic and Legal Aspects," in Haig, ed., *The Federal Income Tax* (Columbia University Press, 1921), p. 7, reprinted in Richard A. Musgrave and Carl S. Shoup, eds., *Readings in the Economics of Taxation* (Irwin for the American Economic Association, 1959), p. 59.

for income tax purposes. The conference participants did not disagree with this conclusion, but some made it clear that in agreeing on the appropriate definition of income they were not necessarily accepting income as the appropriate base for taxation.

The most discussed topic was whether income should be taxed as it accrues, which is implied by the Haig-Simons definition of income, or as it is realized, which is the practice under U.S. law. Under the accrual concept, for example, changes in the value of corporate stock would be recognized each year whether or not the stock was sold. It was generally agreed that a taxpayer receives a monetary advantage when taxes are postponed—he is able to earn interest on the deferred tax. Goode concludes that measures to reduce the advantage of deferring the realization of income should be considered. In discussing capital gains (chapter 4), James W. Wetzler suggests that gains and losses should be taxed only when realized, but he would impose a deferral charge to approximate the taxation of gains and losses as they accrue.

The conference participants did not get into a number of the difficulties in defining income, such as the treatment of gifts. They did, however, discuss including imputed household income (such as the value of housewives' services), changes in capital values due to fluctuations in interest rates, and the value of government services. One participant believed that it would be better to make even a rough approximation of the imputed earnings of the spouse who remains at home rather than to make no imputation, but there was little support for this view.

Changes in the interest rate at which expected future yields are discounted is an important source of capital gains and losses. For example, if the market interest rate declines, outstanding bonds with a fixed coupon increase in value. This does represent an immediate increase in the consumption power of the owners. If, however, the owners are intending to live off the interest income stream, they are in some sense worse off. As long as they hold the bonds, their interest income is not increased. Once the bonds mature, they will find that they are not able to reinvest in comparable bonds with as high a yield. Most participants agreed that, in theory, changes in capital values due to fluctuations in interest rates should be in the tax base.

Some economists have argued that a consistent application of the Haig-Simons definition of income would require that the value of government services be included in the tax base, because some of these services provide satisfactions that resemble those from private consumption. The participants agreed that it is impractical to include the value of all government services. It was generally recognized that there is a great difference between such items as the imputed rental value of a house that has a market value the owner can realize and such benefits from public goods as national defense and general government administration. But the value of specific government payments to individuals, such as cash transfers, presents no valuation problems and should be in the comprehensive tax base.

Personal Deductions

To maintain federal revenues, reduction of the income tax rates for low- and middle-income families would require broadening the tax base by eliminating or pruning the personal deductions—for medical expenses, taxes, interest, charitable contributions, and the like—and including most employee benefits and transfer payments in the tax base. The conference participants had considerable difficulty with the idea of slashing personal deductions. Much of the discussion focused on the specifics and merits of the various deductions. Although many of the deductions were regarded as either unnecessary or too generous, simply eliminating all of them received little support. In fact, the only point of full agreement was that the gasoline tax deduction should be eliminated.

The relative merits of deductions versus credits were discussed at some length. A deduction reduces the income subject to tax and thus provides a tax saving equal to the taxpayer's marginal tax rate times the amount of the deduction. Tax credits, on the other hand, are offset against the amount of tax liability otherwise owed; the tax saving does not depend on the taxpayer's marginal tax rate. The participants generally agreed with John F. Due, the author of the paper on personal deductions (chapter 2), that a deduction is appropriate where the purpose of the tax allowance is to refine the definition of income; a tax credit may be appropriate where the purpose is to provide an incentive for certain types of expenditures. It is not always clear whether a deduction or a credit would be appropriate for the particular allowances now in the law. Most participants favored a deduction for medical expenses in excess of a reasonable floor, in order to limit the deduction to extraordinary expenses. A credit was regarded as more appropriate, however, if the purpose of the allowance is to provide partial medical insurance through the income tax.

Proposals for reform of the personal deductions—floors, credits, and vanishing deductions or credits—often conflict with the goal of tax simplification. Credits are inherently more complex than deductions because taxpayers who do not itemize their personal deductions would have to keep records to claim the credit. Credits also require slightly more arithmetic, and rules must be established for the order in which they can be claimed, since some tax credits can be carried back to prior tax years or carried forward to future years. One participant, noting the recent trend toward new tax credits, facetiously suggested that the major tax reform in the future might be the introduction of the standard tax credit for taxpayers who do not want to itemize their credits.

Placing floors under various itemized deductions would complicate the tax return. Floors would also provide an incentive to bunch deductions in alternate years, or every third year, so as to avoid the effect of the floor as much as possible. Vanishing credits and deductions are even less attractive than floors, since they add considerable complexity and generate concealed increases in marginal tax rates.

One participant questioned the basic article of faith of most comprehensive tax base proponents, namely, that broadening the tax base would permit tax rates to be reduced dramatically. The conventional reasoning assumes that the various tax incentives for certain types of expenditures are not replaced by direct expenditure programs. To the extent that direct expenditure programs are substituted, revenue would not be available to finance the marginal rate reductions. The same participant also pointed out that the recent literature on optimal taxation calls into question whether all income should be taxed at the same rate. In the world of optimal taxation, different kinds of income would be taxed differently, depending on the elasticity of factor supplies.

If personal deductions cannot be slashed, the question becomes what to do with the standard deduction. Increases in the standard deduction switch taxpayers away from itemizing—clearly a major simplification for those taxpayers. An increase in the income range in which the percentage standard deduction applies is equivalent to a reduction in marginal tax rates over that range. For example, with a percentage standard deduction of 16 percent of adjusted gross income, a taxpayer in the 25 percent nominal tax bracket is really in only a 21 percent (25 × 0.84) effective tax rate bracket, since he is taxed on only 84 cents of each dollar. Removing the ceiling from the percentage standard deduction achieves much of the equity and efficiency gains that can be achieved by putting a floor under itemized deductions. The revenue cost of converting taxpayers to the standard deduction may be quite high if the increase in the standard deduction provides a tax reduction for taxpayers already using it.

Employee Benefits and Transfer Payments

The discussion of my own paper on employee benefits and transfer payments (chapter 3) centered primarily on the appropriate tax treatment of private pensions, social security, and means-tested transfer payments. Most participants agreed that other employee benefits, such as premiums for group term life insurance and transfer payments, should be included in a comprehensive income tax base. The discussion focused on the most difficult conceptual issues.

Under present law, employer contributions to private pension plans are deductible by employers when paid, even though they are not considered current income to employees. Earnings on the accumulations in pension trusts also are not taxed currently. Benefits paid by pension plans are considered taxable income, subject to the tax-free recovery of any contributions made by the beneficiaries to the pension plan.

My conclusion was that employees should be taxed currently on employer contributions if they are vested. Pension benefits in excess of amortized contributions should be taxed when received. Pension fund earnings should remain nontaxable, but the benefits should be taxable to the extent that they exceed contributions (amortized over the life expectancy of the beneficiary). This would ensure that the earnings of pension funds are treated as favorably as the accrued capital gains of individual investors.

It was pointed out that there are various degrees of vesting and that taxation of benefit rights when they vest may trigger large increases in tax liabilities. Some participants favored allowing employers to claim a tax deduction only when benefits are taxable to the employee. This would be simpler than the proposal in chapter 3, and it would ensure that employers receive a tax deduction only when employees recognize income. Another alternative would be to impose a withholding tax on employer contributions to pension plans, which would then be allowed as a credit when the employee later reported pension income. The withholding tax would be set at a rate to offset, on the average, the benefits of tax deferral inherent in the present system of taxing pensions. In addition, it was pointed out that cumulative averaging (which is discussed below) would reduce the deferral advantage of private pensions. One participant argued that Congress intended to provide an incentive for nondiscriminatory retirement programs outside social security. A value judgment must be made on whether this incentive should be eliminated or reduced.

There was even less agreement on how social security should be treated. If viewed as unearned transfers, benefits should be taxed in full with no recognition of previous employer or employee contributions. A common arrangement in a number of countries is to tax benefits but permit employees to take a tax deduction for any contribution they make. Unlike present law, this scheme would reduce federal revenues.

If viewed as insurance, social security benefits should be treated in the same way as private pensions. On this basis, employees would be taxable on both employer and employee contributions, and benefits (other than health and death) would be taxed to the extent that they exceeded amortized contributions.

The general conclusion was that it is difficult to separate the transfer and insurance aspects of social security.[2] Until this issue can be sorted out, it would be virtually impossible to agree on how social security should be taxed. Nevertheless, there seemed to be a consensus that social security is undertaxed now regardless of whether it is viewed as insurance or a tax-transfer program.

The conclusion in chapter 3 is that transfer payments made under programs with stringent means tests, such as supplemental security income and aid to families with dependent children, should not be included in the base of the comprehensive income tax. The means tests already subject benefits to tax rates of 50 to 100 percent, and presumably the benefit levels are set so as to meet certain disposable income targets. If the benefits were taxed, the benefit levels would have to be increased to meet the target levels of disposable income.

2. For a detailed discussion of these issues, see Alicia H. Munnell, *The Future of Social Security* (Brookings Institution, 1977), chap. 3.

On the other hand, many of the conference participants felt that welfare programs with stringent means tests should be included in the tax base. Unless they are included, families receiving payments under these programs may be better off than other families who only receive fully taxable income.

Capital Gains and Losses

Under present law half of net long-term capital gains are included in the tax base and gains are taxed only when realized, not as they accrue. Capital losses can be offset only against capital gains and, in the case of individuals, a limited amount of ordinary income. The treatment of capital gains is the major tax preference benefiting high-income families. Its elimination would permit substantial reductions in marginal tax rates in the upper brackets.

The Haig-Simons definition of income implies accrual taxation of capital gains and losses. In chapter 4, Wetzler rejects this approach as unworkable because of the serious problems of valuating assets that are not sold frequently. Instead, he proposes to tax capital gains in full when realized or when transferred as a gift or at death and to permit full deductions for capital losses. In addition, a deferral charge might be introduced to neutralize, on the average, the advantage of tax deferral.

The discussion focused primarily on simplification, the treatment of losses, the deferral charge, and gains at death. Most of the participants accepted repeal of the 50 percent exclusion for capital gains and constructive realization for property transferred by gift or at death but were quite skeptical about the deferral charge and full deduction for losses.

A major simplification of the tax law would be achieved if the distinction between capital gains and ordinary income were eliminated. Wetzler's proposal would greatly reduce the tax advantage of capital gains but would not lead to much simplification. Repeal of the 50 percent exclusion alone would simplify the tax law and the tax form, but the deferral charge would add complications. It would still be necessary to distinguish between transactions giving rise to the deferral charge and transactions giving rise to ordinary income.

The definitional problems and the administrative difficulties associated with capital gains would be largely eliminated if the realization principle were retained and capital gains were fully taxed (without a deferral charge), and losses could be offset against other income.[3] Several participants felt that the simplification achieved under this scheme would be purchased at too high a price. Taxpayers would have an incentive to realize losses and to defer gains and would continue to have the advantage of tax deferral. The resulting whipsaw effect might require limiting the deductibility of losses to gains, reintroducing the complexity of a definitional distinction between capital gains and ordinary income. One participant, however, suggested that the deductibility of losses would have to be limited only for marketable securities. Other assets now giving rise to capital gains are either already provided ordinary loss treatment or do not present much opportunity to time losses for tax advantages. Full taxation of capital gains and full deductibility of capital losses, except those from marketable securities, would simplify the definitional problems and would eliminate the possibility of playing losses against gains to the detriment of the Treasury. The deferral advantage would remain, but this would be the price to pay for maximum simplification.

The deferral charge if properly constructed would neutralize the advantage of tax deferral on the average, but many taxpayers would view it as inequitable. Consider corporate stock that has been stable in price for nine years and takes a big jump in the tenth. A taxpayer who has held the stock for ten years would be subject to a large deferral charge. Another taxpayer who has held the stock for only a year would not be subject to the deferral charge.

In constructing an appropriate deferral charge, consideration must be given to the interest rate to be used. One discussant suggested that it would be reasonable to look at the federal government borrowing cost over the holding period. One can also argue that the marginal borrowing cost of the average taxpayer should be used if the purpose of the deferral charge is to make the taxpayer indifferent about whether he realizes or defers the gain.

Although the deferral charge is supposed to reduce or eliminate the advantage of tax deferral, several participants believed that because of investor psychology it might actually increase lock-in. The deferral charge would encourage taxpayers to hold assets with very large encumbered tax liabilities, even though these liabilities would

3. Some complexity would still remain. Presumably all realizations would not be recognized—for example, corporate reorganizations and sales of homes.

ultimately have to be paid at the time of death. Simple arithmetic, however, demonstrates that a deferral charge reduces or eliminates the tax advantage of delaying the realization of gains. The present value of the tax on the gain is little affected by when the gain is realized or by whether the gain is taxed at death.

Participants generally supported taxing unrealized gains on property transferred by gift or at death. This would tax the right person, and it would be simpler to administer than the carry-over-of-basis rule provided by the Tax Reform Act of 1976.

Homeowner Preferences

Economists have long recognized that housing is favored under the federal income tax. Homeowners may exclude the imputed rental value of their homes from income. In addition they are permitted to deduct mortgage interest payments and property taxes in determining taxable income. Rental housing is also favored to the extent that the owners are permitted to depreciate the properties for tax purposes more rapidly than the actual decline in economic value. On balance the federal income tax favors homeownership over rental housing. Thus the tax system induces investment in housing and distorts housing decisions toward homeownership.

In chapter 5 William F. Hellmuth suggests that a theoretically pure income tax would include in the tax base the imputed net rent from the ownership of a home or other durable assets. At the same time, he recognized that to do so would be impractical. One of the discussants characterized taxing imputed net rent as the last step on the stairway to the paradise of a comprehensive income tax. Another participant, however, pointed out that most of the measurement problems associated with taxing imputed net rent—depreciation and repairs and maintenance—are essentially the same as those that arise in taxing income from business assets. But even he agreed that treating each homeowner as a business would not serve the purpose of simplification. Businesses may be able to handle the complexities of income measurement; the average homeowner cannot, and he may have difficulty understanding why income is being imputed to him.

If imputed rent is not to be included in the tax base, the issue becomes whether equity and efficiency would be improved if the itemized deductions permitted homeowners were repealed. Under present law the mere fact of homeownership often provides the floor that permits a taxpayer to take advantage of other itemized deductions, and this further magnifies the advantage of homeownership. If the taxpayer did not own a home, he would most likely claim the standard deduction. On the other hand, the existence of the standard deduction reduces the value of the deductions for homeowners.

The elimination of the mortgage interest deduction would introduce a tax distortion between homeowners who have a mortgage and those who do not but would reduce the distortion between homeowners with a mortgage and renters. On balance, elimination of the mortgage interest deduction would probably reduce tax distortions, although complex tracing rules would be required to prevent wealthy families from borrowing against other assets to finance a purchase of a home. Alternatively, the deductions for interest payments could be limited to the amount of investment income reported for tax purposes.

The elimination of the property tax deduction in itself would distort the choice between various state and local taxes unless all taxes were no longer deductible. Repealing the deduction for all state and local taxes received little support, however.

During the discussion of homeowner preferences several participants pointed out that tax preferences become capitalized. The elimination of preferences then results in windfall losses. For example, eliminating the homeowner preferences might result in a sharp drop in home values, particularly the most expensive homes owned by high-bracket taxpayers who benefit most from the tax preferences. Most participants agreed that transition rules would be needed to minimize these windfall losses. There was some feeling, however, that in the past Congress has adopted transition rules that are too generous.

Several participants suggested that if the homeowner preferences remain intact, a tax deduction might be extended to renters as a means of reducing the difference in the tax treatment of homeowners and renters. This might also refine the measure of ability to pay as it applies to taxpayers who maintain a separate household and to those who do not. But the proposed renter deduction received little support.

Taxation of the Family

The proper unit of taxation under the income tax was probably the most difficult issue discussed during the conference. The problem is basically one of conflicting objectives. On the one hand, a major policy objective of U.S. tax law since 1948 has been that married couples with the same income should pay the same tax, regardless of how the sources of the income are split between the husband and wife. On the other hand, many contend that the tax system should be neutral in its treatment without regard for the taxpayers' choice of marital status or living or sharing arrangements.

Michael J. McIntyre and Oliver Oldman, the authors of the paper on this subject (chapter 6), as well as some participants, contended that although the Haig-Simons definition of income does not *determine* any particular method of taxing the family, it provides some guidance as to the appropriate taxable person or taxable units. The reasoning was as follows: if consumption plus change in net worth is the appropriate definition, it seems equally appropriate that the taxpayer on any particular item of consumption or savings should be the person who did the consuming or saving.

McIntyre and Oldman's reasoning was not generally accepted. Most of the participants affirmed the traditional viewpoint that the Haig-Simons definition of income simply defines the tax base and does not give any guidance in deciding who should be taxed on the income.

Under present law the income of husbands and wives is aggregated and tax is paid under the wide-bracket joint-return rate schedule; the income of children (or other dependents) is not aggregated with that of the parents but is taxed separately under the rate schedule for single persons. Single individuals rightly contend that if they were to marry someone with little or no income, their taxes would go down because they would be able to use the tax rate schedule for married couples filing jointly. At the same time, when husbands and wives earn nearly equal incomes, they rightly contend that they would pay less tax if they were not married and if each were permitted to use the rate schedule for single persons. They would also be permitted two separate standard deductions (which is more generous than the standard deduction allowed if they are married) and a number of less important tax benefits. For married couples in which one spouse is the source of all or almost all of the couple's income, marriage generally provides a net tax benefit, especially at middle- and upper-middle-income levels.

One solution to the conflict of objectives would be to replace the progressive rate schedules with a proportional rate. A per capita allowance—either a deduction or a tax credit—would provide some degree of progressivity in average tax rates. One conference participant advocated this solution, but his suggestion was ignored, presumably because it would sacrifice too much of the progressivity of the income tax, particularly at higher income levels.

Some participants, who believed that marital status or living arrangements are too fragile a thing on which to hang important tax consequences, suggested that the federal income tax should move to mandatory separate returns. It was pointed out, however, that under mandatory separate returns, married couples would still have a tax advantage over two single individuals. The married couple would be able to shift between them their property income, earnings in community property states, and possibly itemized deductions to achieve a kind of averaging that would not be available to a single person.

Other participants favored reducing the "tax penalty" on two-earner families by permitting them to claim a tax deduction or credit based on the earnings of the spouse with the lesser earnings. This approach can eliminate or moderate the "marriage penalty" on such families. It would keep the household as the basic unit of taxation, but like the proposal for mandatory separate returns, it would no longer ensure that two families with the same income paid the same tax. An important reason for retaining the household as the basic filing unit is that it would surely be the basic unit of any negative income tax. The positive and negative tax systems can only be integrated if the filing unit is the same under both systems.

An ideal solution to the problem would be to impute income to married couples with only one working spouse to reflect the value of domestic and other services performed and leisure enjoyed, but this route was generally considered too impractical for serious consideration. One participant suggested that a second-best alternative would be to permit a separate tax deduction for each full-time earner, with the deduction scaled down for part-time earners. This approach would improve tax equity between one-earner and two-earner families and also between no-earner and one-earner families, but if the deduction were large enough to offset the current tax advantages on unearned and imputed income, it would result in either a massive revenue loss or a large increase in the tax on property income.

Decisions about the tax treatment of the family raise efficiency issues as well as fairness issues. For example, the labor supply of wives to the market as opposed to the home is much more elastic than that of husbands. This means that the inefficiency resulting from the progressive tax on wages is much greater in the case of wives than of husbands. On efficiency grounds a strong case can be made for decreasing the tax on the earnings of wives and increasing it on the earnings of husbands. If one follows this efficiency logic, however, one would end up with a highly differentiated tax system that would strike most people as unjust, unworkable, and having no obvious appeal. Most participants agreed that fairness, rather than efficiency, was the primary concern for tax policymakers in the taxation of the family.

The Measurement of Business Income

Income under the Haig-Simons definition as applied to a business firm is equal to the change in net worth plus any distributions to the owners less any capital contributions received by the firm. It can be more simply defined as the change in net worth plus any *net* distributions to the owners.

In chapter 7, E. Cary Brown and Jeremy I. Bulow point out that in a world of perfect capital markets the increase in the value of the firm can be determined by market values. When capital markets are imperfect, however, business income can be measured only imperfectly. The basic problem is matching income and expense: when should income be included in the tax base and when should capital expenditures be deducted?

Many participants found it difficult to discuss the measurement of business income without dealing with inflation and the relationship between corporate and individual income taxes, but under the ground rules of the conference these topics were ruled out of order.[4] One participant observed that Congress may go easy on the measurement of business income because there are no tax adjustments for inflation and because of the burden of taxation on corporate income when there is a separate corporate tax.

---

4. Brookings held a conference in 1975 on inflation accounting for tax purposes. See Henry J. Aaron, ed., *Inflation and the Income Tax* (Brookings Institution, 1976). For a discussion of integration of the individual and corporate taxes, see George F. Break and Joseph A. Pechman, *Federal Tax Reform: The Impossible Dream?* (Brookings Institution, 1975), pp. 90–104; and Charles E. McLure, Jr., "Integration of the Personal and Corporate Income Taxes: The Missing Element in Recent Tax Reform Proposals," *Harvard Law Review*, vol. 88 (January 1975), pp. 532–82.

Considerable concern was expressed about the present tax rules for depreciation. Most participants felt that tax depreciation should be made simpler and more certain. Some thought that guideline lives should be made mandatory and should reflect actual economic lives. Under present law, taxpayers have the option of using the asset depreciation range system with a range of tax lives for each class of assets or of selecting tax lives based on "facts and circumstances." Although recognizing that there probably is no objective way to measure depreciation, some participants believed that the present rules are too generous. In recent years the United States has moved toward expensing capital assets. If expensing were ever adopted, this would be equivalent to making the present value of taxes zero on the marginal investment.

It was pointed out that the amount of depreciation claimed for tax purposes far exceeds the amount claimed for financial reporting. But very little support was expressed for the proposal to require taxpayers to limit the claim for tax depreciation to that claimed for financial reporting.

One participant argued that the expensing of research and development expenditures provides an incentive that may be justified because of positive externalities. He also suggested that because of negative externalities, advertising expenditures should not be expensed.

It was pointed out that human capital is treated more favorably than investments in machinery and equipment under present law. Investments in machinery and equipment must be capitalized and written off over their useful life. The bulk of human capital is financed out of forgone earnings; since forgone earnings are not taxed, investments in human capital are, in effect, expensed.

On the question of when income should be recognized, several participants indicated that the cash method and the installment method of accounting may provide unrealistic measures of business income. Some concern was expressed about the ability of firms to choose the timing of when income is recognized by selecting the most advantageous methods of depreciation and inventory accounting and by realizing gains and losses on assets.

The adoption of cumulative averaging would leave the tax burden of an individual invariant to the timing of recognition of income and expenses for tax purposes. If cumulative averaging were accompanied by taxation of unrealized capital gains on assets transferred by gift or at death, it would also eliminate the need for a separate tax on corporate income. Under this method the taxpayer would have to compute his adjusted cumulated income for the period to date and the present value of past tax payments. The taxpayer would then compute the total tax liability from a table that would depend on the number of years the taxpayer had been averaging. The current payment due is simply the difference between this total tax liability and the present value of past taxes.[5] Except for the necessity of keeping cumulative records, averaging along these lines would not be complicated for the taxpayer and would be simpler than the deferral charge proposed for capital gains. Most critics of cumulative averaging, however, believe that taxpayers would not be able to understand it, and thus it is probably not feasible. Although most of the participants believed that its legislative prospects are dim, cumulative averaging does provide a conceptual basis for discussing many of the issues raised by comprehensive income taxation.

Priorities for Tax Reform

In an effort to summarize the conclusions of the conference, the authors of each paper were asked to indicate their highest priority for tax change, whether the adoption of the change would require a change in direct expenditures, and whether the change would contribute to tax simplification. The suggestions included repealing the deductions for state gasoline and state-local sales taxes; including unemployment insurance benefits in the tax base; eliminating the 50 percent exclusion and the alternative tax for capital gains; limiting the deductions for the property tax and for interest (other than business interest) in excess of investment income; modifying the income splitting arrangement; and taxing capital gains on accrual. The authors of the papers on capital gains and business income gave the reduction or elimination of the capital gains preferences the highest priority.

According to the authors, not all of the revenue that might be

5. For a fuller description of cumulative averaging, see William Vickrey, *Agenda for Progressive Taxation* (Ronald Press, 1947), pp. 172–95. See also William Vickrey, "Cumulative Averaging after Thirty Years," in Richard M. Bird and John G. Head, eds., *Modern Fiscal Issues: Essays in Honor of Carl S. Shoup* (University of Toronto Press, 1972), pp. 117–33.

gained from eliminating tax preferences could be used for rate reduction. Unemployment benefits would have to be increased so that the one-earner family with no property income would have no reduction in disposable income. Part of the revenue from fuller taxation of capital gains might be needed to reduce the government deficit to offset any adverse effect on national saving. Limitations on the property and sales tax deductions would probably require an expansion of grants-in-aid to state and local governments. The revenue might also be used to finance a step toward integrating the individual and corporation income taxes.

Although the emphasis in Congress is shifting toward greater simplicity, there was substantial agreement that comprehensive income taxation in its purist form would provide little simplification. In fact, some of the most far-reaching proposals advocated by the authors—accrual taxation of capital gains, modification of income splitting, and limitations on the deductibility of interest—would add considerable complexity to the tax law. On the other hand, some aspects of comprehensive income taxation, such as the elimination of itemized deductions, would simplify the filing of tax returns. Comprehensive income taxation would also reduce the complications faced by tax lawyers and would simplify tax planning. Undoubtedly a trade-off exists between equity and simplification, but there is considerable difference of opinion about where the line should be drawn.

Despite the theoretical shortcomings of the present income tax, the participants agreed that tax experts can be too critical. Although the present U.S. income tax has numerous shortcomings when evaluated on the highest standards of equity and economic efficiency, it is considerably better than any other alternative. It is a progressive tax that the vast majority of taxpayers generally regard as equitable. While some of the participants favored the introduction of a consumption tax, none recommended less reliance on the individual income tax in favor of any other tax now in the federal tax system.

The Yield of a
Comprehensive Income Tax

JOSEPH J. MINARIK*

THE PURPOSE of this appendix is to provide a yardstick for the measurement of effective rates of tax under a comprehensive income tax system, to determine the potential yield of such a tax under present rates, and to illustrate the degree to which the tax rates can be reduced under the comprehensive system and still raise the same revenue as the present income tax. The first section explains the difference between comprehensive income and adjusted gross income, the income concept used in the present income tax. The second section presents estimates of the revenue yield of an entire comprehensive tax package. This is followed by a discussion of the effects of eliminating most of the itemized deductions in current law. The final sections illustrate the distributional consequences of various tax rate schedules and personal exemptions and standard deductions, combined with the comprehensive income tax.

A Comprehensive Measure of Income

Comprehensive income (CI) is more comprehensive than adjusted gross income (AGI), which is the base for the current personal income

* The author would like to thank Robin Mary Donaldson, Richard Booth, and Wing Thye Woo for computer programming assistance. Henry J. Aaron, Joseph A. Pechman, and Emil M. Sunley, Jr., provided helpful discussion. Any errors are the responsibility of the author.

tax. CI includes virtually all of AGI and has the following additional elements:

Capital gains. One-half of long-term capital gains is excluded from AGI. This preferential treatment is sometimes claimed to protect such gains from overtaxation due to inflation and the extra "bite" of progressive rates in a single year on gains accumulated over several years. As has been argued elsewhere in this volume, the overtaxation of capital gains is more than offset by the benefits of tax deferral until realization, and the specific problems mentioned here could best be dealt with through specific tools such as inflation indexing and income averaging. In designing a comprehensive measure of income, moreover, it is important to include all resources made available to the filer during the accounting period. CI includes all realized capital gains in full, rather than the alternative approach of including gains as they accrue.

Excluded dividends. Under 1976 law, the first $100 of dividend income was excluded from AGI ($200 on a joint return if each spouse had dividend income of $100 or more). This exclusion is claimed to encourage stock ownership and to offset somewhat the so-called double taxation of distributed corporate income. For the purpose of measuring effective tax burdens, however, all dividends should be included in income. Accordingly, the dividend exclusion is restored to CI.

Interest on state and local securities. Interest on state and local government securities is currently tax exempt. This exemption provides a subsidy to the states and localities, because the interest rates on such securities are lower than they would be otherwise, but the cost to the Treasury Department is greater than the subsidy. The most likely policy remedy is to offer states and localities the option of issuing taxable bonds, for which the federal government would pay a partial interest subsidy. For purposes of assessing tax burdens, however, tax-exempt interest should be included in the income concept in full, even though only a portion of such income would be included in the tax base under an optional taxable bond proposal. CI therefore includes all tax-exempt state and local bond interest, but for calculating tax liabilities such interest is reduced by the 86 percent of the total that is assumed to remain tax exempt.

Life insurance interest. Interest earned on life insurance policies is included in AGI only when it is realized (that is, at the maturation of the policy) and only to the extent that it exceeds the insurance company's loading charge and the cost of the insurance protection associated with the policy. Such interest is therefore favored with both tax deferral and a partial (in most cases a full) tax-free status upon realization. Life insurance interest is included in CI as it accrues, and without offset for loading or insurance costs.

Capital gains on homes. The tax law in 1976 excluded capital gains on principal residences from taxation if the proceeds of the sale were reinvested in homes within eighteen months. In addition, persons over sixty-five years of age could exclude capital gains on the first $20,000 of the sales price ($35,000 in 1977 and later years). CI includes all realized gains from home sales.

Constructively realized capital gains. The accrued appreciation of property that changes hands at death or by gift is untaxed at present.[1] To remedy this defect, the taxation of such gains as if they were realized has been frequently proposed. Such constructively realized gains are included in CI; assets whose appreciation is included are stocks, bonds, and homes.

Imputed rent on homes. The owner of a home receives "income" from it in the form of housing services, in the same sense that the owner of a bond receives income in the form of interest; the only difference is that the income from the home is nonmonetary. That income can be estimated by subtracting from the gross rental value of the home the expenses of operating and maintaining it (including depreciation, repairs, interest paid on mortgages, and property taxes). CI includes net imputed rent computed in this way.

Employee fringe benefits. Under 1976 law, an employer's contribution toward his employees' health or life insurance policies is not taxable to the employees. CI includes the amount of insurance premiums paid on behalf of employees. Another insurance program that should be included in income is prepaid legal insurance, but it is too new and too small to estimate accurately.

Employer contributions to pension programs are also an issue in income taxation. The tax on such contributions is now deferred until benefits are paid upon retirement. In CI, however, these contributions are considered as income when they are made, and benefit payments of such principal are not included. Benefit payments of interest earned on such contributions over the working year are included in income, however.

Social insurance. Worker social security payroll taxes were taxed under 1976 law; benefits and employer taxes were not. All the contributions of the self-employed were taxed. Social security encompasses several different insurance programs and any reasonable approach to the

1. This situation has been modified somewhat by the Tax Reform Act of 1976. Accrued gains on property transferred at death or by gift are not subject to the income tax, but the cost basis for the recipient now remains the basis of the donor, whereas before the act this was true only of gifts. Gains passed on through bequest would avoid tax in perpetuity under prior law; they would avoid tax under present law only if they were not realized by sale.

measurement of income and taxation must consider each program separately.

Retirement and survivors' benefits account for 75 percent (4.375 percent/5.85 percent) of the employee and employer social security payroll taxes, 78 percent (6.185 percent/7.9 percent) of the self-employed payroll tax, and about 75 percent of all benefits. The tax treatment of *contributions* for retirement purposes is much the same as that for private pensions—employee contributions are taxed while employer contributions are not—but the tax-free status of social security *benefits* contrasts sharply with the taxation of all but previously taxed capital under private pensions. This unequal treatment is exaggerated by the progressive benefit calculation formula for social security and by the substantial "minimum benefit" paid to retirees with very short work histories. CI includes both employees' and employers' contributions for retirement purposes and taxes only the amount of the benefits that exceeds the contributions made by, and on behalf of, the employee.

The tax treatment of survivors' insurance contributions is the same as the private life insurance analog, with employee contributions taxed and employer contributions tax free, but here the treatment of benefits is tax free in both cases. Taxing benefits in this case would have the same appeal as any other plan to tax widows and orphans, but including the insurance premium paid by employers in income is as reasonable in the public case as it is in the private; this practice is followed in CI.

Disability insurance is a relatively recent addition (1954) to the social security program; it accounted for 10 percent of payroll tax revenues in 1976 and 11 percent of benefits. Employee contributions to disability insurance are taxed and employer contributions are not, as would be the case with private insurance plans. The most commonly favored plan of tax reform would exclude contributions for this insurance from the tax base and would include benefits in full, treating disability insurance as a tax and transfer rather than as an insurance program. This approach would minimize the use of disability insurance as a source of tax-free income by those with other sources of income. CI follows this pattern by including disability insurance benefits in the tax base but excluding employer contributions for the insurance. Employee contributions are included in CI.

Medicare is the most recent addition to social security benefits. It constituted 15 percent of payroll tax revenues in 1976 and 15 percent of benefits. Again, tax treatment is the same as for private plans, with employee contributions taxed but employer contributions and benefits untaxed. (Of course, there is no real private analog to a public health insurance system where premiums are paid during working years for benefits to be received after retirement.) While the benefits of Medicare should certainly be captured in the tax base, taxing recipients of Medicare services would have the unfortunate effect of taxing the sick on in-kind income that cannot be related to taxpaying ability. Alternatively, the Medicare contributions through the payroll tax could be included in the tax base, with the benefits remaining tax exempt. CI includes employer as well as employee Medicare contributions and continues to exclude benefits.

Veterans' compensation and workmen's compensation. Government payments to veterans in the form of pensions, which are currently nontaxable, are included in CI. Workmen's compensation benefits are paid from state or private insurance funds contributed by employers. Under CI such benefits, rather than the insurance premiums that support them, are taxed in order to prevent their use as a source of tax-free supplemental income.

Transfer payments. All transfer payments are included in the comprehensive tax base. It must be understood, of course, that the personal exemption and standard deduction will shield the poor from taxation, regardless of their income sources; including transfers in the tax base will only affect those whose transfer receipts are large or who have other sources of income. Transfer receipts included in comprehensive income are aid to families with dependent children, supplemental security income, general assistance, and the bonus value of food stamps.

Medicaid, the means-tested program of medical insurance, is far more difficult to categorize for tax purposes. While participants in the program are better off than nonparticipants, all else being equal, the "income" from the program cannot be used to pay taxes. Taxation of those who receive services, as opposed to those who are enrolled, is clearly unsatisfactory; the medical services in case of illness are far less than a perfect substitute for health, and so the recipients are worse off after the services are received than they were before the illness. For this reason, Medicaid benefits are included in comprehensive income for measurement purposes but are not included in the tax base for later calculations.

The Distributions of CI and AGI Compared

With this broadening of AGI, CI encompasses a substantially larger base for taxation. Table A-1 shows the distribution of AGI by classes of AGI, together with the distribution of CI within the same classes. CI on the average is 27 percent greater than AGI, with tax returns in the lowest and highest classes having CI as a greater than average proportion

Table A-1. Distribution of Adjusted Gross Income and Comprehensive Income, by Adjusted Gross Income Class, 1977[a]
Income classes in thousands of dollars; amounts in billions of dollars

Adjusted gross income class	Adjusted gross income		Comprehensive income		Ratio of comprehensive income to adjusted gross income
	Amount	Percent of total	Amount	Percent of total	
0–2.5	18.75	1.58	87.91	5.84	4.69
2.5–5	40.78	3.44	60.84	4.04	1.49
5–7.5	59.15	4.99	78.40	5.21	1.33
7.5–10	81.59	6.88	102.92	6.84	1.26
10–15	207.10	17.46	253.41	16.83	1.22
15–20	226.34	19.08	272.57	18.10	1.20
20–25	167.73	14.14	199.11	13.23	1.19
25–30	110.19	9.29	129.49	8.60	1.18
30–50	149.30	12.59	174.64	11.60	1.17
50–100	64.12	5.41	74.33	4.94	1.16
100–200	32.05	2.70	37.11	2.46	1.16
200–500	17.33	1.46	20.54	1.36	1.19
500–1,000	3.85	0.32	4.93	0.33	1.28
1,000 and over	7.71	0.65	9.33	0.62	1.21
All classes	1,185.99	100.00	1,505.54	100.00	1.27

Source: Brookings 1970 MERGE File, projected to 1977. Figures are rounded.
a. For definition of comprehensive income, see text.

of AGI. Table A-2 shows CI and AGI distributed by classes of CI; the conclusions about the relationships between the two variables are unchanged.

Another question of some interest is how the various additions to AGI affect the final amounts of CI by income level. Table A-3 shows that individual components added to AGI vary in their effect on the different income levels. Transfer payments go largely to people in the lower income levels, for example, while excluded capital gains are concentrated in the upper income brackets. Imputed rent on homes is of the greatest relative importance in the low and middle brackets. Social security benefits in excess of past contributions are concentrated in the lower brackets, while employer social security contributions are received in proportion to wage and salary income over most of the income range.

Table A-2. Distribution of Adjusted Gross Income and Comprehensive Income, by Comprehensive Income Class, 1977[a]

Income classes in thousands of dollars; amounts in billions of dollars

Comprehensive income class	Adjusted gross income		Comprehensive income		*Ratio of comprehensive income to adjusted gross income*
	Amount	*Percent of total*	*Amount*	*Percent of total*	
0–2.5	8.49	0.72	13.76	0.91	1.62
2.5–5	25.89	2.18	48.83	3.24	1.89
5–7.5	43.07	3.63	71.75	4.76	1.67
7.5–10	58.61	4.94	82.83	5.50	1.41
10–15	158.97	13.41	203.57	13.52	1.28
15–20	193.10	16.28	239.25	15.89	1.24
20–25	182.21	15.37	223.22	14.82	1.23
25–30	140.35	11.84	170.19	11.30	1.21
30–50	220.97	18.64	267.13	17.74	1.21
50–100	84.83	7.15	101.13	6.71	1.19
100–200	35.70	3.01	42.08	2.79	1.18
200–500	20.06	1.69	24.67	1.64	1.23
500–1,000	4.74	0.40	6.40	0.42	1.35
1,000 and over	8.76	0.74	11.30	0.75	1.29
All classes	1,185.74	100.00	1,506.09	100.00	1.27

Source: Brookings 1970 MERGE File, projected to 1977. Figures are rounded,
a. For definition of comprehensive income, see text.

Effect of Broadened Tax Base on Aggregate Revenues

Of course, taxing the larger income base of CI will result in greatly increased tax revenues. Table A-4 shows the revenue that would be collected if the CI income concept were substituted for AGI but the deductions in the present tax law remained the same.[2] Total revenue would increase by $71.9 billion, or 43.5 percent. The distribution of these additional tax liabilities is also of interest; taxes are increased more than average for incomes up to $25,000 and for those from $500,000 to $1 million, in keeping with the findings on the changes in the tax base in tables A-2 and A-3.

2. As much as possible, changes in tax liability were insulated from the effects of provisions in the tax law that are keyed to the amount of AGI. For example, the medical expense deduction was carried over from the calculation based on AGI, and the refundable earned income credit was eliminated from the analysis.

Table A-3. Components of Comprehensive Income Expressed as Percentage of the Total, by Comprehensive Income Class, 1977[a]
Income classes in thousands of dollars

Comprehensive income class	Adjusted gross income	Imputed rent[b]	Transfers[c]	Social security benefits	Employer social security contributions	Employee benefits[d]	Capital gains[e]	Other	Total comprehensive income
0-2.5	61.8	2.8	11.1	16.4	3.1	3.9	0.6	0.3	100
2.5-5	53.0	2.3	17.0	22.3	2.0	2.3	1.1	-0.1[f]	100
5-7.5	60.0	1.7	15.5	17.0	2.3	2.7	1.1	-0.3[f]	100
7.5-10	70.8	1.4	11.3	9.2	2.9	3.4	1.3	-0.3[f]	100
10-15	78.0	1.2	6.4	4.1	3.6	4.7	1.4	0.7	100
15-20	80.6	1.0	4.0	2.1	3.9	5.7	1.3	1.5	100
20-25	81.5	0.9	2.7	1.3	3.8	6.7	1.5	1.7	100
25-30	82.4	0.8	1.9	1.0	3.4	7.1	1.8	1.6	100
30-50	82.7	0.7	1.3	0.8	2.7	8.0	2.1	1.7	100
50-100	83.9	0.5	1.0	0.6	1.3	6.8	3.8	2.1	100
100-200	84.8	0.6	0.2	0.2	0.5	3.7	5.5	4.5	100
200-500	81.4	0.6	0.3	0.1	0.2	2.4	8.5	6.6	100
500-1,000	74.0	0.5	0.0	0.0	0.1	1.3	17.5	6.5	100
1,000 and over	77.7	0.1	0.0	0.0	0.0	0.5	17.9	3.8	100
All classes	78.7	1.0	4.4	3.6	3.0	5.8	2.1	1.5	100

Source: Brookings 1970 MERGE File, projected to 1977. Figures are rounded.
a. For definition of comprehensive income, see text.
b. Imputed rental value of owner-occupied homes net of property taxes, mortgage interest, and operating expenses.
c. Aid to families with dependent children, supplemental security income, general assistance, unemployment compensation, workers' compensation, bonus value of food stamps, and insurance value of Medicaid.
d. Employer-paid premiums to life, health, and disability insurance and employer contribution to pension funds.
e. Excluded half of long-term capital gains and the dividend exclusion.
f. Negative numbers are adjustments for the excess of life expectancy recovery of employee contributions to pension plans over nontaxable pension benefits.

Table A-4. Revenue from Broadening the Tax Base and Reducing Personal Deductions, by Comprehensive Income Class, 1977[a]

Income classes in thousands of dollars; amounts in billions of dollars

Comprehensive income class	1976 tax law	Comprehensive income base, present deductions		Adjusted gross income base, limited deductions		Comprehensive income base, limited deductions	
		Amount	Percent increase	Amount	Percent increase	Amount	Percent increase
0–2.5	*	0.0	−100.0	*	118.0	*	143.1
2.5–5	0.4	1.0	156.7	0.6	58.3	1.7	323.3
5–7.5	1.8	3.6	101.1	2.5	39.5	5.1	184.1
7.5–10	3.6	6.3	74.3	4.9	35.0	8.2	125.2
10–15	13.1	20.3	55.0	17.2	31.3	25.0	91.0
15–20	19.3	28.6	48.4	24.2	25.6	33.5	73.6
20–25	21.5	31.5	46.5	26.0	20.9	36.2	68.6
25–30	19.1	27.5	43.4	23.1	20.6	31.8	66.0
30–50	37.3	53.3	42.6	45.5	21.8	62.4	67.0
50–100	20.9	28.4	35.8	26.7	27.6	34.9	66.5
100–200	12.4	15.4	24.4	16.1	30.4	19.4	56.7
200–500	8.9	11.4	28.8	11.1	25.6	13.8	55.5
500–1,000	2.2	3.3	46.9	2.9	32.0	4.0	81.5
1,000 and over	4.8	6.6	37.8	5.8	22.4	7.6	58.9
All classes	165.3	237.2	43.5	206.7	25.0	283.5	71.5

Source: Brookings 1970 MERGE File, projected to 1977. Figures are rounded.
a. For definition of comprehensive income and items included in limited deductions, see text.
* 0.05 or less.

Limitations on Personal Deductions and Credits

A truly comprehensive income tax would have far fewer permissible personal deductions together with the broadened income definition described above. If the deductions were distributed in some rough proportion to income, their reduction would not greatly affect relative tax burdens (although this would of course raise the aggregate yield of the tax).

Some of the most prominent candidates for elimination among the many personal deductions now in the law are:

Homeowner preferences. Homeowners now enjoy deductions for both mortgage interest and property taxes. One possible change would be to tax imputed rent and allow mortgage interest and property taxes to be deducted as costs of obtaining that income. This treatment is the same as that used in the national income accounts regarding home ownership.

Interest. All personal (nonbusiness or nonincome-producing) interest is deductible for purposes of the federal income tax. The mortgage interest deduction falls into this category, and the balance is composed largely of credit card and consumer installment interest. The deductibility of such interest could be terminated.

A second class of interest deductions is investment interest, that is, interest paid on borrowings used to purchase investment assets. Such interest is a cost of obtaining income and is legitimately deductible. The law in 1976 limited deductibility to $10,000 a year plus the sum of net investment income in order to prevent tax shelter abuses.[3] The application of this rule is difficult because the distinction between personal and investment interest is not always clear.[4] One way to simplify this deduction would be to eliminate all distinctions between personal and investment interest and to reduce the limitation on the interest deduction to investment income plus $5,000.

A third type of interest is noninvestment business interest. Such interest is also a cost of obtaining income and is deductible in calculating net business income. Protection against tax-sheltering manipulations in this area is provided by regulations. No change in the law is contemplated here.

State and local taxes. Apart from property taxes, state and local income, sales, and gasoline taxes are deductible for federal income tax purposes. For purposes of the comprehensive income tax, the deductibility of all personal tax payments is terminated.

Medical and dental expenses. The law in 1976 permitted a deduction for half of the premiums paid for medical insurance up to $150. In addition, medicines and drugs in excess of 1 percent of AGI, the balance of insurance premiums, and medical and dental expenses were deductible to the extent that they exceed 3 percent of AGI. A possible revision would allow the deduction of the excess of total medical, medical insurance, and drug expenses over 5 percent of AGI.

These simplifications in the personal deduction structure would add significantly to the income tax base. Table A-4 shows the total increase in revenue due to the elimination or modification of the deductions. It can be seen that total revenues would be increased by $41 billion (25 percent) over those received under 1976 law. Coupling the comprehensive base with this limited deduction system would make the total in-

3. The potential abuse would be the manipulation of borrowing to accelerate and exaggerate interest expenses and thereby shelter nonbusiness income from taxation.

4. For example, a person with $50,000 cash could buy a $50,000 home outright and borrow $50,000 to buy bonds (an investment loan), or he could buy the bonds with cash and the house through a mortgage (a personal loan). The distinction between these two cases is more artificial than real.

crease in revenues $118 billion, or 72 percent of liabilities under 1976
law.

Possible Comprehensive Tax Systems

There are two basic approaches to handling the additional revenue
generated by comprehensive income taxation. One is to use the additional revenue to fund subsidy programs with the same objectives as the
"tax expenditures" under 1976 law; the second is to reduce marginal tax
rates to return the additional revenue without affecting the progressivity
of the 1976 tax law. This section contains estimates of tax burdens by
income class under several possible tax systems assuming that all added
revenues are returned to the taxpayers, with varying effects on progressivity.

All the tax systems discussed here utilize the augmented CI tax base
and the sharply curtailed personal deduction system introduced earlier.
There remain decisions on the personal exemption, standard deduction,
and rate schedules to complete the tax system. A $1,000 exemption is
used. No additional exemption is provided for the aged and the blind,
unlike 1976 law. The standard deduction is $3,000 for single persons
and $4,000 for married couples filing jointly (half of that value for
separate returns).

The choice of a rate schedule involves a decision on income splitting
as well as on the rates themselves. The 1976 tax law allowed a married
couple to file a joint tax return under which their tax was the same as it
would have been had they filed separate returns with their income
divided equally. Single persons had their own tax rate schedule, which
was identical to the separate schedule for married couples except that its
rates were somewhat lower, between $4,000 and $44,000 of taxable
income. A fourth schedule was available for heads of households (those
who are not married but have dependents living with them) that yielded
taxes almost exactly halfway between those of the joint and single schedules for married couples. An alternative to this four-schedule system
would be to use only one schedule and to allow the personal exemptions
and deductions to differentiate among the different types of taxpayers.
Both the 1976 four-schedule system and a one-schedule system are used
in the quantitative estimates below.

Two of the simulations here are intended to leave the progressivity of
the income tax unchanged in the sense that the tax liabilities of classes
of taxpayers ranked by CI remain approximately unchanged. At the
same time, however, the ranking by CI is not the same as the ranking

by AGI because of the many exclusions in the latter income measure. This means that a taxpayer who had a comparatively low AGI because he benefited from the exclusions could be ranked relatively higher in the population when CI is the measurement criterion and would be paying approximately the same taxes as those at his CI (rather than AGI) level. Another factor to consider is the inevitable effect of comprehensive taxation on the relative liabilities of married and single taxpayers. The reduction of homeowner preferences and the elimination of income splitting systematically favor single persons, especially those with low incomes (because they are even less likely to own homes than other singles). Therefore any comprehensive tax that maintains current progressivity among marrieds will not do so among single persons and vice versa, and any scheme that maintains progressivity among all units independent of family attachments will have systematic effects on progressivity among both married and single taxpayers considered separately.

The first tax system calculated here has current progressivity among joint tax returns. It utilizes a four-schedule system, and thus progressivity varies somewhat from the patterns of returns filed by single persons and heads of households in 1976. Rates for this system run from 10 percent in the lowest bracket to 44 percent in the highest. The second system is identical to the first, except that it uses only one tax schedule and maintains progressivity among all units regardless of their household situations. Its rates run from 13 to 43 percent. The third system is identical to the first except that the rates have been redrawn to yield a more progressive tax system; they range from 7 to 48 percent. The fourth system is identical to the second except that it has been altered for a more progressive effect; its rates run from 10 to 47 percent. The fifth system is less progressive than the 1976 tax system. Because it utilizes one constant tax rate, any distinction among rate schedules for different types of households is meaningless. It uses a tax rate of 17.7 percent.

Table A-5 shows the tax liabilities of the five tax systems by income class. Systems 1 and 2 have the intended effect of nearly replicating liabilities in 1976, while the other systems have predictable effects. Systems 3 and 4 reduce tax liabilities in the lowest classes and raise those at the top by about 10 percent. System 5 is substantially less progressive than the 1976 system.

Changes in Individual Tax Liability

It should be apparent from these results that the tax rate schedule can be drawn in such a way as to obtain virtually any desired average progressivity once the enlarged tax base has been defined. But it is not

Table A-5. Revenue under Five Comprehensive Tax Systems, by Comprehensive Income Class, 1977[a]
Income classes in thousands of dollars; amounts in billions of dollars

Comprehensive income class	1976 tax law	System 1		System 2		System 3		System 4		System 5	
		Amount	Percent change	Amount	Percent change	Amount	Percent change	Amount	Percent change	Amount	Percent change
0–2.5	*	0.0	−100.0	0.0	−100.0	0.0	−100.0	0.0	−100.0	0.0	−100.0
2.5–5	0.4	0.1	−66.8	0.2	−56.8	0.1	−75.2	0.1	−66.8	0.2	−41.2
5–7.5	1.8	1.5	−14.5	1.7	−3.6	1.2	−32.2	1.4	−24.7	2.4	31.2
7.5–10	3.6	3.4	−5.5	3.7	1.4	2.9	−21.5	2.9	−19.1	5.0	37.0
10–15	13.1	12.9	−1.4	13.2	0.9	11.0	−16.3	10.9	−17.1	17.5	33.4
15–20	19.3	19.4	0.9	19.4	0.5	17.4	−9.8	16.8	−12.7	25.2	30.6
20–25	21.5	21.6	0.4	21.3	−0.7	20.4	−4.8	19.7	−8.5	26.5	23.4
25–30	19.1	19.2	0.5	19.4	1.1	18.9	−1.5	18.8	−1.9	22.0	14.8
30–50	37.3	37.5	0.4	37.5	0.4	38.3	2.7	40.3	8.0	37.6	0.7
50–100	20.9	21.0	0.4	20.9	−0.2	23.5	12.2	23.5	12.2	15.7	−24.8
100–200	12.4	12.7	2.7	12.3	−0.1	14.1	13.7	13.6	9.8	6.8	−45.2
200–500	8.9	8.9	0.8	8.7	−1.7	9.8	10.4	9.5	7.7	4.0	−54.4
500–1,000[b]	2.2	2.6	15.5	2.5	12.7	2.8	26.2	2.7	23.3	1.1	−51.2
1,000 and over[b]	4.8	4.8	0.3	4.7	−2.0	5.2	9.4	5.1	7.1	2.0	−59.0
All classes	165.3	165.7	0.3	165.5	0.1	165.5	0.1	165.3	0.0	165.9	0.3

Source: Brookings 1970 MERGE File, projected to 1977. Figures are rounded.
a. For definition of comprehensive income and explanation of five comprehensive tax systems, see text.
b. Because the present tax rate schedule stops at $200,000 of taxable income, only one tax rate determines most of the tax liability for upper-income taxpayers. Eliminating the many tax preferences pushes more taxpayers into the highest bracket and increases the liability of those with a CI of $500,000 to $1 million, while having less effect on those with higher incomes. To maintain present-law progressivity under a comprehensive tax, more tax rate brackets above $200,000 may be necessary.
* 0.05 or less.

Table A-6. Changes in Individual Tax Liabilities under Comprehensive Tax Systems 1 and 2, by Comprehensive Income Class, 1977[a]

Comprehensive income class (thousands of dollars)	Number of increases (thousands)	Mean increase (dollars per taxpayer)	Number of decreases (thousands)	Mean decrease (dollars per taxpayer)
		System 1		
0–2.5	0.0	0.0	5.7	48.4
2.5–5	1,357.9	40.4	3,313.0	98.3
5–7.5	3,862.7	124.6	4,402.6	168.7
7.5–10	3,719.9	223.3	4.954.1	208.3
10–15	6,513.8	328.1	9,653.9	240.7
15–20	5,849.8	447.6	7,896.4	310.4
20–25	4,371.8	573.3	5,620.6	431.2
25–30	2,813.2	737.3	3,412.2	580.6
30–50	3,479.4	1,155.3	3,839.7	1,003.4
50–100	736.4	3,424.7	814.2	3,007.2
100–200	148.4	12,225.3	164.3	9,007.4
200–500	39.7	34,570.5	44.1	29,550.8
500–1,000	6.4	87,826.8	3.2	68,500.7
1,000 and over	2.6	311,297.2	3.3	236,948.2
All classes	32,902.0	662.4	44,127.5	484.4
		System 2		
0–2.5	0.0	0.0	5.7	48.4
2.5–5	1,394.9	52.7	3,276.0	92.8
5–7.5	4,072.1	142.1	4,193.2	153.6
7.5–10	3,926.8	244.3	4,747.2	191.4
10–15	6,897.4	334.9	9,270.3	236.7
15–20	5,969.1	437.2	7,777.2	322.0
20–25	4,326.3	554.0	5,666.0	450.6
25–30	2,928.5	724.4	3,296.9	578.9
30–50	3,561.6	1,129.4	3,757.5	1,033.4
50–100	756.3	3,254.4	794.2	3,148.1
100–200	134.3	12,160.3	178.4	9,227.5
200–500	38.3	33,181.1	45.6	31,106.3
500–1,000	6.2	84,144.0	3.4	70,367.0
1,000 and over	2.5	293,986.9	3.4	248,433.3
All classes	34,014.4	638.0	43,015.1	500.8

Source: Brookings 1970 MERGE File, projected to 1977. Figures are rounded.
a. For definition of comprehensive income and explanation of five comprehensive tax systems, see text.

possible to control changes in the tax liabilities of individual filers. To assess the magnitude of these changes under a comprehensive tax system, a detailed analysis of systems 1 and 2 was undertaken.[5] Table A-6 shows

5. These two systems were chosen because they were drawn to replicate the progressivity of the tax law in 1976. Because the other systems were explicitly designed to change progressivity, changes in individual liabilities can only be expected.

that in both systems tax decreases outnumber tax increases by almost a 4–3 margin. This is fairly predictable because tax "avoiders" are relatively few in number, while large numbers of taxpayers take the standard deduction or have small itemized deductions and therefore would benefit from the elimination of preferences. Within the group with tax increases, a substantial minority, almost one-fourth, were not taxable under 1976 law but are made taxable under the comprehensive law. This group is concentrated at lower incomes and consists largely of recipients of transfer payments that are not now taxable. A much smaller group of taxpayers is made nontaxable by the reformed law; this group consists largely of those households whose income was included in AGI and who would benefit from the larger personal exemption and standard deduction.[6]

While there is a relatively large group of taxpayers who would face tax increases under the comprehensive income tax, some of these increases are small enough to be insignificant. Table A-7 shows the frequency of tax increases greater than both $100 and 10 percent of tax liability under 1976 law.[7] This distinction shows that about one-third of those with tax increases face only small additional liabilities either in dollar or percentage terms. There remain, therefore, 22 million taxpayers under system 1 and 24 million under system 2 who face relatively large tax increases; this is about 30 percent of the total population.

To determine the characteristics of these taxpayers, the entire population was first searched to determine the average tax burden under 1976 law at different income levels.[8] This analysis revealed that 24 percent of those who would face large tax increases under system 1 paid from 1 to 25 percent less than average effective tax rates for their income class

6. A very small subgroup in this category (only 500 taxpayers) consists of taxpayers who avoided the regular tax under 1976 law but were subject to the minimum tax and whose preferences slip through the net of the general definition of comprehensive income. The exact characteristics of this subgroup are hard to determine. For example, some taxpayers avoid ordinary tax by amassing large interest payments or business losses; the computer sample of tax returns provides only the total amounts of such payments or losses, which is not at all helpful in determining whether such expenses should be deducted from income.

7. These criteria were applied jointly because an increase in tax liability from $1 to $5, for example, appears huge in percentage terms but is insignificant to the taxpayer; similarly, an increase from $100,000 to $105,000 is impressive in dollar terms but probably would not change the life-style of the $300,000 household paying it.

8. This analysis controlled for variations in family size through the calculation of *standard taxable income* (STI), which is defined as CI less one $750 exemption for each taxpayer and dependent and less the standard deduction allowed under 1976 law. Average effective tax rates were calculated for each of 105 STI classes as a fraction of STI.

Table A-7. Significant Individual Tax Increases under Comprehensive Tax Systems 1 and 2, by Comprehensive Income Class, 1977[a]

Comprehensive income class (thousands of dollars)	System 1		System 2	
	Number of significant increases (thousands)	Mean increase (dollars per taxpayer)	Number of significant increases (thousands)	Mean increase (dollars per taxpayer)
0–2.5	0.0	0.0	0.0	0.0
2.5–5	0.0	0.0	163.4	115.9
5–7.5	1,996.4	197.8	2,400.2	208.0
7.5–10	2,715.3	288.0	2,992.4	305.3
10–15	4,896.4	420.0	5,251.4	424.6
15–20	4,309.9	583.7	4,449.8	565.8
20–25	3,164.3	755.7	3,132.7	730.3
25–30	1,929.2	1,013.1	2,001.5	995.2
30–50	2,466.0	1,540.9	2,556.2	1,484.8
50–100	563.3	4,296.3	562.8	4,175.0
100–200	115.3	15,239.3	110.2	14,425.1
200–500	32.4	41,367.8	31.0	40,051.8
500–1,000	5.5	99,830.4	5.2	97,656.4
1,000 and over	2.2	352,154.3	2.1	346,670.6
All classes	22,196.3	934.6	23,658.8	873.1

Source: Brookings 1970 MERGE File, projected to 1977. Figures are rounded.

a. Significant tax increases are defined as both greater than $100 and greater than 10 percent of tax liability under the law in 1976. For definition of comprehensive income and explanation of comprehensive tax systems, see text.

under 1976 law; 26 percent paid taxes that were 25 to 50 percent less than the average effective tax rate for their income class would dictate, and 47 percent paid at least 50 percent less. In other words, a substantial fraction of those who would have sizable tax increases under a reformed tax are those who pay substantially less tax than the average for their income classes because of the preferences in 1976 law.

Another way of looking at the same question would be to examine the changes in taxes of taxpayers grouped according to the relationship of their taxes under 1976 law to the average for their income class. Table A-8 shows that the comprehensive tax would discriminate quite well according to current liabilities. Only 2 percent of those who now pay above-average taxes would have significant increases under the system 1 comprehensive tax, while 37, 85, and 74 percent, respectively, of the three groups with below-average tax liabilities in table A-8 would have tax increases. On the other hand, 94 percent of those who now pay above-average taxes would have tax decreases, while only 30, 6, and 2 percent, respectively, of those in the below-average tax groups would have tax cuts.

Table A-8. Change in Tax Liability under Comprehensive Income Tax Systems 1 and 2 for Taxpayers Paying More or Less than the Average Effective Tax Rate under 1976 Law
Thousands

1976 law in relation to average for each income class	System 1[a]			System 2[a]		
	Number of tax decreases	Number of tax increases	Number of signifi- cant tax increases[b]	Number of tax decreases	Number of tax increases	Number of signifi- cant tax increases[b]
Taxes greater than average	39,045.4	2,560.9	682.9	39,866.4	1,739.8	155.9
Taxes between 100 and 75 per- cent of average	4,388.3	10,101.4	5,319.6	2,653.3	11,836.4	6,252.2
Taxes between 75 and 50 per- cent of average	412.2	6,400.5	5,769.2	271.7	6,541.0	6,063.2
Taxes less than 50 percent of average	286.5	13,839.1	10,424.6	228.6	13,897.1	11,187.5

Source: Brookings 1970 MERGE File, projected to 1977. Figures are rounded.
a. For details of comprehensive tax systems, see text.
b. Significant tax increases are defined as both greater than $100, and greater than 10 percent of tax liability under the law in 1976.

Moderating Individual Tax Increases

To reduce the number of taxpayers facing significant increases under the comprehensive income tax, it would be necessary to reduce average tax rates. This could be done generally (that is, by reducing all tax-payers' taxes) or selectively (that is, by some device that reduces only the taxes of those who face increases). Four general devices will be considered here—nonrefundable $100 and $200 tax rebates and credits equal to 5 and 10 percent of tax liability—and one selective device—allowing the taxpayer to choose the lower of his comprehensive income tax or the 1976 tax.

The simplest way to avoid tax increases under a comprehensive tax would be to allow those who face increases to pay their tax under the old law. This course eliminates any possibility of raising individual tax liabilities, but it has two disadvantages. First, it allows those who make most use of tax preferences, the target of the comprehensive tax, to continue. Second, it is expensive in terms of lost revenue. Table A-9 shows the result of permitting the taxpayer to choose the comprehensive tax or the old law; aggregate revenues are reduced by $21 billion under system 1. It would be possible to raise the tax rates under the comprehensive tax to recover some of this revenue, but this would drive more taxpayers back to the old law and defeat the purpose of the comprehensive tax.

**Table A-9. Revenue of Comprehensive Income Tax Systems 1 and 2,
by Type of Tax Cuts and Comprehensive Income Class, 1977**[a]
Income classes in thousands of dollars; revenue in billions of dollars

Comprehensive income class	Optional comprehensive tax	$100 rebate	$200 rebate	5 percent credit	10 percent credit
		System 1			
0–2.5	0.0	0.0	0.0	0.0	0.0
2.5–5	0.1	0.0	0.0	0.1	0.1
5–7.5	1.1	0.8	0.4	1.5	1.4
7.5–10	2.6	2.6	1.9	3.3	3.1
10–15	10.8	11.3	9.7	12.3	11.6
15–20	16.8	18.1	16.7	18.5	17.5
20–25	19.1	20.6	19.6	20.5	19.4
25–30	17.2	18.6	18.0	18.3	17.3
30–50	33.5	36.8	36.0	35.6	33.8
50–100	18.5	20.9	20.7	20.0	18.9
100–200	10.9	12.7	12.6	12.1	11.4
200–500	7.5	8.9	8.9	8.5	8.0
500–1,000	2.0	2.6	2.6	2.4	2.3
1,000 and over	4.0	4.8	4.8	4.5	4.3
All classes	143.9	158.6	151.9	157.5	149.2
		System 2			
0–2.5	0.0	0.0	0.0	0.0	0.0
2.5–5	0.1	0.0	0.0	0.2	0.2
5–7.5	1.2	1.0	0.5	1.7	1.6
7.5–10	2.7	2.9	2.1	3.5	3.3
10–15	10.9	11.6	10.0	12.5	11.9
15–20	16.8	18.0	16.6	18.4	17.4
20–25	18.9	20.3	19.3	20.3	19.2
25–30	17.2	18.7	18.1	18.4	17.4
30–50	33.5	36.7	36.0	35.6	33.7
50–100	18.4	20.7	20.6	19.9	18.8
100–200	10.7	12.3	12.3	11.7	11.1
200–500	7.4	8.7	8.7	8.3	7.8
500–1,000	2.0	2.5	2.5	2.4	2.2
1,000 and over	3.9	4.7	4.7	4.4	4.2
All classes	143.8	158.2	151.4	157.2	148.9

Source: Brookings 1970 MERGE File, projected to 1977. Figures are rounded.
a. For definition of comprehensive income and explanation of comprehensive tax systems, see text.

Alternatives to the selective approach above would be general tax cuts, or "sweeteners," added to a mandatory comprehensive tax. The general approach has the advantage that it upholds the principle of comprehensive taxation, but its disadvantages are that it cannot conceivably prevent all tax increases and that attempts to get closer and closer to that target will be increasingly expensive. Table A-9 shows that a $100 rebate

Table A-10. Number of Significant Tax Increases under Comprehensive Tax Systems 1 and 2, by Type of Tax Cuts and Comprehensive Income Class, 1977[a]
Income classes in thousands of dollars; all other numbers in thousands

Comprehensive income class	No tax cut	$100 rebate	$200 rebate	5 percent credit	10 percent credit
		System 1			
2–2.5	0.0	0.0	0.0	0.0	0.0
2.5–5	0.0	0.0	0.0	0.0	0.0
5–7.5	1,996.4	771.7	285.4	1,883.5	1,766.9
7.5–10	2,715.3	1,621.1	1,032.9	2,535.8	2,393.0
10–15	4,896.4	3,741.5	2,829.2	4,451.3	4,048.6
15–20	4,309.9	3,466.3	2,761.3	3,722.2	3,214.7
20–25	3,164.3	2,678.0	2,215.4	2,656.4	2,177.4
25–30	1,929.2	1,697.5	1,459.0	1,572.6	1,280.9
30–50	2,466.0	2,249.4	2,039.7	1,982.0	1,573.8
50–100	563.3	544.2	530.1	456.0	374.7
100–200	115.3	115.1	114.7	101.0	83.7
200–500	32.4	32.4	32.2	29.4	25.6
500–1,000	5.5	5.5	5.5	4.9	4.3
1,000 and over	2.2	2.2	2.2	1.8	1.5
All classes	22,196.3	16,924.9	13,307.8	19,396.9	16,945.1
		System 2			
2–2.5	0.0	0.0	0.0	0.0	0.0
2.5–5	163.4	0.0	0.0	132.1	101.0
5–7.5	2,400.2	1,018.1	417.5	2,269.8	2,162.1
7.5–10	2,992.4	2,047.9	1,286.4	2,859.4	2,722.4
10–15	5,251.4	4,014.0	3,105.2	4,798.4	4,360.3
15–20	4,449.8	3,554.6	2,884.2	3,851.3	3,360.7
20–25	3,132.7	2,632.3	2,167.5	2,609.4	2,172.4
25–30	2,001.5	1,764.2	1,545.6	1,654.3	1,347.3
30–50	2,556.2	2,345.6	2,130.1	2,061.7	1,620.6
50–100	562.8	552.0	539.7	462.2	388.2
100–200	110.2	110.0	109.8	93.7	77.7
200–500	31.0	30.9	30.7	27.8	23.8
500–1,000	5.2	5.2	5.2	4.6	4.0
1,000 and over	2.1	2.0	2.0	1.6	1.4
All classes	23,658.8	18,076.9	14,224.0	20,826.4	18,342.0

Source: Brookings 1970 MERGE File, projected to 1977. Figures are rounded.
a. For definition of comprehensive income and explanation of comprehensive tax systems, see text.

for each tax return would cost $6.7 billion in lost revenue, while table A-10 shows it reducing the number of significant tax increases by only 5.3 million, or 24 percent. A 5 percent reduction in all taxes, at approximately the same revenue cost, would reduce the number of significant increases by 2.8 million, or 13 percent. Higher-cost attempts at the same objective would meet with little more success: a $200 rebate reduces the number of significant tax increases by 8.9 million (40 percent) and a 10 percent tax reduction by 5.3 million (24 percent).

These results indicate that a tax cut to prevent large increases due to a transition to a comprehensive tax would be most effective as a fixed dollar amount per return, rather than as a percentage of tax liability. Even at that, however, it would cost the Treasury Department in excess of $1,000 to reduce the increase of one return to an insignificant level. Allowing taxpayers to use the old law if it lowered their tax liability would be quite expensive in terms of lost revenue.

Married versus Single Taxpayers

This section will briefly illuminate the issue of the relative tax burdens of married couples and single taxpayers, using results from systems 1 and 2.

System 1 was designed, as a first step, with a joint tax rate schedule that replicates the distribution of tax liabilities for married couples under 1976 law. The tax rate schedule for single taxpayers is then determined by the legal requirement that the tax liability of a single taxpayer with taxable income equal to that of a married couple shall not exceed that of the couple by more than 20 percent and that it shall be kept as close to that level as possible. If this principle is maintained and the joint tax liabilities of married couples are held constant, however, the total re-formed tax liability for single persons will exceed that under 1976 law. This is so because upper-income single persons are heavier-than-average users of tax preferences.[9] In contrast, low-income single persons benefit from tax reform because their use of preferences is less than average. When this overall increase in the liabilities of single persons is returned to all taxpayers through rate reductions (as it must be to maintain the 20 percent principle in the law), the tax liabilities of married taxpayers and low-income single persons are reduced and those of upper-income single persons are raised, as shown in the first half of table A-11. This result indicates that if the legal provisions regarding the relative burdens of married and single taxpayers are unchanged, comprehensive income taxation will systematically redistribute tax burdens. If results on the order of those presented in the first half of table A-11 are not attractive, then the rules of the game will have to be changed together with the broadening of the tax base.

One possible alternative is to eliminate the rate advantages of income splitting and to use a single tax schedule, relying on personal exemptions and deductions to provide the differentiation between the liabilities of

9. This is not surprising, because the current tax schedules subject single persons to quite high marginal tax rates at comparatively modest taxable income levels (50 percent at $32,000, 70 percent at $100,000).

Table A-11. Tax Liabilities of Married Couples and Single Persons under 1976 Law and under Comprehensive Tax Systems 1 and 2, by Comprehensive Income Class, 1977[a]
Income classes in thousands of dollars; tax liabilities in billions of dollars

	Single persons			Married couples		
Comprehensive income class	1976 tax law	Comprehensive tax	Percent change	1976 tax law	Comprehensive tax	Percent change
System 1						
0–2.5	*	0.0	−100.0	*	0.0	−100.0
2.5–5	0.4	0.1	−66.7	*	0.0	−100.0
5–7.5	1.5	1.3	−13.0	0.2	0.1	−49.7
7.5–10	2.4	2.2	−8.6	0.8	0.7	−12.7
10–15	5.6	5.4	−4.0	6.3	5.9	−5.4
15–20	4.1	4.4	7.1	14.2	13.8	−2.8
20–25	2.7	3.0	9.9	18.0	17.7	−1.9
25–30	1.8	2.0	11.0	16.8	16.5	−1.6
30–50	3.1	3.3	8.8	33.7	33.4	−0.8
50–100	1.9	2.2	16.3	18.6	18.3	−2.1
100–200	1.0	1.5	45.1	10.9	10.7	−1.6
200–500	0.8	1.0	30.4	7.6	7.5	−1.2
500–1,000	0.2	0.3	42.9	1.9	2.1	11.7
1,000 and over	0.3	0.4	34.6	4.3	4.1	−3.3
All classes	26.0	27.4	5.3	133.2	130.8	−1.8
System 2						
0–2.5	*	0.0	−100.0	*	0.0	−100.0
2.5–5	0.4	0.2	−56.7	*	0.0	−100.0
5–7.5	1.5	1.5	−3.6	0.2	0.1	−34.6
7.5–10	2.4	2.3	−6.8	0.8	0.9	6.8
10–15	5.6	5.1	−9.1	6.3	6.5	3.5
15–20	4.1	3.8	−7.5	14.2	14.4	1.4
20–25	2.7	2.6	−5.9	18.0	17.9	−0.5
25–30	1.8	1.8	−4.4	16.8	17.0	1.0
30–50	3.1	2.8	−7.4	33.7	33.9	0.8
50–100	1.9	1.9	−0.8	18.6	18.5	−0.6
100–200	1.0	1.4	30.6	10.9	10.5	−3.1
200–500	0.8	0.9	23.6	7.6	7.4	−3.2
500–1,000	0.2	0.3	37.8	1.9	2.1	9.3
1,000 and over	0.3	0.4	31.0	4.3	4.1	−5.5
All classes	26.0	24.9	−4.1	133.2	133.2	0.0

Source: Brookings 1970 MERGE File, projected to 1977. Figures are rounded.
a. For definition of comprehensive income and explanation of comprehensive tax systems, see text.
* 0.05 or less.

married and single persons. This was the course followed in system 2. Table A-5 shows that the liabilities under system 2 followed those under 1976 law quite closely; this is true because the rate schedule was drawn to replicate precisely this distribution of tax liabilities among all taxpayers. The second half of table A-11, however, shows that this constant overall distribution is in fact the sum of altered distributions among married and single persons. Virtually all classes of single people have their taxes reduced; only the one-tenth of 1 percent with comprehensive incomes in excess of $100,000 face systematic increases. In contrast, most classes of married persons with incomes below $50,000—those who profit most from income splitting—face tax increases; married persons with incomes above $50,000 would have tax reductions on the average.

Conclusions

This appendix was prepared as a supplement to, and not as a substitute for, the issue-oriented papers in this volume. It contains examples of tax systems that are not necessarily in complete accord with the recommendations of the authors of the papers in this volume or with those of other tax experts. Taken within its limits, however, it establishes several conclusions that may be important to decisions on comprehensive tax reform:

—A broadening of the tax base to include the major types of income not now subject to tax (mainly transfer payments and capital gains) would greatly increase the revenue potential of the income tax. The elimination or reduction of the personal deductions would likewise add considerable revenue potential.

—When compared with adjusted gross income, a comprehensive income tax base would raise taxable income most at the extremes of the income scale.

—A comprehensive income tax could raise the same revenue as the current tax, with both significantly lower rates and generous relief for low-income persons.

—The comprehensive income tax base is neutral with respect to the distribution of tax burdens. Rate schedules can be redesigned so as to have virtually any desired effect on progressivity.

—While a relatively large number of taxpayers would face tax increases under a comprehensive income tax, most of them now pay significantly lower-than-average taxes for their income class. Small sacrifices of tax revenue are unlikely to significantly reduce the number of taxpayers facing increases.

—Comprehensive income taxation does not provide a magic answer to the problem of relative taxation of married and single persons. In fact, the present relationships would be altered unless explicit steps were taken to prevent it.

Conference Participants

with their affiliations at the time of the conference

Henry J. Aaron *Brookings Institution*
William D. Andrews *Harvard Law School*
Walter J. Blum *University of Chicago Law School*
Michael J. Boskin *Stanford University*
David F. Bradford *U.S. Treasury Department*
Gerard M. Brannon *Georgetown University*
Harvey E. Brazer *University of Michigan*
Roger E. Brinner *Data Resources, Inc.*
E. Cary Brown *Massachusetts Institute of Technology*
Michael Bruno *Harvard University*
Jeremy I. Bulow *Massachusetts Institute of Technology*
Edwin S. Cohen *University of Virginia Law School*
Sheldon S. Cohen *Cohen and Uretz*
Charles Davenport *Congressional Budget Office*
John F. Due *University of Illinois*
Ann F. Friedlaender *Massachusetts Institute of Technology*
Harvey Galper *U.S. Treasury Department*
Richard Goode *International Monetary Fund*

Daniel I. Halperin *University of Pennsylvania Law School*

William F. Hellmuth *Virginia Commonwealth University*

Frederic W. Hickman *Hopkins, Sutter, Mulroy, Davis and Cromartie*

Jerome Kurtz *Wolf, Block, Schorr and Solis-Cohen*

Donald C. Lubick *Hodgson, Russ, Andrews, Woods and Goodyear*

Michael J. McIntyre *University of Virginia Law School*

Charles E. McLure, Jr. *Rice University*

John K. McNulty *University of California Law School*

Joseph J. Minarik *Brookings Institution*

Peggy B. Musgrave *Northeastern University*

Richard A. Musgrave *Harvard University*

John S. Nolan *Miller and Chevalier*

Benjamin A. Okner *Congressional Budget Office*

Oliver Oldman *Harvard Law School*

Harry A. Olsher *Fund for Public Policy Research*

Joseph A. Pechman *Brookings Institution*

Bernard M. Shapiro *Joint Committee on Internal Revenue Taxation*

Eytan Sheshinski *Harvard University*

John B. Shoven *Stanford University*

Emil M. Sunley, Jr. *Brookings Institution*

Stanley S. Surrey *Harvard Law School*

William Vickrey *Columbia University*

Alvin C. Warren, Jr. *University of Pennsylvania Law School*

James W. Wetzler *Joint Committee on Internal Revenue Taxation*

Melvin I. White *Brooklyn College of the City University of New York*

Laurence N. Woodworth *Joint Committee on Internal Revenue Taxation*

Selected Bibliography

General

Bittker, Boris I., and others. *A Comprehensive Income Tax Base? A Debate*. Branford, Conn.: Federal Tax Press, 1968.

Blum, Walter J., and Harry Kalven, Jr. *The Uneasy Case for Progressive Taxation*. Chicago: University of Chicago Press, 1953.

Break, George F., and Joseph A. Pechman. *Federal Tax Reform: The Impossible Dream?* Washington: Brookings Institution, 1975.

Eisenstein, Louis. *The Ideologies of Taxation*. New York: Ronald Press, 1961.

Feldstein, Martin. "On the Theory of Tax Reform," *Journal of Public Economics,* vol. 6 (July-August 1976).

Goode, Richard. *The Individual Income Tax*. Rev. ed. Washington: Brookings Institution, 1976.

Haig, Robert M., ed. *The Federal Income Tax*. New York: Columbia University Press, 1921.

Harberger, Arnold C. *Taxation and Welfare*. Boston: Little, Brown, 1974.

Pechman, Joseph A. *Federal Tax Policy*. Third ed. Washington: Brookings Institution, 1977.

———, and Benjamin A. Okner. "Individual Income Tax Erosion by Income Classes," in *The Economics of Federal Subsidy Programs*. Part 1: *General Study Papers*. Joint Economic Committee. 92 Cong. 2 sess. Washington: Government Printing Office, 1972. Brookings Reprint 230.

Report of the Royal Commission on Taxation. 6 vols. Ottawa: Queen's Printer, 1966.

Simons, Henry C. *Federal Tax Reform.* Chicago: University of Chicago Press, 1950.

————. *Personal Income Taxation.* Chicago: University of Chicago Press, 1938.

Smith, Dan Throop. *Federal Tax Reform: The Issues and a Program.* New York: McGraw-Hill, 1961.

Stern, Philip M. *The Rape of the Taxpayer.* New York: Random House, 1973.

Surrey, Stanley S. *Pathways to Tax Reform: The Concept of Tax Expenditures.* Cambridge: Harvard University Press, 1973.

U.S. Department of the Treasury. *Blueprints for Basic Tax Reform.* Washington: Government Printing Office, 1977.

U.S. Office of Management and Budget. "Tax Expenditures," Special Analysis F, in *Special Analyses, Budget of the United States Government, Fiscal Year 1978.* Washington: Government Printing Office, 1977.

Vickrey, William. *Agenda for Progressive Taxation.* New York: Ronald Press, 1947.

Willis, Arthur B., ed. *Studies in Substantive Tax Reform.* Chicago: American Bar Foundation and Southern Methodist University, 1969.

Personal Deductions

Andrews, William D. "Personal Deductions in an Ideal Income Tax," *Harvard Law Review,* vol. 86 (December 1972).

Bittker, Boris I. "Income Tax Deductions, Credits, and Subsidies for Personal Expenditures," *Journal of Law and Economics,* vol. 16 (October 1973).

Commission on Private Philanthropy and Public Needs. *Giving in America: Toward a Stronger Voluntary Sector.* Washington: The Commission, 1975.

Feldstein, Martin. "The Income Tax and Charitable Contributions." Part 1: "Aggregate and Distributional Effects," *National Tax Journal,* vol. 28 (March 1975).

Kahn, C. Harry. *Personal Deductions in the Federal Income Tax.* Princeton: Princeton University Press for the National Bureau of Economic Research, 1960.

Tax Institute of America. *Tax Impacts on Philanthropy.* Symposium. Princeton: Tax Institute of America, 1972.

Capital Gains

Bailey, Martin J. "Capital Gains and Income Taxation," in Arnold C. Harberger and Martin J. Bailey, eds., *The Taxation of Income from Capital.* Washington: Brookings Institution, 1969.

Bhatia, Kul B. "Accrued Capital Gains, Personal Income and Saving in the United States, 1948–1964," *Review of Income and Wealth,* series 16 (December 1970). Brookings Reprint 200.

Brannon, Gerard M. *The Effect of Tax Deductibility on the Level of Charitable Contributions and Variations on the Theme; The Lock-In Problem for Capital Gains: An Analysis of the 1970–71 Experience; Buildings and the Income Tax.* Washington: Fund for Public Policy Research, 1974.

Brinner, Roger. "Inflation, Deferral and the Neutral Taxation of Capital Gains," *National Tax Journal,* vol. 26 (December 1973).

———, and Alicia Munnell. "Taxation of Capital Gains: Inflation and Other Problems," *New England Economic Review,* September-October 1974.

David, Martin. *Alternative Approaches to Capital Gains Taxation.* Washington: Brookings Institution, 1968.

Diamond, P. A. "Inflation and the Comprehensive Tax Base," *Journal of Public Economics,* vol. 4 (August 1975).

Holt, Charles C., and John P. Shelton. "The Implications of the Capital Gains Tax for Investment Decisions," *Journal of Finance,* vol. 16 (December 1961). University of Wisconsin, Social Systems Research Institute, Reprint 14.

———. "The Lock-in Effect of the Capital Gains Tax," *National Tax Journal,* vol. 15 (December 1962).

Seltzer, Lawrence H. *The Nature and Tax Treatment of Capital Gains and Losses.* New York: National Bureau of Economic Research, 1951.

Homeowner Preferences

Aaron, Henry J. *Shelters and Subsidies: Who Benefits from Federal Housing Policies?* Washington: Brookings Institution, 1972.

———. *Who Pays the Property Tax? A New View.* Washington: Brookings Institution, 1975.

Goode, Richard. "Imputed Rent of Owner-Occupied Dwellings under the Income Tax," *Journal of Finance,* vol. 15 (December 1960).

James, Franklin J. "Income Taxes, Homeownership and Urban Land Use." Processed. Washington: The Urban Institute, 1976. (See especially chapters 2, 3, and 6.)

Laidler, David. "Income Tax Incentives for Owner-Occupied Housing," in Arnold C. Harberger and Martin J. Bailey, eds., *The Taxation of Income from Capital.* Washington: Brookings Institution, 1969.

Sunley, Emil M., Jr. "Tax Advantages of Homeownership versus Renting: A Cause of Suburban Migration?" in National Tax Association, *Proceedings of the Sixty-third Annual Conference on Taxation.* Columbus, Ohio: NTA, 1971.

U.S. Congress. Joint Economic Committee. *Federal Subsidy Programs.* 93 Cong. 2 sess. Washington: Government Printing Office, 1974. (See especially pp. 1–14; 87–94.)

White, Melvin and Anne. "Horizontal Inequality in the Federal Income Tax Treatment of Homeowners and Tenants," *National Tax Journal,* vol. 18 (September 1965).

Taxation of the Family

Bittker, Boris I. "Federal Income Taxation and the Family," *Stanford Law Review,* vol. 27 (July 1975).

Groves, Harold M. *Federal Tax Treatment of the Family.* Washington: Brookings Institution, 1963.

International Fiscal Association. *Studies on International Fiscal Law.* Vol. 57a: *The Income, Fortune and Estate Tax Treatment of Household Units,* Twenty-sixth International Congress on Fiscal and Financial Law. Rotterdam: IFA, 1972.

Oldman, Oliver, and Ralph Temple. "Comparative Analysis of the Taxation of Married Persons," *Stanford Law Review,* vol. 12 (May 1960).

Organisation for Economic Co-operation and Development. *The Treatment of Family Units in OECD Member Countries under Tax and Transfer Systems,* A Report by the Committee on Fiscal Affairs. Paris: OECD, 1977.

Pechman, Joseph A. "Income Splitting," in *Tax Revision Compendium.* U.S. Congress. House Committee on Ways and Means. Washington: Government Printing Office, 1959.

Index

Aaron, Henry J., 11n, 17n, 18n, 30, 182, 184n, 189n, 191n, 194n, 195n, 256n, 273n, 277n
Accretion concept of income, 7, 8, 30, 261
Accrual taxation, for capital gains, 11–12, 117, 154, 161, 262; constructive realization versus, 120–21
Adjusted gross income (AGI), 49, 100; compared with comprehensive income, 277–82, 287–88; contributions relative to, 50; Haig-Simons guidelines for inclusions and exclusions from, 29; personal deductions relative to, 50, 51, 59, 61; standard deductions relative to, 55
Advertising, capitalization of expenses for, 249–50, 255
AGI. See Adjusted gross income
Alexander, Sidney S., 242n
Alimony payments, deductibility of, 54
Allocation of resources. See Resource allocation
Alternative rate, for capital gains: legislative history of, 116n; proposed repeal of, 125, 150, 151
American Institute of Certified Public Accountants, 254n
Andrews, William D., 2n, 16, 17, 234
Asset depreciation range system, 249, 255

Assets: accrued versus realized income from, 250–52; depreciable, 244, 247, 251–52; determining business income through value of, 243–46, 253; factors affecting productivity of, 245
Austin, John S., 168n

Bailey, Martin J., 141n, 193n
Bale, Gordon, 53n
Benefit rule, 213–15, 217, 220, 228, 239
Benefits, employee: in AGI versus CI, 279–81; amount of employer contribution to, 76; disability insurance, 88, 280; disability pensions, 84–85; fringe, 77, 90–92, 113; group health insurance, 86; group prepaid legal service, 89–90; group term life insurance, 85–86; inequities in tax exemptions for, 76–77; proposed excise tax on interest from plan reserves, 110; proposed taxation of, 75–76, 104, 106, 114; retirement, 77–84; sick pay, 84–85; supplemental unemployment, 89, 109; workmen's compensation, 86–88
Bhatia, Kul B., 141n
Bird, Richard M., 21n, 275n
Bittker, Boris I., 17, 18n, 27, 30n
Black-lung benefits, 101–02
Blinder, Alan S., 52n
Booth, Richard, 277n

305